LIVING ON YOUR OWN

THE COMPLETE GUIDE TO SETTING UP
YOUR MONEY, YOUR SPACE, AND YOUR LIFE

LIVING ON YOUR OWN

THE COMPLETE GUIDE TO SETTING UP
YOUR MONEY, YOUR SPACE, AND YOUR LIFE

PIERRE A. LEHU

Fresno, California

Dedicatated to my parents, Pierre and Annette Lehu,
for lovingly kicking me out of the nest.

Published by Quill Driver Books
An imprint of Linden Publishing
2006 South Mary Street, Fresno, California 93721
(559) 233-6633 / (800) 345-4447
QuillDriverBooks.com

Quill Driver Books and Colophon are trademarks of
Linden Publishing, Inc.

ISBN 978-1-61035-212-3

135798642

Printed in the United States of America
on acid-free paper.

Library of Congress Cataloging-in-Publication Data

Lehu, Pierre A.
  Living on your own : the complete guide to setting up your money, your
space, and your life / Pierre Lehu.
    pages cm
  Includes index.
  ISBN 978-1-61035-212-3 (pbk. : alk. paper)
  1. Home economics. 2. Life skills. 3. Finance, Personal. I. Title.
  TX147.L435 2014
  640--dc23
                                                    2013045033

CONTENTS

Part Three: How to Take Care of Yourself

Part Four: How to Take Care of Your Money

INTRODUCTION

When you buy a new electronic gadget, do you ever bother to read the instructions? Maybe you do, but I suspect most of us just plug it in and hope it works. I know I'm like that. I always assume I'll be able to figure out how to operate the device once I turn it on. And it seems that most of the time this fly-by-the-seat-of-your-pants approach works out pretty well.

Except when it doesn't. While there are a lot of "smart" gadgets these days, most other aspects of life aren't so user friendly. When you're living on your own for the first time, this realization can hit hard—there's so much to learn and be aware of, but what are the rules and where are the instructions? Why didn't anyone ever tell you all this stuff? How are you supposed to know that the dyes in certain clothing can stain your other clothes in the washing machine? Or that there are more germs in your kitchen sink than in your toilet bowl? Or that when you verbally request the power company to hook up power to your apartment you've just entered into a *legally enforceable* contract?

Taking care of the basic, day-to-day necessities of life involves a little bit of knowledge on a wide range of subjects. Sure, you can research the answers piecemeal on the web, but the fact is that when you're new to living on your own, you may not even know what questions to ask.

The purpose of this book is to ask and then answer those questions—not all of them, because that would be impossible, but enough to give you a solid foundation to proceed with your life and to do further research if you need to. *Living on Your Own* is designed to be a step-by-step learning program, with four major parts:

How to Find the Right Place to Live: This part explains everything you need to know about creating a budget and conducting a smart search for your new home.

How to Take Care of Your Home: You will learn the ins and outs of dealing with utility companies, becoming competent at basic home maintenance, doing the laundry and dishes, and handling all the other household tasks you'll one day become an expert at.

How to Take Care of Yourself: Living on your own won't be much fun if you don't take care of your mind and body, so this part of the book covers the basics of eating well, staying happy, and learning to interact with your roommates and neighbors.

How to Take Care of Your Money: You may not have a lot of it right now, but it's never too early to learn how to wisely use and grow your money. And it's just as important to understand how to avoid getting into trouble with the IRS.

Life doesn't come with a manual, but you might think of this book as a starter kit of sorts. I've experienced everything described in this book, either directly myself or through watching my two children move out and live on their own. As I witnessed their questions and struggles, and remembered having the same issues when I moved out of my parents' home, I started wondering, "How come nobody ever writes all this stuff down?" That's how *Living On Your Own* came into being.

Although I recommend reading this book cover to cover, I realize that's not what most people will do. And that's OK, because if you run into an issue that has you throwing your hands up in dismay, you can turn to the appropriate chapter. But as I mentioned earlier, many times we aren't even aware of the questions to ask as we navigate our way through the obstacle course of life. So I encourage you to at least thumb through the pages to familiarize yourself with the book's contents.

And after that, go enjoy this wonderful time in your life. Make smart decisions, keep on learning, and have a whole lot of fun as you set off to conquer the world.

— Pierre A. Lehu

PART ONE:

How to Find the Right Place to Live

1 CAN I AFFORD TO LIVE ON MY OWN?

Simple Steps to Creating a Budget That Works

LOOK BEFORE YOU LEAP

This book will try to answer all your questions about living on your own, everything from big topics such as how to pay the rent to lifestyle satisfaction issues such as how to get your dishes sparkling clean. But before we get to all that, you have to ask yourself the very first and most important question: **"Right now—can I afford to live on my own or will I crash and burn?"**

The good news is that there's a straightforward way for you to answer this crucial question: You need to take a realistic look at your financial situation by assembling a personal budget and doing a bit of math. Sure, it involves a little bit of work, but your personal budget will be a critical key to successfully living on your own. It will tell you how much it's going to cost you to live on your own every month, which you can then compare to how much money you'll have coming in through your earnings or other sources. If the two numbers are fairly close and you'll be pulling in a bit more money than you'll be spending, you can go ahead and make the jump. But if your money supply won't meet your expenses, then it's on to Plan B, which, more likely than not, means you're staying put.

It's true that until you actually do move out on your own, the numbers you enter into your budget will be a bit rough around the edges (Chapter 2, which involves conducting some research, will help you firm up these numbers). But if you make sure to pad the expenses—and trust me, they'll be higher than what wishful thinking will encourage you to put down—then you should arrive at a budget you can trust when making your go/no-go decision.

Think of Your Budget as Your Friend and Advisor

You may think that making a budget is worse than doing an eighth grade science project, but this chapter will demonstrate that it's really not at all difficult to do and that the sense of control you get from doing a budget feels good. More than that, it gives you peace of mind. Competence, control, and peace of mind—not a bad combination, is it? And all achievable through the financial clarity of a simple budget.

Plus, creating a budget can actually involve some fun moments. Why? Because this number-crunching assignment comes with a built-in reward—a brief trip to fantasyland. I know this sounds strange, but hear me out: To make a realistic budget, you have to picture yourself in a new environment, an environment that you get to customize (to one degree or another) to your *personal* liking. So you say to yourself, "Here I am in my new apartment. Let's see, where am I going to put the TV?" True, as soon as the word television pops into your brain, the budgeting process requires you to consider the cost of purchasing a TV (not to mention paying your monthly cable bill!), unless you already own one. But whether or not a TV fits into your budget right now, at least for a moment or two you can fantasize about watching your own TV in a place of your own without having to share the remote or DVR. Maybe this visualization also has you lounging comfortably on that particular sofa you've been eyeing at Ikea, or that used recliner in the window of the little furniture shop down the street.

And should your budget eventually inform you that you have to put your dreams on hold for a while, at least you'll be proud to know you were smart enough to look before you leaped. Or perhaps your budget shows that you *can* move out now, but only if you compromise a bit. Let's say you prefer to live alone, but the numbers make it clear you can't afford that option—you may decide it's OK to give up some privacy and live with a roommate or two for a while. Or perhaps you discover you're not financially ready to go anywhere at all. At least you'll still have a bed on the old homestead to wake up in until that day comes when you are ready to move out.

CAUTION While it's great to fantasize, you don't want to allow yourself to indulge too much in fantasies that have no basis in reality. The reason for this is that when you're faced with the stark reality of your financial situation, the resulting emotions may be overwhelming to you. So as soon as the thought of moving out comes along, start the budget-making process. It will help keep you and your fantasies grounded as you work toward your goal.

FYI Many apartment landlords will require that your income be three times greater than the monthly rent. That's why it's common for first-time renters to have a co-signer assist them with qualifying for the lease.

BASIC BUDGETING CONCEPTS

Income

Before you delve into actually creating your budget (that comes a bit later in the chapter), you need to have a firm understanding of several basic concepts about budgeting. Since your budget can be summed up as your income minus your expenses, let's start with the top line of that all-important equation—your income.

Income is all about how much money you have coming in to your life each month. Your income outlines the parameters of your life—at least when it comes to spending money. Let's assume you haven't just graduated from an Ivy League school and landed a plum job on Wall Street, or come into a big inheritance, or just won the lottery. You're going to be like most people, meaning your budget is going to face limits based on how much money will be coming in combined with any savings you may already have. Now if you have a lot of savings, a collection of first-edition comic books that you're willing to part with, or are willing to take out loans, you could at some point subsidize your budget with non-income dollars. But unless this is part of your initial plan, it's better not to consider these options when making out a budget. If something happens down the road that alters your plan, that's one thing, but when you're starting off, by far the safest approach is to try your best to stick to a budget that is supported by your income, not your savings. This will prevent your long-term financial picture from resembling one of your three-year-old niece's "paintings."

In most cases, calculating your income is pretty straightforward. For example, if you're an hourly wage worker, you'll know with a fair bit of precision how big your paycheck will be every two weeks. And if you receive a salary, you'll know exactly what you'll be taking home each pay period. Or if you're in school you may receive a grant check or student loan disbursement on a regular basis, typically for the same amount every time, allowing you to know how big the check will be and when it will arrive.

The accuracy of your budget planning is going to depend on how regular your income is. If you're waiting tables, then your income will go up and down depending on how generous your customers are with their tips. Or you may be in a situation where you get to work overtime now and again but don't know how often that will happen in the future. Plus, you might get some chunks of money during special times of the year, like a Christmas bonus or some checks from relatives on your birthday—but they're not in a fixed amount or even guaranteed to come at all. How do you figure these variables into your budget? The smart approach is to be on the conservative side when you estimate how much of this variable income you'll receive.

If your income flow is choppy, think about making a contingency plan. What might a contingency plan be? Perhaps a second part-time job for a short period or a loan from your family. Or a list of expenses you can do without for a while. The one thing you want to avoid is accumulating credit card debt, because the interest rates are so high.

WORD TO THE WISE

If you are an hourly worker, it may be wise to be a bit conservative in estimating your hours for your budget, because you never know when you'll hit a minor bump in the road that might cause you to miss a few hours of work. If you regularly work 7.5-8 hours a day every pay period, you may want to assume you'll log just 7 hours per day when working on your budget. If you're still covering expenses, then you'll have the comfort of knowing you actually have a small income margin (of half an hour to 1 hour per day) accruing to help you deal with the unexpected, such as having to take unpaid leave to pick up Aunt Sally from the airport this Tuesday at 10 A.M.

DOWNLOADS

If you're in school, check out the handy Student Budget Planner spreadsheet at **SquawkFox.com**. There's also the very helpful HoursTracker app for iPhone and Android; it allows you to track the hours you work, input regular deductions, and get a good estimate of how much your check will be each pay period. And there are many more apps like it. Find the one that works best for you. If you need help budgeting in expense categories, **GoodBudget.com** allows you to assign a dollar amount for each category and track how much you've spent on those categories during the month. It has both a desktop and a smartphone app. For more apps like this, google "best budget apps" to review expert recommendations. Tip: Look for apps that can sync to your phone and your computer so you can access your budget at your desk or on the go. There are also lots of free downloadable budget templates and sheets to help you fill in a potential monthly budget. **Office.com** has a basic one for Excel, as does Google Docs in its templates gallery (**drive.google. com/templates**). You can also google "best personal budget worksheet" to get some recommendations. Consider reviewing and downloading several; then create your own worksheet tailored to your needs.

What Are Your Expenses?

A budget must include a line for every possible monthly expense you're going to have. Some will be obvious, like rent and food. Others, unless you've lived on your own before, can creep up and surprise you if you don't do a thorough job of researching them all out.

Here's one example. Let's say your local cable company advertises that it can provide cable, Internet, and telephone service for a fixed monthly fee of $99. Do you put $99 in your budget spreadsheet under "cable"? No, you don't, and the reason *isn't* that this package will expire at the end of a certain period and the rate will then rise dramatically—though that's obviously something you want to plan for as well. The $99 advertised rate doesn't include the taxes and other fees that will get tacked on to that flat rate. With these added costs, $99 can quickly become $109 or $119, depending on where you live. And if you add in premium channels, your monthly cable company bill might climb to, say, $209. So don't put down the lowest cost number you can find in an ad for a particular expense unless you're sure about it. Instead, call the cable company and find out what the final cost is actually going to be. Get it itemized.

This is just one example of an unexpected expense, and there are plenty more lurking out there. No one expects you to predict every single one of them. But the more diligently you try to figure out the true cost of each expense ahead of time, the more accurate your budget will be and the better job it will do in helping you figure out where and how you can afford to live.

Key Monthly Expenses

Not all expenses are equal. Your key monthly expenses are those essential things that you need to survive on your own, things such as rent, utilities, and food. It's important to budget for these things first. (Then, if there's money left over, you can figure out what kind of cable or Internet package you can afford!)

Many of your monthly expenses will be easy to calculate because they are **fixed**, meaning they will be for the same amount every time. For example, if you'll have to take public transportation every day and you know the monthly fare, that's a fixed cost. Once you select where you'll be living, the rent will become a fixed cost, too; but until you pick the place, that particular cost will remain unknown (although you should still try to have a ballpark figure in mind for initial budgeting purposes).

Other monthly expenses are **variable**, meaning they will fluctuate a bit each month. Consider your electric bill, which may be higher in summer because you're running an air conditioning unit. (By the way, many electric and gas companies will allow you to set up a payment plan that will balance your payments out so that you're always paying the same monthly amount.) Variable expenses can still be estimated with a fair degree of accuracy, and you'll gain experience doing so the longer you pay them. When starting out, play it safe by budgeting for the higher end of the likely range for each variable expense to make sure you're covering your costs.

Your key monthly expenses will include some or all of the following:

- rent (and probably renter's insurance)
- utilities such electricity, gas, telephone, cable
- transportation to get you to and from work/school (bus/train fare or gas for the car)
- food
- health insurance (which may be partially or entirely subsidized by your employer, your parents, your school, or the government)
- car insurance (if you have a car)
- loan payments (student, car, other)
- credit card payments
- water or trash (if billed separately from rent)
- taxes (if not automatically deducted)
- bank fees
- contribution to a retirement account (not absolutely necessary, but a good idea if you can manage it)

If you're not sure how to calculate some of these expenses, don't be afraid to ask. Your friends and relatives could be a big help and save you time. For example, if you know people living on their own in the city you plan on residing in, ask them how much they pay for electricity and gas every month. At least you'll have some ballpark figures to put into your budget.

A handful of your key expenses won't be monthly, but you still need to budget for them. This is particularly true if you own a car: You've got your annual auto registration fee, which can come as an unpleasant surprise if you're not prepared for it; your car insurance payments may well be biannual; it would be smart to assume a certain amount of car maintenance expenses on a quarterly or biannual basis. If you're in college, you'll have registration, tuition, and book expenses each semester.

To avoid wrecking your budget when these occasional bills come in, I strongly recommend that you budget for such key expenses on a *monthly* basis. How do you do this? Just take the total for the year of each such line item and divide by 12. This gives you a monthly amount. Put that amount in a savings account each month so that when the payment eventually comes due you'll have the money you set aside specifically for that expense ready for use.

Lifestyle Expenses

Once you have a decent idea of what your monthly income is and you have a pretty solid grasp of your key monthly expenses (both fixed and variable), you'll know more or less how much money you'll have left over on a monthly basis. This pool of money can be spent at your discretion on "lifestyle expenses"—those things that are important in order to enjoy a satisfying overall quality of life.

The range of possible lifestyle expenses is far too vast to put down in its entirety, so for now we'll just take a look at the starter list below. Hopefully, these items can stimulate your thought process when it comes to putting down your discretionary expenses into your budget. This can be particularly helpful while you're still in the planning stages. As I mentioned earlier in this chapter, it's a good idea to not underestimate how expensive living on your own can be.

- smartphone/cell phone (This is really more of a key monthly expense as opposed to a discretionary expense; but you *could* live without one for a month or two if you absolutely had to.)
- cable TV and/or Netflix
- car/public transportation/bike for nonessential purposes
- air conditioning/heating or electric fan
- buying lunch/brown-bagging lunch
- personal grooming
- discretionary shopping for clothing, books, etc.
- trip to visit the parents or vacation with a friend
- gym
- dining out/bars/cafés
- live entertainment/sporting events/movies
- club dues or hobby expenses
- pet expenses (food, toys, vet visits)
- pharmacy or personal supplies
- household supplies

As with your key monthly expenses, some of your lifestyle expenses will be fixed (like your gym membership bill) and easily calculable, while others will be variable. For the variable expenses, such as eating out, try to put down a budget number that's as realistic as you can manage. This can be a bit challenging at times, but it's well worth the effort. Your budget—even when it comes to your flexible expenses—has to be realistic; otherwise it's not going to be a valuable tool you can depend on.

And it's important to keep in mind that things don't always go as planned. Cars break down, the price of coffee goes up, and so on. That's why a key to successfully living on your own is to put aside some money for items that no one ever wants to spend money on but sometimes are forced to. For example, a cash reserve come in handy if you don't have medical insurance and you need some medical attention, such as urgent dental work. Or if that pair of old shoes you've been hoping you could wear for another three months unexpectedly gives out, you're going to want to have some funds ready to buy another pair.

On the happy side, having some money in reserve can allow for the occasional unexpected pleasure. Let's say you suddenly hear from your friend that your all-time favorite band is coming to town. Tickets are $65, but there's no way you're going to miss this concert. Wouldn't it be nice to have a little money set aside to pay for this?

Because of possibilities like these, you don't want the margins of your budget to be razor thin. Too much padding may not be realistic, but having no padding at all is just asking for trouble. Remember, you're doing this exercise before you actually have to spend a dime, so if you have to adjust some fixed expenditures in order to make room for the flexible ones, the time to make these decisions is before you sign on the dotted line anywhere.

WORD TO THE WISE

Because of the possibility of needing some added funds somewhere along the line, you should establish an emergency fund—money set aside for dealing with unexpected problems (or opportunities!). Even if you don't have a penny in that fund when you first land in your new place (which is possible, as you'll see below in the Start-up Costs section), you'll still want to insert a dollar amount in your monthly budget that you'll set aside for that purpose. The key is to just get started and do your best. In time, try to work your way up to saving 10% of your take-home income each month, until you've got an emergency reserve that can pay for three months of rent.

START-UP COSTS

Your start-up costs are a special set of budgetary items you might accidentally omit (if you weren't reading this book, in any case). These costs occur only once—just before and during your move—but they can be substantial. If you're moving into a college dorm, most of those costs will be laid out for you by the college, such as the choice of meal plans. If you're moving into your own place, the biggest start-up cost is likely to be the deposit your future landlord will require, which will be at least one month's rent but could be two. So if your rent is going to be $1,000 a month, you may have to fork over $3,000 when you sign the lease—your first month's rent plus two months' deposit. (And there may be a pet deposit on top of all that.)

You may incur some transportation expenses as you travel to move to your new apartment. If you're fortunate enough to already own some larger items of furniture to take with you that won't fit into the back of your car, you may need to hire a rental truck or even sign up a moving company. Other moving expenses may include boxes, tape, packing foam, fuel, pizza, etc.

Setting up your new digs will also involve costs. You may need to buy some major items like a bed or refrigerator, or basic furniture. If so, spend your time looking for good deals and consider buying used. If the place needs painting, you could hire a painter, or you could do it yourself for a lot less money. But if you intend to split the living room in half by putting up a wall in order to fit in a roommate, the landlord will definitely hire a professional to handle this job and then charge you for it. There may be utility hookup and deposit costs; investigate these.

And do you plan to buy renters' insurance to protect your personal property? Some landlords insist that you do, and it's a good idea in any case. Rates can be as low as $10–$15 a month, and you should be able to get it through your car insurance provider.

If you move to another state and have a car, you'll have to register it. And if you were on your parents' auto insurance policy, you'll probably need to get your own insurance. If you're moving far enough away, you may need to put aside some money to travel to the new city in order to find a place to live. And that task will probably require at least two trips, the second to go back and sign the paperwork.

CAUTION If you're going off to college, don't forget the cost of textbooks. Trust me, this single expense could break your budget into smithereens. Often your best bet here is to take a look at various online booksellers. This could save you a lot of cash compared to your school's bookstore.

Finally, there's a long list of essential household supplies that you should consider when figuring out your start-up costs:

- sheets
- towels
- pots and pans
- basic kitchen supplies
- pantry stock
- bathroom items (*do not* forget the shower curtain!)
- cleaning, laundry
- power strips and extension cords
- lamps

The good news here is that you can get some of these items from family. However, if you're the fifth kid in your household to be moving out, the cupboard is probably already bare of such necessities, in which case you'll have to factor in buying basic supplies.

Finally, there's one final start-up cost to consider: taking time off from work. Have you discussed this with your manager? Do you have vacation time to cover it? Will you have to take two or three days of unpaid leave? It's best to get this angle figured out well in advance to make sure you can get the time you need.

SquawkFox.com has a good First Apartment Essentials Checklist. Google it! And also check out the site's printable Moving Checklist Planner, which DOWNLOADS begins six weeks before your move through moving day. Another great site is **MyRegistry.com**, where you can register links to items you'd like to have bought for you by loving and thoughtful family members. The list can be for any occasion—like a first apartment—and can link to items on any shopping site on the web. It is an easy way to tell friends and family what you still need in your new place.

LIVING ON SAVINGS

Yes, your budget can include a column for the money in the bank you already have that you intend to spend down in order to live on your own. Is that always a dumb move? Definitely not. Let's say that the job opportunities in your hometown are nil, which means there's no way to land the type of job you really want without moving to where the job market is healthier. But the only job you're sure you can land when you get there would be flipping burgers at a fast-food restaurant, which won't pay the rent. If you have some savings, and are fairly certain that after a few months of pounding the sidewalk searching for a job in your chosen field you'll find one, then it would make sense to take such a leap of faith. But in that scenario, one of the most important factors in your budget becomes time. You'll need to figure out exactly how long your savings are going to help you get by.

Why is this so important? The most glaring example is that you don't want to sign a one-year apartment lease if your savings are going to run out in six months. It would be sad to have to move back home in order to be able to afford to eat, but a whole lot sadder if you were still paying rent someplace you can't afford to live.

 WORD TO **THE WISE** Skipping out on a lease is not a good idea. Even if you move a couple of states away so that your landlord will probably not be able to take you to court, your credit rating will be destroyed, and that's something potential employers look at. A poor credit rating could be harmful to your future earning potential for years to come.

Doing the smart budget preparation we're discussing in this chapter will save you from making a big mistake, but the greater likelihood is that it will help you to make the *right* decisions in the early stages of this great adventure of yours—so that you won't risk having to move back home to your parents having run out of money.

FOUR ROOKIE BUDGET MISTAKES

While creating a budget is a relatively straightforward exercise, there are some rookie mistakes that you need to watch out for. The worst one is overlooking taxes. Let's say you got a new job and you're told that your salary is going to be $40,000 a year. You may think that you then have $40,000 to spend every year, but that's far from true. Out of that money will come taxes, including federal income tax, any state or city taxes (the percentage of which will depend on where you live), and FICA taxes (Social Security and Medicare). There's a good chance that some $10,000 of that $40,000 will never reach your pocket. So make sure you know how much money you'll actually be taking home before attempting to create a budget. (More on taxes in Chapter 19.)

TaxFoundation.org has a state tax lookup tool on its front page and an easy-to-follow Federal Tax Rate Chart under "Tax Basics." Also, **PaycheckCity.com** has free payroll calculators for both salaried and hourly workers to help you better understand your paycheck.

WORD TO THE WISE

"The only difference between death and taxes is that death doesn't get worse every time Congress meets." –Will Rogers

The second most common mistake people make in creating a budget is ignoring the role of spending cash for small purchases. Everyone has little expenditures that occur almost every day, from transportation to buying a cup of morning joe, that can quickly add up. You have to allot for those little payments or else your budget will end up being way off base. The best way to get a handle on these costs is to download one of the numerous helpful phone apps that can track these expenses for you.

The third rookie mistake involves credit cards, and it can be a budget buster if you don't watch out. If you intend to use credit cards, then you have to take into account future interest payments. (If you're in the habit of paying off your credit card in full every month or you stick to a debit card, good for you—interest rates are not an item you need to be concerned about.) Credit cards can be helpful tools because they allow you to defer when you pay for things. But there's a price for this convenience: interest payments. Credit card interest rates can easily be 25%, so that if you buy something for $100 on credit and don't make more than the minimum payment every month, you'll actually still owe the entire $100 principal by the end of the year. Since each month you have to make at least the minimum payment on your credit card, you have to include that in your budget, too. These are rough numbers, but the point remains the same. If you're not going to pay for things right away, then there's a cost for doing so that you have to include in your budget.

FYI Even if you have no intention of charging any of your expenses, and so don't really need to worry about interest charges in your budget, it may be a good idea to get a credit card anyway. One can be very helpful in getting you through the occasional short-term emergency expense. Let's say you depend on your car to get to work and it develops a major problem that will take a few days to get fixed. If you don't have enough savings to pay for the repair, then charging that cost on a credit card may save your job. And you'll definitely need a charge card if you need to rent a car for a few days.

You can also keep track of your credit card expenses with smartphone budget apps that can keep track of interest, payments, and balance—often with the same app that you use to budget your checking account. With many apps, checking, savings, and credit card accounts can all be entered as three separate accounts.

And the biggest money mistake you can make is to create a budget and then ignore it. If it turns out you spend more than you make because you didn't update your budget as needed, you're going to be in for some rude surprises. So while you don't want to become a penny pincher, you also don't want to bury your budget at the bottom of a drawer never to be consulted. By regularly checking what you're actually spending against what you've budgeted, you'll be able to spot problems before they happen.

Your Budget

Now it's time to create your budget. Use the format below to begin the budget-making process, adjusting it to suit your needs.

Most personal budgets include pretty much the same items, but it's also possible that you may need to include something that other people may not. For example, if you have a health condition that requires daily treatment, like diabetes, you'd need to include either the cost of your medications or the cost of health insurance. Many young people forgo health insurance figuring they're healthy and will always remain so, but in some cases that's just not possible.

Again, some of your numbers may be vague right now, but don't worry about it. As you work your way through Chapter 2, which tells you how to go about researching where to live, you'll be able to come back to your initial budget and firm it up with some more accurate numbers, particularly with regard to rent, utilities, and transportation.

There are dozens of free web-based tools and calculators for your computer or apps for your phone that do a great job of helping you manage your budget, all without the possibility of an embarrassing computation error. **Mint.com** is a great place to start. And if you prefer to work offline, many online tools also offer downloadable copies of a budget template. If you have Microsoft Excel, go to **Office.com** and check out its downloadable budget templates, which offer the convenience of having the formulas already entered.

SAMPLE BASIC PERSONAL MONTHLY BUDGET

(Note: The number below are only *example* numbers. Your numbers may be very different.)

Projected Income	Budget
Main source of income (job, student loan, etc.)	$1,100.00
Secondary income, if any (part-time job)	$400.00
Other income, if any (money from parents?)	$100.00
Total Income:	**$1,600.00**

Key Monthly Living Expenses	Budget
Rent/Mortgage	$600.00
Utilities:	
Gas	$20.00
Water/Trash (included in rent)	$0.00
Electricity (average)	$40.00
Groceries	$155.00
Phone	$65.00
Subtotal Key Monthly Living Expenses:	**$880.00**

Stop here. Can you afford this apartment?

Regular Monthly Obligations	Budget
Health Insurance and Co-Pays	$95.00
Debt #1 — Student Loan	$100.00
Debt #2 — Credit Card	$40.00
Debt #3	$0.00
Basic Transportation:	
Public Transportation	$0.00
Car Payment	$0.00
Auto Insurance	$50.00
Fuel	$40.00
TV/Internet	$60.00
Prescriptions/Pharmacy	$0.00
Subtotal Regular Monthly Obligations:	*$385.00*
Total Living Expenses and Obligations:	**$1,265.00**

Stop here. Can you afford this?

SAMPLE BASIC PERSONAL MONTHLY BUDGET, CONT.

Discretionary (Lifestyle) Expenses per Month	Budget
Homeowners'/Renters' Insurance	$0.00
Gym Membership	$0.00
Clothing/Personal Grooming	$20.00
Dining Out	$40.00
Entertainment	$50.00
Savings	$100.00
Retirement	$0.00
Giving/Charity/Tithing	$0.00
Storage Rental	$0.00
Pet Expenses	$0.00
Laundromat	$20.00
Miscellaneous	$0.00
Subtotal Discretionary Expenses:	*$230.00*

Annual or Biannual Expenses	Budget (per month)
(Take the total estimate for the year and divide by 12 (or 6). This money should be put in savings each month to be available for annual or biannual payments.)	
Auto Registration	$10.00
Auto Maintenance	$20.00
Auto Club Membership (AAA)	$0.00
Taxes	$40.00
Club or Group Dues	$0.00
Hobby Expenses	$0.00
Miscellaneous	$0.00
Subtotal Annual/Biannual Expenses:	*$70.00*
Total Monthly Expenses:	**$1,565.00**
Balance (your total income minus all expenses):	**$35.00**

Do you have enough money to spare? Have you budgeted for putting some money away? Are you comfortable with this outlay and this margin for emergencies? Now you have a clearer view of whether you are prepared to live on your own.

MONEY SAVER Use this budget-making process as a good opportunity to calculate ways you can stretch your budget. For example, if you've gotten used to buying a mocha latte for $5 on your way to work every day, figure out how much you could save if you bought a thermos and made your own latte at home each morning. If your budget seems a little shy of what you need and there's no more loose change to dig out from under the couch pillows, try cutting back on purchasing ready-made foods. By preparing your own food you can give yourself a real financial boost, not to mention learn a handy skill!

PIERRE SAYS When I was a student spending my junior year in Paris, my only source of income was the money my parents were sending me every month. I pinched pennies, eating at the government-subsidized student restaurant religiously, no matter how bad the food. After a time, I actually started to build a nest egg. Someone was supposed to lend me a car to go to Italy at the Easter break, but then the offer was pulled at the last second. I said . . . well forget what I actually said . . . but in any case, I took my savings and bought an old Renault, which I used not only to go to Italy and back, but also to travel around Europe that summer. I didn't know what my goal was going to be when I started socking away whatever I could, but I was sure glad that I had the dough when I needed it.

A Quick Note about Long-Term Savings

In addition to saving some money for emergencies, as mentioned earlier, you should try to save some money long-term. I realize this may seem like an impossible goal at the moment, but it's still worth a try. Most people understand the basic benefits of slowly building up a nest egg, but there are certain short-term benefits, too. Consider this: Remember that you have to plan for taxes for any income you make? Well, you're entitled to skip paying taxes on the part of your income that you save in certain qualified retirement accounts. (You have to pay the taxes eventually, but not until you're retired, so it's not something you have to worry about for a while.) The big advantage of putting money into a retirement account is that you collect interest on your savings, including the amount that you otherwise would have paid in taxes.

TO LEAP OR NOT TO LEAP

In all likelihood, living on your own as compared to living under the family roof is going to require some sacrifices. If the list of what you'd have to give up is too long or painful, then maybe you'd prefer not to make this leap just yet. A horrible thought? It all depends, but if that's the conclusion you reach, the effort you put into making a budget won't be a total loss because now you'll have a set of realistic goals. You'll know that you have to either find a way of getting a job that pays more, or save a lot more while living with your parents so that when you do move out you have some funds to lean on.

It may be a good idea to show your budget to a trusted advisor, such as your parents or a good friend who has been through this process before. They will help to make sure that you haven't forgotten anything that will throw your numbers way off track. But in the end, you're the one who is going to have to decide whether or not this budget-making process has led you to the moment to spread your wings. To help you make this important decision, here are some questions that you'll want to think about if you're staring at your budget and all you see is a big question mark superimposed on it:

- Is this budget realistic or am I kidding myself?
- Would I be better off staying home for a while longer to bulk up my savings rather than live under conditions that would be less than ideal?
- Can I survive on a tight budget or will having to crimp my lifestyle make living on my own not worth it?
- Will working so hard to make money to pay day-to-day expenses force me to push off other goals I've dreamed of, like working on a political campaign or visiting all 50 states?
- What happens if I make this move and then discover it's not going to work out? How would I feel if I was forced to move back home?
- Is moving back even an option or will my parents have rented out my room?

As you can see, the questions you have to ask yourself are a mixture of both the practical and the philosophical. This is a time to get to know yourself a bit better. Some people know at a young age what they want to be when they grow up, while others never figure it out. You may not have thought of using a budget as the impetus to contemplating your entire future, but it's not so much the budget itself as this moment in your life that dictates this self-examination of where you may be headed.

An Inspirational Note

At this point in the chapter, you're well aware of the practical benefits of creating and sticking to a budget. And the emotional payoff of disciplined budgeting—a sense of purpose and control, a peace of mind—are equally important. But just in case you need a bit more inspiration, let me leave you with a few parting thoughts.

What's most painful about a budget is that it is going to highlight your financial limitations. You'd love to have a car, but if your budget is screaming "No way!" that can admittedly be frustrating. It's one reason why making budgets isn't up there with watching a movie or playing Frisbee.

But a budget also allows you to focus on goals. Not just vague ones, but distinct goals with dollar signs attached to them. Goals that move your life forward. If you figure out exactly how much a certain car would cost you, at least you'll know how much more you need to earn in order to get that car. If you decided to wait tables on weekends in order to save up for this car, you'd know how many months that would take, and how many weekends a month you may have to work to maintain car ownership once you acquired it. Most people who succeed in life have goals, and if you look at a budget as a goal-making machine, you'll have taken a big step toward achieving your much bigger goal: successfully living on your own.

CHAPTER **2** **HOW TO CHOOSE YOUR NEW NEIGHBORHOOD**

Safety, Lifestyle, Location

MAKING THE RIGHT CHOICE

So the decision has been made and you're definitely going to fly off on your own. Good for you. Even if you hit some rough patches, you can't live under your parents' roof forever. Now comes the fun but hard part. Fun because you're on your way to making your vision of living independently come true. Hard because realizing this goal will take a lot of heavy lifting on your part, and I'm not just talking about the pile of boxes containing your life's possessions.

Living on your own is one of the biggest decisions of your life, and it won't be a cakewalk because, unless you're very lucky, it will mean making a series of compromises about where you live, the money you spend, and the quality of your life. This chapter will help guide your thoughts and clarify your wants and needs as you go through the process of deciding where to live.

BUDGET

If you read Chapter 1, you already know the most important factor in deciding where you're going to live is your overall budget. Your initial budget probably had a number of question marks on the expense side. Now—as you get out there and start to narrow your focus and get a better sense of costs—remember to go back to your initial budget and pencil in more exact numbers, particularly when it comes to your rent. As you research places to live and your budget clarifies what you can afford, be sure to stay realistic; otherwise you could make a mistake you can't afford (for long). Leave some wiggle room because as time goes by the odds are that either the prices of what you budgeted for some items will go up or else some unexpected expenditure will arise that will eat into your finances.

LOCATION, LOCATION, LOCATION

If you didn't already know this, the price of real estate is strongly dependent on location. The odds are the neighborhood you most want to live in will be popular with many other people, which pushes up the prices—perhaps beyond your budget's reach. This dose of reality can feel like a slap in the face because it means that wherever you end up living will almost certainly not be your first choice—you'll probably have to compromise (a word you'll see a lot in this chapter).

Does that mean you shouldn't even bother looking in your preferred neighborhood in order to avoid disappointment? No, as long as you maintain the right attitude. It's sort of like buying a lottery ticket. If you do it feeling that your only option is jumping off a bridge if you don't win, then you're better off keeping the couple of bucks in your pocket. But if it's done in the right spirit, it's OK. The same is true with finding your dream place to live. It's possible you'll get very lucky and find the perfect place in terms of location and size at an affordable price. But what you mustn't do is waste too much time looking in neighborhoods that are out of your league.

WORD TO THE WISE   Once you've moved your search to neighborhoods you can afford, it's a good idea to list all the potential positive and negative factors in each area you look at. Your list should include things like safety, transportation options, cost versus size, solo living or sharing, and shopping convenience. This little exercise will help you pinpoint your two or three best living options.

SAFETY, THE NUMBER ONE FACTOR

Why is safety the number one factor you should examine? It's one thing to *say* you could put up with living in an unsafe neighborhood, but quite another to actually feel threatened while going to and from your place. It's even worse to feel unsafe while inside it.

Safety is also going to be your family's number one issue. They've undoubtedly provided you with a safe environment and they're going to be very uncomfortable worrying about your safety. Yes, it's your life, but they're a big part of it and so they have an important stake in your health and happiness.

   Your first place to look when deciding a neighborhood's level of safety is the local police department's crime map, which is probably available online. If that doesn't really give you what you need, you can also stop into the local precinct and ask questions about a particular block or even building.

Touring a neighborhood can also tell you a lot about it. If on a commercial avenue you observe lots of boarded-up stores, with the few that are open selling mostly items like liquor and cigarettes, and with the staff secured behind two-inch-thick, floor-to-ceiling plexiglass plates, don't waste your time! Look somewhere else. But even if the area doesn't show any obvious signs of crime, I recommend you take a stroll (rather than drive) down several blocks during both the day and the evening. Take note of anything that makes you uncomfortable. Without prying into people's privacy, pay attention to things such as litter, yard maintenance standards, alley maintenance, cars (their general condition, bumper stickers, orderly parking), and patios (are they well maintained or messy?). If the neighborhood is kept up at a level you are comfortable with, you're probably ready to look at it more closely for a specific apartment or building.

PIERRE SAYS When you get to the stage where you are seriously considering a particular neighborhood, you can take an even deeper look at safety by asking the residents whether they feel safe. Stop people on the street and say you're thinking of moving there and get an opinion. I've found that most people will cooperate, and you'll probably pick up some useful info, like how well the buses run, to cite one possibility. It's helped me in the past, and it helped my daughter in 2013 when she moved to Jersey City, which got badly flooded during Superstorm Sandy. Her questions weren't so much about crime, in this case, but about just how badly the floods had affected the block she was looking at. She wanted to get the opinion of folks who lived there and had experienced the impact of that terrible storm.

Even in a safe neighborhood, you can't ignore the possibility of being a victim of crime. To increase your safety, examine potential living places for any safety weaknesses, like an unsecured window overlooking a fire escape (not that fire escapes are bad things!).

One cheap form of protection is a timer for one or two lights. While professional burglars won't be fooled by a light that always goes on and off at the same times, they probably wouldn't be targeting your place anyway because they'd think it doubtful you'd have much worth stealing. (Replacement costs to you of stolen goods might be considerable, but a thief will get next to nothing for used electronic equipment.) Amateur thieves, on the other hand, are more likely to skip an apartment with a light on—they won't have been casing your place, and they're probabably just looking for a quick hit.

 It's always worth investigating the cost of renters' insurance, even if you're moving into a safe, low-crime neighborhood. Being in a safe neighborhood won't help you if your possessions are destroyed in a fire.

The costs of gates and better door locks, not to mention alarms, can be considerable. Rather than pretend you don't need any additional security equipment, mention it to your parents. They may be more than willing to offer up the cash just to give themselves some added peace of mind. If you have parents, relatives, or friends who live nearby, consider giving them a spare set of keys. This could be a lifesaver if you get locked out at 3 A.M. when an all-night locksmith will probably charge you $250 to help you get back inside.

A NEIGHBORHOOD'S LIFESTYLE IS ALSO IMPORTANT

A NORC is a naturally occurring retirement community—that is, a neighborhood where a lot of old people live. If you're planning on writing the Great American Novel in your new digs in your spare time, then maybe having a lot of old people as neighbors who go to bed at 9 P.M. would be a good thing. But on the other hand, if you'd prefer to come home to an area where there are busy cafés or a couple of pubs frequented by people your age, then a NORC might not suit your lifestyle.

So, have you thought about which lifestyle factors are most important to you in a neighborhood? If you're a gym rat, then having a nearby place to work out could be key. If you have no intention of having a car, then an area's "walkability" is a factor. Are there good grocery stores, restaurants, and shops within walking distance? Is "bikeability" important to you? If so, is a prospective neighborhood sufficiently bike friendly with plenty of safe bike lanes on the streets? A vegan might want a good vegan restaurant nearby. If you eat a gluten-free diet, are there good eating options in the area? List your lifestyle goals in order of importance and use the list when checking out a particular neighborhood.

To get one of the characteristics in a neighborhood that is most important to you may mean giving up something else. A hipster neighborhood might be a lot of fun, but it's probably going to be on the noisy side and perhaps offer less privacy (in which case, getting a place where your bedroom doesn't face the street might be the solution to getting a good night's sleep). A creative, craft-oriented section of the city could be just what you're looking for, but it could also be on the poor side and perhaps suffer from street crime. Face it, unless you have an unlimited budget, there are going to be trade-offs when examining each neighborhood. Deciding how to factor all of them into your decision-making process will be your biggest challenge. By spending the time needed to choose wisely, you're more likely to end up falling in love with your new neighborhood; when that happens, overlooking its few faults will come naturally.

When you've reached the point of considering a specific apartment, make sure to check that your cell phone works in it. Since fewer people are signing up for landlines, being able to receive and place calls in the place where you live is vital.

TRANSPORTATION

The shorter your commute the better, but in most instances the places with the shortest commutes are the most popular and therefore the most expensive. If you're sure your commute from a particular neighborhood is going to be 30 minutes or less, then there's not much to worry about, unless the cost of transportation is a major factor. But if you're going to have a long commute, don't sign on the dotted line for a particular place until you've actually experienced the commute and talked with some of the other commuters. There may be some particular quirks about a certain commute that will make it much longer than you think—perhaps a persistent traffic snarl at 8:15 every morning, or a difficult bus-to-train transfer. A twenty minute walk to the train might be fine on a spring day, but will be miserable in the heart of winter if you have to do it day after day.

 When figuring public transportation costs, make sure to find out the cheapest options. There are often monthly passes of some sort that will reduce the normal fare.

Keep in mind that time isn't the only factor when judging a commute. If you're sure to get a seat, you can make productive use of your commuting time. But if you're going to be squeezed like a sardine, you'll be unable to do anything but listen to music on your phone. Also, the more transfers you have to make, the more likely you'll encounter screw ups. This could be a problem if you have a boss who doesn't tolerate anyone being late for work.

If you have a car, then parking is going to be a major concern. If you'll have to spend 20 minutes every night in a desperate hunt for a parking spot near your apartment, you'll rue moving into that neighborhood. And the only way to find that out may be to actually try parking at what you estimate would be your normal arrival time.

On a similar note, I definitely recommend actually *doing* the commutes in both directions at the approximate time you'd do them, leaving from the apartment and returning there from work/school. It will help you understand things like rush hour, the heaviness of pedestrian or bike traffic, slow lights, bad transfer connections (on a bus), dangerous streets (on a bike), and so on. Plus, doing this will help you spot *good* things, like services you can use on your way to and from work/school: dry cleaners, gyms, grocery stores, etc.

COST VERSUS SIZE

While you're checking out your number one neighborhood, be sure to note the size of the apartments you visit. You want to develop a sense of what 300 square feet of living space feels like so that if you see an ad for such a place, you'll know whether or not it's acceptable to you. Assuming you're on a fixed budget with regard to rent, one of the deciding factors will be the trade-offs between added space and longer commuting time.

Keep in mind that even if you don't cook now, the odds that you'll be doing so will grow as the cost of eating out depletes your wallet. So rather than shrug off the fact that a potential living space has pitiful cooking facilities, bear in mind that such a deficiency could cost you a lot of money in the long run.

If you know you're getting certain furniture for your new place, remember to factor that in as you look at places to live. For example, if having your grandmother's bedroom set is really important to you, then you're going to need a one-bedroom place and not a studio.

LIVING SOLO OR WITH A ROOMMATE

The most common way to reduce your living costs is to share your space with other people. If you've already been down that road in college (and learned that sharing space with strangers is much different from sharing space with family members), then you know whether you can deal with this sort of living arrangement. If you've never experienced it, then you have to think more carefully about whether you can adapt to living with roommates.

Having roommates in college can be different from having them when you're in the workforce. In college, if you feel like getting away from your living quarters for a while, you'll typically have a multitude of options, such as libraries and coffee shops. That may not be the case if you're sharing an apartment in a city.

There are several ways of going about this process. The first is to look for a place where one or more people are looking for a new roommate. Or, a riskier gambit is to move by yourself into a place that you can afford in the long run only by living with a roommate, and then start looking for that roommate the moment after you've signed the lease. Finally, you could seek out someone else in your position and team up to look for a place to live.

The first method is probably the most common and easiest to do, particularly if your belongings are minimal and you're pretty flexible about the amount of space you need. Websites like **Craigslist.org** will give you many options to choose from. The nice thing about this approach is that you immediately get a sense of the space you'd be sharing. The downside is that you probably don't know the current residents very well and can't be sure if you'll all get along. Of course, if you only have a single roomful of stuff to deal with, moving out probably won't be too painful, should it come to that.

Moving into a place you really like but can't afford is a bit of a gamble—especially if you're picky about whom you live with, as the process of finding a roommate can take a long time. In this scenario, you could get stuck paying a lot more rent than you planned on until you find a suitable roommate. But if you have a little extra cash, this option might be attractive because it gives *you* control, over both where you live and the roommate you end up living with.

 CAUTION In the above scenario, keep in mind that it won't be just the rent that you'll have to be fully responsible for, but the full one or two months' security deposit. Be very careful when reading the lease to make sure that the landlord will allow your future roommate to be added to the lease.

The third method usually involves people who are already friends (although this isn't always the case). One benefit of this approach is that you can split up the apartment exploration work, making the search process less time consuming than if you were doing it all yourself. But the key advantage of selecting your roommate in advance is that you know that you're compatible with him or her. Of course, there are people who make great friends but lousy roommates, so you have to be a little more choosy with roommates than friends because you're going to be spending a lot more time with them. Your life isn't a situation comedy, and in real life someone's annoying habit could really get under your skin. Keep in mind that any bad habits that you might have could also impact this relationship, so take a good look in the mirror so that you don't start off on the wrong foot.

If you have problems reaching agreement on an apartment with the person or people you plan on living with, this might be a sign of difficulties to come, and you should rethink your roommate selection.

CAUTION

Do not sign a lease without first reading the material in Chapter 3 on leases. These are legal documents that cannot be treated lightly. If you find a great place to live, you may have no choice but to sign a lease that's all to the landlord's benefit, but at least don't do so until you understand the rights you may be signing away.

So Many Choices

There's a better than even chance that what you're going to face is a situation where not all the pieces fall nicely into place and no particular living situation stands out. Rather, you'll be faced with several choices. Each will have different advantages and disadvantages, and making the decision of where to go won't be easy.

After considering all of your options in terms of price range and type of apartment you're looking for, you should have a very clear idea of what your deal breakers are in terms of neighborhood, safety, and lifestyle. If you know what you can't live without and what you can compromise on, spotting the neighborhood that's going to be right for you becomes a much easier process.

While you're the one who's going to be living in your new space and you have the final decision, don't hesitate to ask for advice from family or friends who've gone through similar experiences. It's so easy to miss the obvious mistake, especially when you're faced with a great number of different options. Asking for advice doesn't mean that you have to take it, but if someone else helps you to avoid making a big mistake, that advice would be worth quite a lot.

What Are Your Neighborhood Deal Breakers and Must-Haves?

Since few people will find a neighborhood that is absolutely perfect for them, consider what your highest priorities are for where you would like to live and be willing to compromise on the other things. If you can identify two or three neighborhood deal breakers, you'll trim down your search considerably.

Here are some potential deal breakers to consider:

- unaffordable rents for your budget
- continuing violent crime (a pretty big deal breaker for most people)
- continuing petty and property crime: vehicle break-ins, amateur thefts, vandalism (Some people can deal with this in exchange for other benefits in a neighborhood; can you?)
- neighborhood noise: traffic, sirens, people out and about at night
- lack of transportation choices, few bus routes, no bike lanes
- lack of accessibility: few nearby services, grocery stores, parks, etc.
- general messiness, sidewalk litter, unkept yards
- lack of street lighting
- lack of parking options
- graffiti and tagging

On the positive side, have you thought about your neighborhood *must-have* list? What neighborhood benefits are you looking for? Some things to consider are:

- affordable rents to fit your budget
- low crime rates and high security
- quiet and privacy
- culture and entertainment: restaurants, theaters, galleries, clubs, cafés, lots of social activity
- walkability, bikeability, lots of bike lanes
- outdoor options: parks, trails, lots of yards and community spaces
- proximity to services: gym, grocery, pharmacy, shops, salons, etc.
- easy commute to work/school

What are you willing to trade off for what you want most? What set of compromises will allow you to land a place of your own? If you're looking to live on your own for the first time, try to avoid rushing into anything. Don't settle on the first place you look at. Make sure that at the very least you visit and research several potential neighborhoods and places to live before making your choice. Before long, you'll get a better sense of what works for you and what doesn't. And continue to refine your budget to make sure that you stay on financial track.

Keep at it. It won't take too long before the right place will come along. You'll know it when you see it, and you'll be fully prepared to grab it when the opportunity arises.

CHAPTER 3

NAILING DOWN THE APARTMENT YOU WANT

Now That You've Found It, Here's How to Make It Yours

PROCEED WITH CAUTION

Whether you're dancing up and down because you've found the apartment of your dreams or are sort of down in the dumps because you're being forced by your budget to settle for an apartment that's less than ideal, don't sign on the dotted line until you've read this chapter. Landlords take leases very seriously, which means that you should, too. Yes, they can be filled with barely understandable legalese, but once you sign one it has a powerful hold on you. In general there's not much you can do about what it says, but once you're at the point where a landlord has made up a lease in your name, you do have some leverage. The landlord has probably told others that the apartment is taken and doesn't want to start advertising all over again, so it's possible to squeeze some small concessions at this point. And if there's anything major you overlooked, then you want to know about it before the ink has left your pen, not after it's drying on the page.

THINGS TO LOOK FOR DURING THE APARTMENT WALK-THROUGH

Before signing the lease, you'll want to conduct a careful and formal inspection of the apartment (called a walk-through), typically along with the apartment manager or building owner. The most important "detail" to nail down is to make sure you're getting the right apartment. If you visited apartment 2A, the lease should say that you're getting Apt. 2A. If you only visited a model apartment, make sure you visit the exact apartment you're going to be getting before signing the lease, as it might not be identical to the model you saw. Will management companies pull a fast one like showing you an apartment that has sun shining through the windows and then giving you the one apartment in the complex overlooking a brick wall? It's been known to happen, and the only way you can protect yourself is to insist on seeing the exact apartment that's going to have your name on the door.

Another important reason to inspect your future digs is that you want to make sure that everything functions, so flush the toilet, run the water, and see if the refrigerator is cold, the dishwasher works, etc. Check whether the electrical outlets and light switches function properly. (Don't be shy about bringing along a night-light or your phone charger and plugging it into each outlet to make sure they all work.) If you discover anything that doesn't work properly and will need to be repaired, either before you move in or after, make sure that this is mentioned in the lease. If the landlord agrees to paint or change the carpets or linoleum, make sure that is specified in the lease before you sign it. A verbal commitment isn't worth the hot air it comes to you in.

If you've seen signs of vermin (checking for roach or mouse traps behind the stove is one good way to know what past tenants have experienced), find out whether the landlord is responsible for sending an exterminator regularly and, if so, whether it's in the lease.

Ask if you can get a copy of the lease before the day you are actually going to sign it (for example, you may want to do the walk-through on a Friday and plan to sign the lease the next day). If when examining the lease you don't understand much of it, show it to a lawyer, or at least someone else who has experience with such documents. Leases are legally binding and once you sign it, you're stuck with the terms for the duration of the lease.

WORD TO THE WISE Odds are you're not going to like many of the terms of the lease because they're written by the landlord's lawyer to favor the landlord. Although reading a lease is difficult, because of both the legalese and being confronted in writing with all the ways in which your rights are stripped, it's still important for you to know what you're signing.

Your Walk-through Checklist

During your walk-through, be sure to do the following:

- Check the cell phone reception.
- Ask about the parking situation: garage, stall, or street?
- Review the complex's common areas—what are the hours and activity prohibitions? Are they well maintained?
- Learn about garbage collection. When does it occur? Who's responsible?

- Find out if Internet services are provided? If so, do they work? Or will you have to call either the phone or cable company to see what services are available at that address?

Then carefully check the condition of the items in this next list. Do any need to be repaired or improved? Don't be shy about noting problems; after all, you'll be the one who has to live with them if they don't get fixed.

- Are the electrical outlets modern and do they work? Are there enough? Is there anything in the lease prohibiting using a power strip?
- What's the exterior lighting situation, in both the front and the back of the unit? Are there functioning porch lights and security lights?
- Are the windows, screens, and window locks in good shape? Do they open without difficulty and secure properly?
- What is the condition of the doors, particularly those leading to the outside? Check the latches and locks. Do the doors open and close smoothly? How many sets of keys will you be given? And who has keys to the apartment? Will they let you install your own lock, if you want?
- Does the apartment have smoke and carbon monoxide detectors installed? If so, test them to make sure the batteries are good. And if there's a fire extinguisher, check to be sure the tamper seal is still in place. Is the unit charged?
- If you're unable to test the heating and air conditioning (for example, the heating is off in summer), then make sure the lease states that the landlord must provide both.
- Are there preexisting holes, cracks, or water stains in the walls to take note of? If your lease says that you have to leave the apartment in the condition you found it, take pictures of any existing damage so you won't have to repair it when it's time to leave.
- What's the condition of the floors and carpets? Are there holes or stains, or evidence of severe wear and tear? Again, if you might be held responsible, take pictures before you move in.
- Does the hot-water heater work? How new is it? Where is the pilot light?
- Is there an electrical breaker box or a power meter you should be concerned about?

- How much storage is available inside the apartment (closets, cupboards, etc.)? Is it enough? Do you also get an outside storage space?

The kitchen:

- Check the appliances to make certain they all work.
- Check the drains and the hot water in the sink.
- Check the electrical connection to the oven and the refrigerator.
- Does the refrigerator light function?
- Look inside cabinets and under the sink. Is there water damage or evidence of pests?
- Measure for space to place a microwave and small appliances.

The bathroom(s):

- Check the water pressure and hot water.
- Check all drains to make sure they're not clogged. Is there obvious water damage under the sink?
- Test-flush the toilet with toilet paper.

The living room and bedroom(s):

- Check on the size of these rooms in relation to your furniture. Take measurements and write them down or put them in your phone. You might want to also measure the closets.

 Take a night-light to check outlets, a flashlight to check under the sinks and in dark cupboards, and a measuring tape to measure rooms for your larger items (bed, sofa, desk, bookcases, etc.). Measure your largest furniture items in advance and record them in your phone or on a notepad for later reference. If there are things that need fixing or improving, ask the manager what can be fixed before move-in. Take lots of photos before signing a lease. Keep these photos in your digital archives in case you need them later. Talk to neighbors if you can. Ask about the noise in the building, what the landlord is like, any safety issues, and how other tenants like living in the building.

Common Terminology

Leasing versus renting month by month: A lease is a document that says how long you must stay in the apartment and pay rent. It says lots of other stuff, but that's the key. If you're renting month by month, there's a chance you might not be asked to sign a lease, although most landlords will still require one.

Security deposit: Since some tenants try to skip paying the last month's rent or leave the apartment in such disrepair that the landlord will have to spend a lot of money before renting it again, landlords require a security deposit, usually one or two months' worth of rent. You're supposed to get that back after you've left and the landlord has inspected the apartment and found the condition to be satisfactory.

Cleaning deposit: Some landlords insist that you clean the apartment thoroughly before you leave and ask for a deposit in case you fail to do so.

Walk-through: An examination of the premises before you sign any legal papers.

Pet deposit: If an apartment allows pets, you might be asked for a deposit in case your pet does any major damage to the place.

First and last months' rent: First month's rent is just that, while some landlords will also ask you to pay the last month's rent up front (similar to the security deposit).

ALL ABOUT LEASES

 Know your rights! Check out **hud.gov** and search for "tenant rights" for your state.

Since the main audience for this book is people moving out into a place of their own, your likely first encounter with a legal document will be with a lease. You may not be legally able to sign a lease if you are under 21 in some states and your parents may have to sign for you. But assuming you are old enough, you need to read a lease carefully before signing, and in this section we'll go over what to look for.

In addition to signing the lease, you may be asked to initial every clause, proving that you read it and understand the conditions, which is all the more reason to carefully read the lease and make sure you really do understand all the conditions.

CAUTION To be honest, if good places to live are scarce in the neighborhood you want to move to and you've found a rare vacant apartment, you may not have any choice but to sign the lease that's put down in front of you, no matter how unfair it is.

WORD TO THE WISE Make sure you get a copy of the signed lease from your landlord. Keep your copy in a safe place.

Rent

The first thing to make sure you understand is how much you'll be paying on a monthly basis. Just because you were told the rent was $1,000 a month, for example, doesn't mean a thing if you sign a lease that says it's $2,000, because at that point you're legally bound to pay $2,000. In all probability any differences between what you were told and what the lease says won't have that much of a spread. But if you're going to be on a tight budget, even an extra $100 a month may make a big difference to you, so you need to understand what other charges affect your monthly outlay, which will be spelled out in the lease. For example, a lease will tell you whether any or all utilities are included. If they're not, you'd better be sure of approximately how much these monthly costs will be when deciding whether your budget will allow you to stay in this place.

MONEY SAVER Heating costs can be significant, so if you're fully responsible for them, make sure you are given an accurate estimate of what they are, especially if they won't kick in for a few months until the seasons change. See if you can take some steps to reduce your heating bills by reviewing the apartment's door and window sealing and insulation. (See Chapter 5 for more ideas on reducing energy costs.)

Security Deposit

Your lease will also tell you what security deposit you will owe when signing the lease. It's usually one or two months' rent. If it's two months, and the rent will be $1,000, you'll need to give the landlord a check for $3,000 when signing the lease—so you have to make sure you have that sum in the bank.

You're supposed to get that deposit back when you move out, but the landlord is probably entitled to withhold some of it to repair any damages and won't give you your deposit back until you've left and the apartment's been inspected. Since the landlord may charge you an outrageous price to fix anything broken, you may be better off doing such repairs yourself, as well as taking care not to cause too much damage during your stay. On the other hand, the lease may say that the landlord will deduct certain costs, like cleaning your apartment, no matter what condition you leave it in, in which case you wouldn't want to pay for something like cleaning the carpet if you're going to be charged for it in any case.

 States offer tenants a number of protections, including regulations concerning how landlords must handle security deposits, how eviction notices are handled, and so on. It's well worth your time to become acquanted with the rights granted to renters in your state.

 WORD TO THE WISE As mentioned previously, if you notice any damage in the apartment when first looking at it, take pictures to prove that you didn't cause this damage and so are not responsible. Let the landlord know of this damage and offer copies of the pictures so no questions will arise when you leave. If you and your landlord haven't gotten along, take pictures of the empty apartment after you leave so that you have proof of the condition in which it was left. Keep in mind that since the landlord already has your money, you're in a position of weakness when it comes to such negotiations.

Roommates

If you plan on moving in with roommates, make sure that everyone's name is on the lease. Otherwise if one roommate skips out without paying the rent, you'll be responsible. You might be responsible in any case, per the lease, but at least you'll have a legal leg to stand on when it comes to going after your ex-roommate for the money.

If you think you might want to have a roommate later on, make sure that the lease allows this. If it's a boyfriend or girlfriend, that may not be something the landlord can forbid (depending on state laws), but if it's a paying roommate, then the landlord may be allowed to prevent that. The same is true for subletting. Again, the lease should say what rights you have.

Subletting means that the tenant who signed the lease moves out, possibly for only a limited time until the lease expires, and allows someone else to live in the apartment. That person would pay rent to the tenant, who in turn would pay the landlord. If you are thinking about subletting an apartment from someone, ask to see their lease agreement. If the lease forbids subletting, either don't accept an offer to sublet or at the very least understand the risk that the landlord could throw you out at any time if you do so.

Your lease will be for a specific period of time and all those (you and any roommates) signing the lease are responsible for paying the rent until the lease is up. If you move out before the end of the lease and can prove the landlord rented it out afterward, you might get away with not paying the rent on all the remaining months, but otherwise a landlord would have the right to go after you, including potentially garnishing your wages, even if you no longer live there.

The lease will probably say how much notice you have to give before moving out.

Info about How to Pay the Rent, Pets, Renters' Insurance, and More

The lease will tell you how to pay your rent. It will say by what date it must be paid and to whom to pay it. You should always pay by check in order to have a paper trail to prove that you paid your rent. If the landlord demands cash, which might happen if you are renting a small apartment within a house, then make sure to get a receipt every single month so that you can later prove you paid your rent in a timely manner.

If you have a pet, or plan to get one, make sure that pets are permitted. If you own a washing machine and dryer, the lease will tell you whether or not such equipment is permitted. (Landlords may be afraid of leaks, and if electricity is included in the rent, that may also be a factor in a landlord not permitting certain equipment.)

The lease may require you to take out renters' insurance, which isn't a bad thing to have; in fact, I recommend it. The costs are generally reasonable, but you do need to factor in that cost into your monthly budget.

If you think you may want to stay beyond the term of the lease, you can assume that the new lease will stipulate more money. You should ask whether the terms of that new lease can be included in the current one, so that if you do stay the new rent won't go up more than the percentage specified in the lease.

If you are sure that you will stay in an apartment for longer than a year, you might be better off financially signing a longer lease that will lock in the monthly rent. Many leases have a built-in escalation clause for each year but at least you'll know exactly what your rent increase will be. In all likelihood, if you re-sign a one-year lease, the percentage of increase in rent will be greater than if you sign a multiyear lease to begin with.

If the apartment comes with a parking space, check that details about this are spelled out in the lease. If the apartment comes with a specific parking spot, the location should be noted. If there's a fee for a parking space, the amount should also be specified in the lease.

If you think you may want to add any locks, check to see whether or not that is specifically mentioned. And if this is allowed, do you have to supply keys to the landlord? (This probably isn't a bad idea. For instance, if there's a leak coming from your apartment when you're away, the landlord needs the keys in order to get in to stop it.)

PIERRE SAYS

At the start of my junior year in college, I stayed in a dorm the first few nights and then started looking for a room to rent. I found one in a neighborhood I liked. It was a garret, meaning it was on the top floor overlooking some other nearby roofs and the ceiling slanted down pretty steeply. When I was being shown the room I saw a sink at one end and next to it a curtain. I assumed that behind the curtain was where the toilet was located. Well, I assumed wrong—the toilet was in the hall. Not the end of the world, but it was a rookie mistake not to have checked every nook and cranny before signing on the dotted line.

4 MOVING IN

Get into Your New Place without Losing Your Mind

YOUR PLAN FOR LOW-STRESS MOVING

They say that moving is one of the most stressful things you can do in your life (along with changing jobs and getting married). The sheer number of tasks can feel overwhelming, and many people have a lot of anxiety about making a change, even if it is a positive change. But the problems can be greatly reduced if you have a plan, create a task list and a time line, and stay on schedule. This chapter will help break down the tasks involved in moving into an apartment, so you can stay on track with your goals without suffering over-the-top stress. Be sure to check out the handy-dandy moving task list and timeline at the end of the chapter to help you stay on top of it all.

TIMING YOUR MOVE

While it might not be obvious, one of the trickiest parts of moving is the timing. Leases, for the most part, expire and begin at the end or beginning of a month. That may not leave you much turnaround time unless you plan for it. For example, if you're moving into an apartment on May 1 and the old tenant moved out on April 30, you won't have access until the day you move in and there may be things that need to be done to the apartment, some of which you'd like done before all your possessions are in place.

More often than not, though, there is a delay between the former tenant moving out and your available move-in date. Most landlords are required to give the space a deep cleaning and fix any issues noted during a walk-through, tasks which take usually five to ten days. The rent for that first month would be prorated. If you are going to be the one doing the cleaning or fixing up, make sure you negotiate a reduction in the cleaning deposit for the time and effort you are putting in. Overall, this is something that calls for a little bit of research on a state-by-state basis. Knowing what is the responsibility of the landlord before moving in will be helpful.

Prepping Your New Apartment

There may be repairs that need to be made to your new place, especially painting. It's much easier to paint an empty room than one full of furniture. If it's the landlord's responsibility, that's great, but if it's something you'll be doing you will have to figure out when you can do it and how that fits into your moving schedule. Painting is time consuming because walls must be prepared first (holes need to be patched, walls may need sanding, and primer needs to be put down before paint). The prep process will probably take longer than the actual application of paint because your prep work must dry before you can begin painting. So if you're going to be painting the place, plan on getting access to it at least three days before you actually move in order to complete the task.

CAUTION If you're going to have floor work done (sanding and finishing) as well, you need to build in even more time as you can't be doing your wall work while the floors are being worked on and then drying. That's another twenty-four hours that you need, at least.

Timing the Setup of Your Utilities

Another timing aspect of moving is utilities (see Chapter 5 for the full lowdown on dealing with utility companies). Depending on the utility, you may have to be in the apartment to allow a worker in to get things going. Even if all you need is someone to throw a switch somewhere in a central building, you're unlikely to get service within mere minutes of your call for assistance. Prepare to wait. If you're lucky, you may be able to schedule service people from all the utility companies—phone, gas, electricity, Internet, cable—to come on the same day, or during the period you're painting. But that won't happen unless you work the phones very carefully and give utility companies enough notice.

WORD TO THE WISE Call your utility companies several weeks in advance to schedule a service turn-on date at the new address. Get information from your landlord about any special switches required. Ask providers about how long service turn-on takes and the deposits that need to be paid. You don't want any surprises on that score.

CAUTION You may be saying to yourself that you don't need a landline, so no phone company visit, and that you will watch TV on your laptop, so no cable company visit. But if you want to use a computer, you'll need Wi-Fi, and that service will probably be provided by your local phone or cable company. This is where your research about the availability of services at your new address is vital. If you need high-speed Internet but the service isn't available or is slower at that address, you need to know your options.

And there may be other timing issues. For example, if the place you're moving into, or even the place you're moving out of, requires the use of an elevator, when you're allowed to use that elevator(s) to move may be regulated. If there's a freight elevator that can be operated only by a building employee, you will have to reserve time to use it. You won't be allowed to use the passenger elevator to move anything that you can't carry in your arms. Since any tenants moving in or out will probably be moving at the end or beginning of a month, possibly the same time you're moving, they may have already reserved the elevator on the day you need it and then you'll be out of luck. So as soon as you know when and where you're moving, if there's a freight elevator involved, you want to reserve it ASAP.

Timing Your Moving Helpers

Once you've done your research and set everything up for the move, ask for help on the move-in date. Ten to fourteen days before moving, use social media to see who might be available. Private-message your best friends to ask for the favor, but go ahead and put a shout-out on social media to see if other friends and acquaintances are up for helping you. You never know who might think hanging out with you for the day will be fun.

WORD TO THE WISE Don't forget to look at your own schedule! Can you make the move during a single weekend? Do you need to arrange for time off from work or school?

Timing Your Change-of-Address Tasks

Before you move, you'll also want to take care of changing your address. You need to notify your family and friends, your employer and/or school, banks and other financial institutions, clubs and associations, and magazines. You can fill out a change-of-address form at the post office and hand it over to a postal worker. But you can also do this online at **USPS.com**. Or you can go to **www.usa.gov** and get links to the Post Office change-of-address form, as well as the change-of-address links for the Social Security office, driver's license/ID, and voter registration. You have to complete these changes of address at least two weeks prior to your move for them to be in effect by your move-in date.

Be sure to change the address on your bank accounts, credit cards, and various online accounts, such as PayPal or Amazon (especially if you love Amazon's 1-Click option!). You can change all of these things online almost automatically, although your bank may ask for verification, so you might want to call that one in.

PACKING

Of course, before you can move you have to pack up your belongings. It's not that complicated, but there are some pieces of advice that may help you.

Packing Supplies

You're going to need boxes—probably lots of them—so try nearby liquor stores. Their boxes are less likely to have bugs, or their eggs, than those from a supermarket as food attracts insects but closed liquor bottles don't. Department stores and bookstores are also good places to look for boxes.

U-Haul has affordable boxes for sale, and you can return any you don't use for a full refund. U-Haul also recycles your used U-Haul boxes for free when you're done with them, so you don't have to fill up your trash bins with them, thereby avoiding your neighbors' wrath. Bankers boxes can be purchased at any office supply store and are good for small, heavy items like books and files.

DOWNLOADS

The web is full of places where you can get new or used boxes. Check out **UHaul.com/exchange** for any used boxes people may have in your area. If you want to purchase new boxes, there are plenty of online options (for example, **CheapCheapMovingBoxes.com**).

Here's a list of other handy moving items you're going to want to have available:

- marker pens for labeling boxes
- newspaper/newsprint and/or bubble wrap for packaging
- packing tape (Also consider getting a heavy-duty tape dispenser as it makes reinforcing boxes much faster and easier.)
- a box cutter for opening up boxes at your new place
- a hand truck to move stacks of boxes
- a furniture dolly for larger pieces of furniture

You can purchase all of these things at an office supply store, storage facility, or a local vehicle rental company outlet.

Do you have a particularly large or awkwardly shaped piece of furniture you need to move? And does your new place have a particularly tight entryway, or perhaps a staircase to contend with? If so, consider taking a few careful measurements beforehand so that you don't end up lugging Uncle Morton's grand piano across two states, only to discover it can't fit in your apartment!

Out with the Old

Use moving time as an excuse to get rid of stuff you don't want. No point in packing and lugging around things that you never use, is there? Donate clothes that you haven't worn in over a year or put them on consignment. Also take a hard look at your books, hobby and decorative items, games, and electronic equipment. Have a yard sale (or two!) a few weeks before your move-in date—a little extra cash will come in handy and you'll have fewer things to pack. What you don't sell, donate. Toss any items that aren't in good condition. Having less to pack and starting with what you actually need and want helps you feel great about starting your new life with less baggage.

Notes on Packing

Mark the boxes you plan to unpack right away with a big checkmark. And also mark the room they should be placed in: "kitchen," "bedroom," "bathroom," etc. Doing so makes the whole process much easier for your moving helpers, not to mention yourself. And if you won't be unpacking some boxes right away, you may forget what's inside them, so write down the contents of these boxes with a marker pen to help you remember.

Start your packing early. You probably have some things you never or rarely use, and the sooner they wind up in a box the less work you'll have to do right before the actual move. At the very least you can pack up your clothes from the previous season, summer or winter.

Pack room by room. One or two weeks in advance, clear a corner and pack your nonessential items that you won't be using in the next two weeks.

One week before, pack a "go bag" with the items you'll need *during* the move itself: clothes and toiletries (consider getting travel toiletries), the file of moving documents and checklists for the move, essential items like your iPad, phone, books, keys—everything you need to keep your head together. Then proceed to your regular packing, room by room.

Also, pack a "first-to-unpack" box full of the items you'll need as soon as you get there: coffeepot, laptop, shower curtain (if your apartment needs one—you'll hate not being able to take a shower the day after you move!), a blanket and set of sheets, paper plates, cooking and eating utensils, a mug, a small saucepan. This box will help you the day after you move when you are too tired to think about where everything is.

Fragile items need to be carefully wrapped (blankets can be very useful for this), and the boxes that hold them should be marked "Handle with Care."

CAUTION Never assume the bottom won't drop out of a box, especially if you've got fragile or very heavy items in it. Better to add too much tape at the bottom than to stint and find everything on the floor, possibly in pieces.

Transportation

If all you own fits into a couple of duffel bags, then moving day is not going to be a big problem for you. But if you have a lot of possessions, you have a more complicated situation, and your move will require thoughtful planning. The other major factor besides the amount of stuff that needs to be moved is the *distance* your stuff has to travel. If you're moving close by, maybe you can do the move in a smaller vehicle over many trips. If you're moving far away, you'll have to plan more carefully as you'll want to move as much as possible in one trip.

FYI Unlike car rental agencies, which won't rent to young people, U-Haul will rent a trailer to someone as young as 16 (with a valid driver's license, of course); to rent a truck, you only have to be 18.

Consider renting, if needed, regular dollies and appliance dollies. A regular dolly will typically come with the rental of a truck. Appliance dollies—heavy duty and intended to handle washer, dryers, and refrigerators—can be rented for a low price, even if you are not renting a truck.

Of course, if you really have a lot of stuff, including furniture, then you may need a moving company. In calculating how much a moving company charges, bear in mind that they charge for the time it takes their truck to get to where your goods are and then again back to their garage at the end of the day. You also have to budget money to tip the movers.

For young people, getting friends to help move locally *is* often less expensive than hiring movers. Their friends are usually single, child free, and in good shape, and the cost of feeding them pizza isn't very much. Movers tend to come into play with young people when there is some distance to be handled in the move. For a local move, though, two pickup trucks or a rental vehicle and three or four friends can usually handle a small apartment move.

Moving Day

Get a good night's sleep before the day of the move and get up early. Create a game plan for the move. Are you going to be the director of this move or is one of your friends more experienced at directing? One person should be in charge of what goes where so wires don't get crossed.

For a regular apartment move (if there is such a thing), it's usually optimal to have four people total: one to keep packing and organizing inside, one to organize and load the truck, and two to move items from the house to the truck. More than that and they tend to get in one another's way.

Designate an "Alamo" station—the last stand. This is the place (a section of counter or a small table) where you and your moving help can put personal items such as keys, pens and markers, and coffee and other beverages. This is also where your go bag and your "first to unpack" box can wait. These are usually the very last things to leave when everything else has been packed up and is ready to travel. That way, you know where they are.

When everyone arrives, decide where to start moving. Think about how things will go into the vehicles you have and also how they will come out. If everything is going in a moving truck, furniture is usually the last to go in because it is usually the first to come out of the truck and into the new place. If you are moving things over in shifts, perhaps the furniture should go first. Just think "the flow" through and you'll have a good idea where to start. The move doesn't have to be perfect. It just needs to get done. And "done" is beautiful.

When you get everything to your new place, stop what you are doing and set up your bed. You'll regret putting this off until the end of the day. This is also a good time to send someone to the store with some cash to buy you a few basic groceries for tomorrow morning; even if it is just milk and muffins, you'll be glad they are there in the morning.

Feed your crew! Pizza, soda, lots of water. And when the move is done and the last box crammed into your new place, take your helpers out for a bit of fun.

The best way to plan for moving day is to picture yourself at the end of it. Imagine what could have gone wrong and then do whatever you can to prevent that from happening. Was your laptop stolen while it was sitting on the sidewalk and your back was turned? (Make sure it's in a box labeled "kitchen utensils.") Did your best friend cut himself and you didn't have a bandage available? (Buy bandages and cheap work gloves for everyone.) Did one of your friends who swore he was going to help you out not show up? (Have a backup mover ready to call.) Maybe you can't prevent every mishap, but one or more are likely to crop up if you're totally unprepared. So the time you spend trying to prevent anything from going wrong will be time well spent, even if nothing does go wrong.

MOVING CHECKLIST AND TIME LINE

Once you have your move-in date, use this list to organize your moving tasks. Put them on a calendar to help keep yourself on schedule for your move. The closer your move-in date, the more you're going to have to do in a short time, so stay on task!

Phase One: 4–6 Weeks Before

- If using a mover, contact moving companies for estimates. Research online reviews for the moving company that you are seriously considering.
- If you're doing the move yourself:
  - Contact truck rental companies for estimates.
  - Make an assessment of your stuff. Begin to remove clutter and separate items for yard sale, donations, or tossing.
- Start a file of moving paperwork, contact info, and budget and expenses. Also keep on hand any other important documents, such as insurance, birth certificate, academic records, etc.
- If using a mover, schedule moving company.

- If moving yourself, reserve moving truck, ask friends to help, or hire a moving team.
- Obtain and fill out post office change-of-address cards, or do online. Use mail forwarding.
- Make arrangements for storage, if necessary.

Phase Two: 3-4 Weeks Before

- Prepare travel arrangements for yourself and pets, if moving out of the area.
- If needed, reserve elevators for move: See if moving permits are required.
- Order and buy moving materials, such as boxes, bubble wrap, packing tape, and other supplies.
- Start to pack seasonal clothing, sports gear, and other items not in immediate use.
- Schedule all utility services and connections at new home: telephone, cell phone, gas, electricity, water, cable, satellite, Internet.
- Notify family and friends, companies, banks, credit cards, magazines, school/employer, clubs, associations, and so on of new address.
- Hold a yard sale or donate item to charity.

Phase Three: 2-3 Weeks Before

- Arrange child care or pet care for moving day.
- If moving yourself, begin to pack bookshelves, kitchen, bedrooms, and bathroom.
- Hold a second yard sale. (Yes, you still have too much stuff.)
- Prepare for donation or disposal of items not sold during yard sales.
- Return borrowed items (to friends, library). Collect items you've loaned to friends (CDs, books, toys).
- Transfer medical prescriptions (if moving out of the area). Be sure to have enough medication on hand.

Phase Four: One Week Before

- If using a mover, confirm date and time of packing and moving.
- If moving yourself, confirm moving truck. Confirm help with friends or moving team. Pack.
- Confirm travel arrangements for yourself and any pets.

- Pack a travel kit or "go bag":
  - check book, credit cards, cash
  - passports, birth certificates, ID, keys, flashlight, tools, papers for movers
  - cell phone (keep the charger handy)
- Pack your "first-to-unpack" box with items that will be needed right away at new place. Mark "Load Last" on box.
  - disposable dishes, utensils, trash bag
  - bedding, clothing, toiletries, shower curtain, medicine, bandages
  - coffeemaker!
- Transfer all account info to your bank's branch nearest your new residence.

The Day Before

- If using a mover:
  - Let movers pack your belongings.
  - Confirm arrival time of moving van or truck.
- If moving yourself:
  - Confirm pick-up time of rental van/truck.
  - Dismantle beds and large furniture. Continue packing items.
- Disconnect and prepare major appliances for move.
- Set aside items to travel with you (like your go bag and Load Last box) to prevent them from being packed by the movers.
- Print out several copies of directions to your new home to hand out to movers and helpers.

Moving Day

- Drop off pets at prearranged care site.
- If using a mover:
  - Confirm bill of lading and inventory before signing. Keep forms in a safe place.
  - Be sure someone is at the old house to answer questions and keep an eye on things.
- If moving yourself:
  - Create the "Alamo" station for personal items, go bag, and Load Last box.
  - Be sure helping friends and family have lunch.
- Breathe. Moving is stressful.

After the Move

Enjoy your new home, even if things are a bit chaotic. And remember to register to vote if you're in a new district!

 PIERRE SAYS My parents used to move every few years when I was a kid, and I would look forward to each move. To me it was all a big adventure. (After all, they were doing almost all the work.) Since getting married, I've only moved once and my kids hated it, even though we only moved a couple of blocks away! The lesson here is that your attitude toward a move will greatly influence how enjoyable the moving process is. So make a point of being as positive about each step as you can.

Part Two:

How to Take Care of Your Home

5 Utilities

How to Set Up the Services You Need and Save Money on Your Bills

Time to Get Connected!

Once you've signed the lease and your new place is in your name (and you have the keys!), it's time to set up your utilities. Sure, nobody likes paying utility bills, just as no one likes to pay taxes. However, since few people are really willing to go off the grid entirely, utilities are an unavoidable necessity of modern life. On the bright side, you'll get used to dealing with them pretty quickly, and after a while they will fade into the background of your life and become a routine and minor life detail.

Deciding Which Services You Need

Depending on your arrangement, some utilities may be automatically set up for you and you won't have to decide a thing. If you're moving in with people already established in a house or apartment, the basic utilities—such as gas, electricity, garbage, and water—will be up and running. The same is true if you're subletting a place or renting a garage apartment in a private home. In those cases, you shouldn't have to set up your own account for most basic utilities.

CAUTION If you're moving into a place with roommates who already have accounts with the various utilities, then make sure that you understand how much you have to contribute to paying those bills. Most roommates simply divide the bills equally among themselves. But if one roommate is making a lot more use of a particular utility, you may want to know that ahead of time and negotiate.

If you're moving into your own apartment or into a new place with roommates, you'll need to review your lease or rental agreement to find out which items your landlord pays for (if any). Things that are often included in the rental agreement for an apartment are water, garbage, and sewage. On the other hand, landlords renting a house (or a room in a house) usually ask you to pay for these. You will be responsible for opening an account for any utilities that are not covered in your lease, so review it carefully.

Something else to keep in mind: The decision on which companies to use for your utilities may have already been made for you. Most utilities are near monopolies, so you may not have much choice when it comes to services such as gas, electric, water, and garbage. If there's only one provider, then that's the one you're going to use. Furthermore, sometimes there will be only one option for your Internet or cable hookup, depending on your area and the companies that offer services there.

Nobody can be an expert on everything, so don't waste a lot of time researching all the angles of utilities you're not familiar with. I recommend that you consult with a friend or relative who has experience dealing with utility companies and who can help you to make the right decision about which services to choose. If you aren't sure about the kind of Internet service you need, ask friends who use the Internet a lot for work or for games what they would recommend. The same goes for TV and cell phone coverage. The key is to fully understand all your options, not to mention what's on the horizon. Not everyone bothers to keep up with all the latest tech information, but you probably know at least one person who does and who would be happy to advise you. And you can always read consumer reviews or articles online about the services so you can get a full picture of what life with them might be like.

Looking at Utility Services

When you're in the process of investigating services, you'll probably need to poke around and ask a few questions. If you're planning to open a new account with a particular utility, the best thing to do is to check its website or call customer service about what is required to open an account. All utility companies will want some form of ID, such as a driver's license or state ID card, and they may want to see a copy of your lease. Some will want a security deposit.

A utility deposit can be hefty, depending on the specifics of your situation, so remember to plan for this in your budget. As discussed in Chapter 1, your budget is a great tool, but you have to keep it up to date to maintain its effectiveness.

Basic Utilities

Electricity: Contact the electric company directly and ask about the requirements for opening an account, any deposits that need to be made, and how long installation takes. Also, if you're interested, ask if the company offers a balanced payment plan that allows you to pay the same amount every month; this will help you take the guesswork out of your monthly bill and add certainty to your budget.

Gas: Sometimes gas is provided by the same company that provides electricity. If this not the case in your area, you will have to contact the gas company and ask the same questions you asked the electric company.

Water, garbage, and sewer: If your rental unit doesn't include these utilities, contact the local water and waste management department—usually with the city or county government—to inquire about opening an account. Ask about the usual rates for the number and type of garbage containers you will rent (trash bin, recycling bin, and possibly a green bin for yard trimmings). Also ask about deposits and the day(s) that pickup is scheduled for your address.

Additional Utilities

With the following utilities, you'll likely have some choice about the service provider and type of plan and therefore some choice about cost and variety. Think through what you'll actually use regularly and the cost of the plan. Stay within your budget.

Telephone: Today, most people have mobile phones, and more and more are using them as their primary phone. But if you need a landline—for instance, if you plan to work from home and wish to keep personal and business calls separate, or if your cell phone reception is sketchy—calling the telephone company to set up a landline is usually quite simple. Ask about local and long-distance rates, voice mail service if you need it, and any deposit you may need to make.

Internet: You almost always will have several options available regarding Internet service providers, so the key here is to think about *how* you use the Internet. If you are a light Internet user—just checking email and social media and reading a few websites or blogs—you won't necessarily need the fastest Internet in town. Most low- to mid-priced DSL services will suit your needs. But if you stream a lot of video online, play a lot of online games, or download music or programs, you'll need a fast connection to keep your sanity intact. So look into the fastest DSL you can find or into cable Internet, which tends to be the fastest. Faster lines are, of course, more expensive.

And, if absolutely necessary, you can always do without Internet service, at least for a while. A few people still forego the Internet connection, preferring to use their laptops to check the basics at a favorite spot that provides free Wi-Fi.

Television: Television is another utility that offers you many choices, so you may need to conduct some research. And, like the Internet, a lot depends on *how* you prefer to watch TV (if at all).

You can make do with the offerings on free digital television, especially if you aren't much of a TV watcher. If you have an older TV and need a digital converter box, you can find very reasonably priced units at any general electronics department. After that, this option is entirely free.

If you like traditional television with the most up-to-date shows, sports networks, and DVR recording, cable or satellite service is probably for you. But review the service packages before committing. The lower-priced packages may not offer the networks you like, and the higher-priced and premium packages may be unaffordable. Also, be very aware of promotional sign-up deals with cable and satellite companies—the quoted rate is often good for only three to six months, then the bill jumps to the regular price. Sometimes they also have sign-up fees, so always read the fine print on these offers.

 One of the most flexible ways to get your TV is by streaming programs over the Wi-Fi Internet you already have and are paying for. This may be the option for you if you tend to binge-watch television shows one full season at a time or like to watch old movies and TV shows that aren't available on cable. To get these programs, you attach a streaming box to your TV that picks up your Wi-Fi signal and streams video from various services. Check the Internet for streaming boxes that are on the market, such as Roku, Google Chromecast, Netgear, Apple TV, etc. These boxes are a one-time purchase, so there's no monthly bill. Then, you subscribe to entertainment streaming services such as Netflix, Hulu Plus, or Amazon Prime. There are dozens of services to choose from. Some services are free while others such as Netflix cost a small monthly fee. With this option, though, you'll need to keep track of all the fees you owe every month and put a cap on them so costs don't sneak up on you.

Bundling Services

Utility companies often bundle several services together and charge one fee for them. The most commonly bundled services are telephone, Internet, and cable TV. Taking these combined services from one company will cost less than taking them separately.

Here's a piece of basic advice about bundling: The fee for bundled services almost always lasts for a limited period, often one year. The rate could potentially shoot up the next year. Again, read the fine print and think about your budget before signing up.

So, should you or shouldn't you bundle? The answer to that question may depend on which services you need. If you don't need all three, then bundling may not make sense. On the other hand, the word *need* is flexible. Although you could get away without a landline, you might also regret not having one if cell phone service in your area is poor.

One way to decide is to pick one monthly sum that you can safely budget for all your communication expenses. Then see how many services you can obtain with that amount, investigating both bundled and nonbundled options. Having set one price goal will make it easier to choose which options you absolutely need and which you can live without.

 Bundling is certainly more convenient when it comes to bill paying and installation/setup, but do your research first before agreeing to a plan. Find out what your preferred services would cost you separately and then ask the company how much they would cost if they were combined.

STARTING SERVICE AND SCHEDULING SERVICE CALLS

To open a new account and set up service for any utility, you simply call the customer service number and ask about getting service to a new place with a new account. Have the following items and information on hand to make the call go smoothly:

- your driver's license or ID number
- your Social Security number
- the address of your new place (the complete address!)
- the date you wish services to start
- a credit or debit card for any deposit or first payment you'll need to make
- your employment information, such as company name, phone number, and how long you've worked there

Waiting for Services

One thing that you have to get used to when dealing with utilities is waiting for service people to show up. Utilities tend to make appointments for particular *dates*, not particular hours (although they may at least give you a half-day time frame of, say, 8 A.M. to noon). So when you want to turn on service, or if you have a problem later on requiring a technician visit, they will give you the date when someone will be there rather than the exact hour. You may well be forced to wait the entire day, so remember to consider the impact of this loss of work time on your budget.

It pays to plan ahead. If you have service calls looming from two different utilities, try to schedule them for the same day. And figure out what you can do while you're waiting. Perhaps laundry and other household chores? Maybe catching up on calls to distant friends and relatives? Perhaps this would be a good day to organize your socks drawer. You get the picture.

You may also have to get used to being put on hold when calling about an appointment or service issue. Try to be patient and civil with customer service people on the phone. Typically, the more level headed and understanding you are (even if they are completely wrong!), the better your outcome will be with them. Occasionally, you wait an entire day and the utility representative doesn't show up. Even if you're not the complaining type, it's wise to call the day of the appointment to make sure that you're on the calendar, unless the utility has some sort of automatic appointment confirmation system, such as sending you a text message.

Meter Reading and Unexpected Service Calls

Although more and more utilities these days are installing meters that don't require a meter reader to visit your home, it's still fairly common in some areas for companies to send someone out to read your meter. If your building has meters that can be accessed only from the inside, the utility company will ask that you let the meter reader into your home.

Obviously, your first concern should be the legitimacy of all service calls. When signing up for a utility, ask whether the company will send someone out to read your meter. If the answer is yes, then you can expect routine visits from the utility company. If the answer is no and someone appears at your door without an appointment, claiming to represent the utility and asking to be let inside, then you should call the police.

PAYING YOUR BILLS

As mentioned, if you're a new customer, many utilities will ask you to pay a deposit up front before they will turn on service. If you'd like to get this deposit out of the utility's hands and back into your bank account, one way is to make sure that you pay your bills on time. The better your record of payment, the more likely the utility will work with you if you find yourself in a jam and need to pay late once or twice. Also, if you ever move and need to connect with the same utility, it probably won't ask for another deposit, at least if you ask the utility not to charge one.

If possible, set up automatic payments from your checking account for all of your monthly bills and payments. Then note the dates and expected withdrawal amounts in your budget or account register at the beginning of every month. This will prepare you to make the payments on time. If you cannot do automatic payments, set up reminders to pay the bills a few days in advance of the due date.

DOWNLOADS Use the reminders app on your smartphone to set up monthly reminders or use a budgeting app with a calendar that will send reminders to you when things are due. Use your smartphone to advantage to organize your bills. Many utility services have apps that you can use to pay your bill by phone. Also download a bill payment reminder app like Manilla or BillMinder. With these types of apps, you can just input due dates and they will push reminders to you a few days in advance.

What happens if you can't afford to pay your utility bills for a month or two? At some point the utility company will cut off your service, which could leave you literally in the cold and dark. And then when you want service again, you'll be forced to offer up an even bigger deposit before the company will take you back as a customer. Also, if you are several months behind in paying these bills, the utility company can report you to the credit bureaus, which will negatively affect your credit rating. Finally, the company might sell the amount you owe to a debt collection agency, which will then hound you to death until you pay. So the worst thing you can do is to ignore unpaid bills.

By sticking to the budgetary principles discussed throughout this book, you shouldn't run into trouble. But should you see a payment problem looming, be proactive and contact each of the utilities right away. Because they are regulated by the government, they will work with their customers to come up with a solution. They'll help you to figure out a payment plan that you can afford until you can once again start paying in full. For example, some companies will put people on a long-term payment plan to help them catch up on their bills. Customers on such plans pay a fixed amount over six or twelve months that will get them back on track.

PIERRE SAYS Do not be afraid to call utility companies and explain when you're stuck on a bill. Trust me—customer service representatives are trained on how to handle such calls, which frankly aren't that unusual. Most of us have been in a financial tight spot before or know friends who have. Being open and honest goes a long way with utility companies, and you'll feel great relief when you and they have worked out a reasonable plan.

SAVING MONEY

You can save a lot of money right away by making smart choices when signing up for utilities, but there are always plenty of ways to save money in the long term, mainly by establishing good usage habits. Do you leave lights on all the time or turn them off whenever you're not in the room? Do you keep your apartment warm or do you set your thermostat a few degrees lower and throw on a sweater? Even if you don't own the place where you live, it might pay off for you to make some improvements in energy savings. If there are leaks where cold air comes in and your landlord won't fix them, you might be able to cut down on your heating bill sufficiently to make fixing them yourself pay off.

Some utilities provide free energy audits to customers. There are also private companies that conduct such audits for a fee. If you're a renter, it may not pay to hire such a company, but you can conduct a "lite" audit yourself. Walk around your house with a lit candle in wintertime to detect any breezes coming through windows. A cheap canister of caulk could help you to seal such leaks and save you lots of energy.

Here are some more ideas on how to use less energy and cut down on your utility bills:

- Use compact fluorescent energy-saving lightbulbs and turn off lights when you're not in the room.
- Keep your thermostat turned down to the upper 60s in winter and up to the high 70s in summer. And turn it off completely overnight and when you're out of the house.
- Use room-darkening shades or curtains. The heavy material will keep cold drafts from coming into the room in wintertime, and the

reflective backing will deflect heat from the sun in summertime, keeping the room cooler.

- Make certain your computer's sleep mode is set to the most efficient setting. Consider turning your computer off overnight.
- Refrigerators use a lot of power. Keeping the door open for a long time allows the expensive cold air to escape, causing your fridge's motor to run more. So minimize the amount of time the fridge door is open.
- Air-dry dishes instead of letting the dishwasher dry them.
- Hang-dry clothes, towels, and sheets as often as possible to save dryer time.
- Use power strips with switches to easily turn small appliances on and off. A lot of power is used by electronic equipment that never really shuts down even after you've turned it off. If you plug such equipment into a power strip, you can then shut off the electricity to that piece of equipment by flipping the on-and-off switch on the strip, which will stop the "phantom" power usage.

WORD TO THE WISE If you're using a surge protector power strip to protect your equipment from lightning strikes, be aware that it probably won't work if your house gets a direct hit. If you know a thunderstorm is heading toward you, it is better to unplug any equipment you want to protect.

So if you make a point of being careful about energy conservation, you can cut down on your utility bills, but if you don't, they can skyrocket. In particular, remember to be extra alert to energy costs when the seasons change. You won't see the bill for the first month or even two months of cold or warm weather until it's too late to do anything about it. So as soon as the temperature starts to dip or rise, take steps to protect yourself from a spike in energy costs.

6 HOUSECLEANING

How to Impress Your Friends with Your Housecleaning Acumen

KEEPING A CLEAN HOME: ONE OF THE KEYS TO LIVING ON YOUR OWN

When you were a kid playing video games, did you ever wonder why your parents were so often scurrying about the house keeping things clean? What was the point, you probably wondered? After all, the house will just get dirty again (in no small measure because of your activities). Keeping your living space clean is a never-ending battle but one well worth fighting. It's one of the keys to successfully living on your own. In addition to giving you a bunch of great tips, this chapter will explain *why* staying on top of household cleaning is so important. Hopefully, that knowledge will give you the incentive you need to put in the effort. Sure, you probably won't find yourself feeling chipper while doing cleanup, but at least you'll be motivated to power through it and feel proud enough about your home to want to show it off to your friends.

REASONS TO BE TIDY

Let's examine the main reasons why keeping your place clean and tidy can pay big dividends.

Getting Your Security Deposit Back

Your security deposit is probably pretty large, isn't it? It's likely one or two month's rent, or more. Remember—that is *your* money and you deserve to get it back when you move out. By maintaining a decent standard of cleanliness, you can greatly increase the chances of your getting all or most of your deposit back. The key is to stay on top of the cleaning, every day and every week. If you can manage to do this, the final cleanup on move-out won't be nearly so difficult—or costly!

Stopping the Invasion of the Body Snatchers

One major reason to maintain a clean home is to prevent an infestation by bugs because they're . . . gross. If you've never lived through a cockroach invasion, you should feel fortunate. Supposedly, cockroach leavings can cause asthma, but that's not really the reason you don't want them crawling into every nook and cranny of your home. The real reason is that the thought of these potentially germ-carrying creatures sitting on your face while you're sleeping is more nightmarish than a real nightmare. And while bugs such as cockroaches, silverfish, and ants are disgusting, bedbugs will leave you full of bites.

How do you prevent bug invasions? The answer is simple: Get into the habit of keeping your space clean. What attracts bugs is not you (except in the case of bedbugs), but your actions that leave behind sources of food for the filthy little critters. So if you want to live a bug-free existence, keep all food stored in sealed containers or in the fridge. Roaches, for example, can feed off things that aren't food to humans and can go without food for long periods. But since their first choice is to share what we eat, don't lure the bugs into your abode by leaving your groceries out for them.

Preventing a Germ Outbreak

And of course you also have to worry about the bugs you can't see, especially those nasty microbes that can cause illness. You've probably read about the outbreaks of *E. coli* that have sickened hundreds of people and even killed a few. The human body can tolerate a certain amount of contact with germs (most are actually beneficial), but if your cleaning standards aren't up to snuff, then you'll increase the odds of coming into contact with some type of bug that can leave you constantly running for the toilet.

 CAUTION Garbage, dirty dishes, mildewed laundry, moldy bathrooms, and sweaty sheets all attract illness-laden bacteria and vermin. Even if you avoid serious illness in these conditions, your overall health will be affected, making you more prone to getting the flu every year, sinus infections, and skin issues, and generally feeling low on energy. Cleanliness keeps you healthy and working toward your goals!

Impressing Your Guests

Now that we've discussed the "guests" you want to keep *out*—germs and vermin—let's switch to talking about the more pleasant varieties of guests, such as your friends, family, and dates. If your castle looks like a hovel, then instead of wanting to hang with you, guests will want to flee. But if you offer visitors a clean environment, they (and you) will feel more comfortable. This opens up a lot of fun opportunities for great socializing without leaving the comfort of your apartment! And hosting a get-together, a holiday open house, or a romantic dinner is a major signal of an adult lifestyle.

Making a Mountain Out of a Molehill

The last reason to clean regularly is that if you don't, the job becomes so big that it can be overwhelming. If you maintain a certain level of cleanliness and make it part of a routine, then you'll never be faced with having to spend an entire day doing nothing but housekeeping chores. Plus, as mentioned earlier, keeping on top of cleaning improves your odds of getting most or all of your security deposit back.

HOW TO KEEP YOUR HOME CLEAN: THE BASICS

Buying Cleaning Equipment

The good news about cleaning equipment and supplies is that you really don't need a lot of stuff to do a good job. Let's take a look at the essentials:

- broom and dustpan
- mop and bucket
- toilet brush
- cleaning and dust rags
- all-purpose cleaner
- bleach
- small spray bottle
- sponges
- vacuum cleaner (if your apartment is carpeted) or mechanical sweeper

If you feel like upgrading your cleaning arsenal, you can invest in wet and dry cleaning cloths, dusting spray, disinfectant wipes, powdered bleach, toilet bowl cleaner, and glass and mirror cleaner.

Cleaning Bare Floors

Most kitchen floors are made of tile, either vinyl or ceramic, or linoleum, and these surfaces clean up pretty easily. Sweep them frequently with a broom and a dustpan and you'll stay on top of them.

If you get a dustpan with a long upright handle, you won't have to do as much bending as you sweep up your little piles of dirt, dust bunnies, and old pennies.

Beyond sweeping, it's a good idea to occasionally "swab the deck," as the navy would call it, although we'll stick with calling it plain old "mopping the floor." You don't have to use the big, old-style mop. I recommend sponge mops: They take up less room and do a good job. Tip: You will need to replace the sponges, so buy a mop made by a large, brand-name company such as Clorox; this will make finding replacement sponges much easier.

CAUTION If you have a wood floor, don't use too much water when cleaning or you risk damaging your (landlord's) floor. A soap specially made for wood, such as Murphy's Oil Soap, is good to have on hand. You'll also want to apply a sealant, either wax or some other product, to protect it.

It pretty much doesn't matter how often you clean your kitchen floor, if food drops on it, throw the food out. (Yes, this applies even if the food was on the floor for "only" five seconds. Science has debunked that myth!)

Taking Care of Carpets

For the carpeted areas of your home (including floor rugs), you're going to need something other than a broom to pick up the dirt.

The lowest-cost option is a mechanical sweeper. It's got a movable dustbin at the base and a long handle, and as you push and pull it, the brushes inside the dustbin pick up dirt, lint, and whatever else. When you're done you empty the dustbin into the trash. Sweepers also work on wood floors, don't use electricity, don't make much noise while doing their job, and are easily stored.

You might ask, if mechanical sweepers are so great, why do people use vacuum cleaners? The answer is that sweepers do an OK job at cleaning carpets but not a great job. You can go over and over a spot with a sweeper and sometimes fail to pick up that piece of lint staring you in the face. But a vacuum cleaner's suction power will pick up just about anything. Plus, vacuum cleaners usually come with an assortment of handy attachments that can help you pick up dust on a shelf or in between the cushions of a chair.

As with many other things, the more money you spend on a vacuum cleaner, the more versatile it will be. There are two ways of looking at the kind of vacuum you want. The first and most important is to figure out what will fit your budget, which may well mean looking for a basic model. Just be careful that you don't spend money on one that either doesn't get the job done or else will break down the day the warranty expires. The other consideration is to evaluate your needs. If you're living in a studio apartment, a small, less expensive vacuum will probably do. If you expect to live where you are for a long time, you might want to invest in a more elaborate machine that will last for years. Just make sure you have the room to store it.

MONEY SAVER Do a bit of research before you purchase a vacuum cleaner. Go online and check out the reviews so that you get a good idea of a particular product's strengths and weaknesses, as well as whether it offers the features you are seeking.

Getting Rid of Dust

The best way to get rid of dust is to prevent it from building up in the first place. Using floor mats, both inside and outside every door, will help. Shake out the mats now and then, and make sure everyone going in and out uses them. You might also institute a policy of having guests take their shoes off at the door, although not everyone will be happy doing so.

Whenever you open your windows, you're letting in dust. If you run air conditioners (and you can even use them in winter set to "fan" when you feel the need for some fresh air), then the filter will screen out much of the dust, provided you change the filter once or twice a year. Of course ACs use electricity and aren't good for the environment, but for anyone who is allergic to dust or pollen, they are a good way to keep your suffering to a minimum.

CAUTION Dust in electronics, such as computers, can be damaging. You can use a can of pressurized air to blow dust out, though in some cases you might have to take an item apart to get to where the dust has accumulated (don't forget to first unplug the device!).

One way to collect dust is to use your vacuum. That way you know you're sucking up the dust and not just moving it around. Of course most vacuum hoses won't reach high shelves and other awkward places, so a vacuum can't usually do the whole job unless you have one of the smaller ones that you can easily lift.

Lots of people tear up old clothes to make dust rags. Depending on the material, you could leave as much lint as you pick up when dusting with an old rag, though spraying either water or some commercial spray on the surface will greatly improve the results. Microfiber cloths do a great job (much better than the old-style feather dusters) as they attract dust without leaving any lint behind. The one drawback is that the dust clings to them so well that they're hard to clean afterward. But you must clean them; otherwise, the tiny particles they pick up could damage your furniture the next time you dust. A more convenient but less cost-effective option to look into is throwaway cloths, which you can pick up at the drugstore.

If your place is really dusty, wear a mask to keep the dust out of your nose and lungs. You can get one from either a hardware store or drugstore. A mask is particularly important if you're a highly allergic person.

FYI Dust bunnies occur when the various components of dust, lint, hair, dead skin, spiderwebs, etc., clump together due to static electricity. Furry pets aggravate the problem. If you haven't cleaned under your bed in a while, there's a good chance a whole herd of dust bunnies is roaming there. Because dust mites and other parasites can move into your dust bunnies and set up shop, it's best not to let your herd get too large.

The act of dusting usually creates dust, meaning that as you're dusting you stir up the dust, fail to collect it all, and so inadvertently move it elsewhere. That's why it's best to start dusting high places first, so the dust will fall down and you've got a second chance at removing it. And vacuum the room last, so that the machine can collect any dust that's fallen all the way to the floor.

You can place dust collectors such as throw pillows or slipcovers (or even the old sheet you use to cover up how bad your armchair is stained) in the dryer set on delicate for fifteen minutes or so to shake loose and take away the dust. Just don't forget to clean the lint filter after you're finished.

FYI There are products that you spray on furniture that will make it easier for the dust to cling to whatever you are using to wipe it up. Just remember that whenever you use a spray, as opposed to a pump mist, you're putting chemicals in the air that do damage to the environment.

Wiping Hard Surfaces

Some hard surfaces need special attention because of germs. It's not enough to wipe the dust and dirt off with something wet. You need to use a cleaning product that will sanitize as well as clean. If you visit your local grocery, you'll discover a wide range of cleaning products. They all work pretty well so what you select may not matter all that much in the end. Still, I do recommend that you learn a little something about how these products function so that you can make an informed decision.

So what does a cleaning product need to contain to make it better than using plain water? The first type of ingredient is a **surfactant**, which combines with water to emulsify grease and helps to lift the dirt off the surface you're cleaning. Surfactants are the primary agents in household cleaners like laundry detergent, dish and dishwasher detergents, hand soaps, shampoo, and cleaning sprays like 409. They make a good general cleaning agent because they're effective at attaching to soil or germs and separating them from the surface they are stuck on.

A **solvent** is a water-soluble organic compound that dissolves soil, grease, and contaminants that it contacts. Solvents are found in heavy duty cleaning items like stain removers, carpet cleaners, furniture polish, and oven cleaners. They don't just pull the soil away from the surface, they also help dissolve the soil right there.

Chelants are materials that bind with metal ions that are found in soap scum. Chelants work in household cleaners in two ways. First, they are often used in shower or toilet cleaners because they can loosen and dissolve the stains caused by metals in hard water (water that contains a significant quantity of minerals). The other way they work is as an agent in household cleaners to keep the chemicals stable and their potency strong over time.

Many household cleaning products—laundry detergent, dish detergent, bathroom cleaners—use a certain amount of all three of these primary ingredients.

 Do cheaper or generic products work just as well as the brand-name ones? The answer is, apparently they do. According to *Good Housekeeping*, the cleaning and paper products you can get from your nearby dollar store are just as good as the equivalent but higher-priced items at grocery stores or retail giants. Learn more at the Good Housekeeping Research Institute, **www.goodhousekeeping.com/product-reviews/research-institute/dollar-store-dos-and-donts**.

How dangerous is the product you're using? If you really want to know, the government will tell you. Go to **http://householdproducts.nlm.nih.gov/cgi-bin/household/brands?tbl=brands&id=18001012** and see how most products rate with respect to various health factors. You can also find out what to do if you are accidentally injured using one of these products. If you really want to play it safe, don't use any product that has a warning on its label. Plenty of "green" cleaning products are available on the market that can't harm you; exactly how harmful nongreen products are in the long run, assuming you don't do anything stupid like drink them, is not clear.

TIP: Want a cheap, effective cleaning spray? Put some bleach in a spray bottle with plenty of water (dilute to one part bleach, nine parts water), and you have yourself a great cleaner for kitchen counters, tile floors, and other surfaces. It doesn't cost very much at all. Always spray a small area first that's not so visible to make sure that whatever you're cleaning won't lose its color from your bleach solution. On the same note, make sure you're wearing an apron or old clothes when you use it—you don't want any bleach spots on your good clothes! The smell left by bleach is very potent, so leave a window open when using it. Although the smell of bleach may be unpleasant, it nonetheless conveys the message that the room has been cleaned—not a bad aroma to leave behind if your friends or family are coming over.

Making the Bed

What's the point of making a bed when you're only going to unmake it when you go back to bed? That's a common philosophy among many people, young and old alike. But when you're living on your own, it is likely that your space will be limited and at a premium, so having an unsightly lump of unmade bedding all the time will start to get under your skin, even if you are the messiest of individuals.

Psychologists have found that making your bed can actually make you happier. Keeping your surroundings neat reduces confusion and helps you to get a jump-start on the day.

But while there's no rule that says you have to make your bed every day, at some point your sheets are going to get soiled, and so you will have to make your bed with fresh sheets. When it comes to putting on clean sheets you have two options. The first is to wash and dry the ones you have on the bed and put them back on. The second is to make the bed with a spare set of sheets, which gives you a bit of breathing room when it comes to cleaning the first set.

How often you need to change your sheets depends on several factors, most having to do with personal choice. Clearly, if you get all sweaty in bed during summer, you'd want to change the sheets more often than in winter. Once a week is probably average, though if you wait another week or two the only person who'll notice is you. After that, your sheets may start to give off various signs that scream "Wash me!"

If you need to buy bedding, the first thing you need to know is the size of your bed. The standard sizes are single, full (also known as double), queen, and king. Sheets come in two basic varieties: bottom, or fitted, sheets and top sheets. Bottom sheets have elastic edges, particularly at the corners, and are much easier to put on. They won't slide off as easily either. They're called fitted sheets because they fit tightly around the mattress, and they stay in place rather than bunch up underneath you, which can be very uncomfortable. Top sheets don't have elastic edges. They are bigger than bottom sheets because they go over whoever is sleeping. When you make the bed with top sheets, you tuck them in at the foot and at the sides.

Sheets come in a variety of fabrics, including polyester, satin, flannel, and cotton (probably the most popular sheet choice because it feels comfortable in all weather).

 Many college dorms have extra-long single beds, meaning you have to purchase special sheets that won't ever fit on any other bed. If you plan on bringing sheets that you purchased ahead of time, make sure that you know the size of your bed, or the sheets you bring might not fit.

 Before you even consider sheets, you may want to look into buying a mattress cover. Mattress covers are thicker than sheets and protect your mattress from getting stained by anything that would soak through the bottom sheet. Since sheets are subject to potential staining by bodily fluids, spilled drinks, etc., it's not a bad concept to protect a mattress with an absorbent covering that can be washed if it gets badly stained, particularly if you've got a new mattress.

Putting on the bottom-fitted sheet is simply a matter of pulling on all four corners, the last of which will be the most difficult because the sheet will be quite taut at that point. When you have the bottom sheet in place, smooth it out as best you can as you'll be sleeping on it. Even if you don't have the sensitivity of the fairy tale princess with regard to that annoying pea, you still might find sleeping a little easier on a smooth bottom sheet.

Next comes the top sheet. Most top sheets have a large hem at one end, which indicates that end should be at the head of the bed (where the pillows are). If it's blanket weather, lay the blanket on top of the sheet, lift the bottom and end corners of the mattress, and fold the ends of both the top sheet and the blanket under; then do the same for the sides. Don't forget that pillows get pillowcases. If the cover on your pillow has a zipper, put the zipper end into the pillowcase first so that it won't be exposed and cut your face. And now you're done!

 After several surprisingly painful encounters between my toes and my bed's feet while making my bed, I finally got smart and started wearing slippers or shoes when tackling this chore. So now if *you* slam your toes into your bed's wooden or metal supports, don't say you haven't been warned!

Washing the Windows

Washing windows is never an easy job, in part because if you don't do it perfectly, the streaks you leave behind can ruin your hard work. It's best to use products made for washing windows because those are designed to leave the fewest streaks. And a microfiber cloth will also help to ensure that you get the best results. One way to make this chore a little less onerous and more manageable is to do only one room at a time, washing the windows in the other rooms on another day.

 Here's a good window-washing tip: Wipe the inside of the window with a horizontal motion and the outside with a vertical motion (or vice versa). That way, should there be a leftover streak you need to eliminate, you'll have an easier time figuring out which side of the glass it's on.

HOW TO KEEP THE BATHROOM CLEAN

You might think that the bathroom is the most likely spot in the house to find nasty microbes lounging about, but the truth is that the kitchen is their prime habitat. Still, the bathroom is a part of your home that requires a fair amount of cleaning attention. Why? The main reason is water, not to mention steam from a shower or bath (germs love to congregate in places with high humidity and pooled water). Bathrooms also offer lots of crevices, such as the grout between tiles, where microbes can hide out. So while bathrooms are usually small, they present special problems and demand that you be thorough in their maintenance. On the other hand, bathroom are made to be water resistant, at least to some extent, so you can go to town cleaning a bathroom without worrying too much that all the water you use will damage anything.

In a bathroom, it's wise to use a cleaning product that has disinfectant properties. For the floors, use either a mop or sponge. Even if you vacuum to pick up hairs and other dirt, you will still want to wipe the floors with a wet disinfectant. Use a sponge or rag to clean around the sink.

 Swiffer wets are great for bathroom floors, and having on hand a pack of Clorox Disinfecting Wipes in the cabinet for the counters, toilet seat, sinks, and mirrors makes keeping the bathroom clean easier and convenient. Just wipe down with a wet wipe or two a few times a week. It helps keep deep cleaning of the bathroom to a minimum.

If you see mold (black stuff) growing in the grout around tiles, use a cleaner that says it gets rid of mold. You may need to use an old toothbrush to scrub the mold away after allowing the cleaner to work. Read the label to see how long the cleaner may need to sit before you start scrubbing. These products are not good to breathe, so make sure that you leave a window open and, if you're very sensitive, wear a mask. A quarter solution of bleach and water (one part bleach to three parts water) will also do the job and will cost you a lot less. You can use cotton balls immersed in the bleach solution to give a serious soaking to the grout before scrubbing it.

Cleaning Bathtubs and Shower Stalls

Bathtubs can be tricky, depending on what they're made of. For a tub made of porcelain enamel, you can use the same cleaning product that you use on the floor. But a tub made of fiberglass or stainless steel requires special treatment, and you need to consult the instructions that came with it. If you have a rubber mat on the bottom of your tub to keep you from slipping, remove it after every shower or bath or you risk mildew growing beneath it. If that happens, soak it in a solution of one part bleach, three parts water.

If when moving into a new place you see that the tub isn't porcelain, check with the landlord or current tenant about the best way to clean it. Keep in mind that if you damage the tub by using scouring powder, you may be responsible and asked to pay damages when you move out. If you're not sure whether or not whatever cleaner you're using might do damage, test some on a small, out-of-sight area and wait to see what happens.

If you have a stall shower, which tends to stay more humid, it helps to leave the stall door or curtain open so that drying air circulates. Also consider towel-drying the walls to keep mold at bay. If you make it a rule to clean the shower walls after every use, with either soap and water or a special product made for this purpose, they'll stay cleaner and won't present you with a horrible chore. At the very least, try to rinse down any walls that have soap or shampoo on them.

 Keep a spray bottle of quarter-bleach and water mix to spray down your shower every few days after you use it. This will go a long way toward warding off mold and mildew.

Cleaning Toilets

Cleaning a toilet bowl may not be a pleasant job, but it's definitely less gross if you have the proper equipment. Start off buying a toilet bowl brush, which comes in its own little container that can stand on the floor next to the bowl, ready at all times. You'll feel much better knowing that this particular implement does only the job it's intended for. There are products made especially for toilet bowl cleaning; however, pretty much any cleanser thrown in the water will work, unless you have very hard water that leaves stains. Allow the cleanser to soak in the bowl a bit before scrubbing with the brush to loosen any stains, including under the rim. Rinse the brush as you flush and put it back in its container. You can use paper towels, or perhaps a sponge dedicated to the toilet, to clean all the other surfaces.

If you have tough mineral deposits that won't scrub away with a brush, turn off the water to the toilet, flush so that the toilet bowl empties, apply a cleaning product like Lime-A-Way that dissolves these minerals, and then attack the mineral deposits with something stronger, such as a pumice stone or sandpaper. Just be careful that you don't scratch the enamel of the bowl.

If you want to keep the germs in your toilet bowl from spreading far and wide to the rest of the bathroom, put down the lid of the toilet before you flush. If you don't, droplets of toilet bowl water get thrown into the air and wind up all over your bathroom. But if you close the lid, that won't happen—and your toothbrush will thank you.

You can buy products that you hang in the toilet tank which make the water blue. These products probably have some cleaning properties, but in the end you're still going to have to scrub the bowl at least once a week.

Cleaning Mirrors

To clean the bathroom mirror, it's better to use a glass cleaner that won't streak. You can also use a Clorox Wet Wipe. This will leave streaks, but they easily wipe off with a dry hand towel or paper towel. Never use soap and water as that will definitely cause streaks. Tip: Did you know that there are products like Z'Fogless Spray that can keep your bathroom mirror from fogging up after you take a hot shower?

Getting Rid of Hair

Because people comb, brush, and wash their hair in the bathroom, loose hair can be a problem. Hair that falls to the floor can be vacuumed or swept up, but hair that goes down the drain in sinks and bathtubs may gather and cause clogs. (See Chapter 12 on plumbing to understand why this occurs.) You can unbend a wire clothes hanger and insert it into the drain to loosen the clog. You can also buy a plumber's snake, a special long wire that can go deep down into the drain to push through the clog and then can easily be pulled back out. Or else you can buy a chemical drain cleaner like Drāno or Liquid-Plumr. You pour some down the drain, wait for the period described in the instructions, and then pour hot water down the drain. If one treatment doesn't do the job, try again.

Of course these drain-cleaning products won't work if the problem isn't a clump of hair or old makeup, which dissolve under the chemical attack. You may have dropped a hard object into the drain. If so, review Chapter 12 and do your own "excavating," or (have the landlord) notify a plumber.

If you call a plumber after first trying a chemical drain cleaner that didn't work, make sure to let him or her know what you've poured down the drain. These chemicals are potentially dangerous, especially to someone who might be lying down under a sink when they spill out.

Getting Rid of Drip Stains

Do you have a blue-green stain around the drain of an enamel tub? That's the sign of a constant drip. The first thing you should do is to have the drip repaired or else the stain will keep coming back. Once that's done, apply a paste of borax and lemon juice, let it sit for a while, and then scrub it away. There are also products made for this purpose such as Lime-A-Way and CLR. Just be careful as these products are powerful and can damage both the wrong surfaces and you!

 If you ever get the crazy idea that mixing two cleaning products will produce better results, the best advice I can give is *don't!* Certain chemical combinations, such as ammonia and bleach, can create harmful, potentially fatal, fumes. If you have detailed instructions, you'll be safe so long as you follow them to the letter. But don't go mixing up your own cleaning concoctions! It's not worth the risk.

TAKING OUT THE GARBAGE

In the past, garbage was never a fun job, but at least it wasn't complicated. Today, because of recycling, taking out the garbage is more of a science than a simple chore. Since each locality has its own set of rules, you need to check in with the local department of sanitation to find out how to get rid of your trash legally. Also, depending on where you live, you also may need to know *when* to throw out the garbage and recycling. This task usually isn't a problem in large apartment houses where the staff handles this chore. But if it is your responsibility, then you have to know when the garbage is picked up, keeping in mind that different types of garbage may be collected on different days.

In your kitchen, have two different garbage cans: one for waste (discarded food, plastic foam, nonrecyclables) and the other for recyclables (plastic jugs, aluminum cans, plastic, and cardboard wrappings, etc.). Tip: Make the recyclable can the *larger* can. Recyclables take up more space than food waste, so you'll have to take the recyclable trash out more often. Purchase trash bags in bulk, if possible. Typically, the larger the box of bags, the less you're paying per bag.

Get in the habit of taking out the trash regularly—at least twice a week will typically do the job and will keep smells down, bugs away, and the trash bins from overflowing.

WORD TO THE WISE If you have some old or rotten food, you may not want to throw it out right away if it will be sitting in the garbage can for days, stinking up the kitchen. Instead, keep it tightly sealed in the fridge, which will contain the smell. Put this type of trash in the can when you take the garbage out of the house.

Tips for Cutting Down on Garbage

The world is drowning in garbage, so anything you can do to lessen the garbage you create is appreciated. Start with getting some permanent bags to carry groceries and other stuff you buy so that you can turn down the plastic bags that stores offer. Buying fresh produce is not only healthier but reduces the need for packaging that ends up going into the garbage (but if you purchase fresh, purchase only as much as you'll eat and visit the farmers' market regularly—otherwise, the food goes bad in your fridge!). And going paperless in terms of bills and bank statements will cut down on your contribution to your local sanitation engineer.

Invest in some good plastic storage containers to keep leftovers and reuse the containers for as long as possible. And learn to cook for yourself more often—and with an eye to creating leftovers—rather than depend on frozen or store-prepared meals and fast food. This will greatly cut down on the amount of waste you generate per meal. And, of course, try to avoid using disposable plates, cups, and utensils—that is, unless you're throwing a party.

MISCELLANEOUS CLEANING TASKS

Frequently Overlooked Spots

Some places that need to be cleaned are obvious, but there are some others that you need to add to your cleaning routine. For example, the bottom shelf of a refrigerator needs regular and thorough cleaning. The reason is that moisture and condensation tend to gather down there, creating a breeding ground for bacteria.

Cleaning your oven is important because if too much grease has built up along the walls, you could start a fire next time you use the oven. Some ovens are self-cleaning, meaning that you turn a special dial and the oven locks, goes on, and gets so hot that it literally burns the grease off. If you don't have a self-cleaning oven, you can purchase oven cleaners at the supermarket or hardware store. Read the instructions carefully because these are noxious chemicals and you want to limit your contact with them.

Some people carefully clean their flatware or silverware only to put it in a drawer that is anything but clean. Yes, you put only clean items in there, but if you look carefully, you'll see that the drawer itself probably needs cleaning, too. Utensil trays that you can remove from the drawer and wash will simplify this chore immensely.

Lamp shades end up being dust collectors, partially because they're out in the open and also because the heat from the lightbulbs seems to attract dust. You can vacuum them or use a lint brush. The same applies to ceiling fans and miniblinds.

 Do you have a single sock that you don't know what to do with? Once you've given up on ever finding its mate, a sock makes a great dust cloth as you can stick your hand right in it, wet it down, and reach into tight places (such as in between the slats of venetian blinds) much more effectively.

TV screens attract fingerprints and, because of the static electricity, dust. Modern TV, LCD, and plasma screens are easily scratched, so read the instructions to learn how to clean them. The same is true for smartphone, tablet, computer, and laptop screens. Dusting them with a microfiber cloth is usually the way to go. Do *not* apply a cleaning chemical.

When Bugs Attack

Having a can of bug spray to kill any bugs you see may satisfy your immediate urge to zap a visible roach invader, but if you have a bug infestation, it's all the bugs you *don't* see, and which are reproducing at warp speed, that are the main problem. Cockroaches are the most common pest, but if you have an infestation of any type of bug, or worse, mice or rats, then the best thing to do is to call in a professional exterminator. Report the situation to your landlord so maintenance can call the exterminator—and pay for it.

CHAPTER 7 DOING DISHES

Simple Steps to a Cleaner Kitchen

DON'T LET THE DISHES PILE UP!

If I can offer just one piece of advice about washing dishes, it would be this: Don't let them pile up. Why? Because doing the dishes regularly is probably the most basic thing you can do to keep your place clean, bug free, and low stress. Sure, washing dishes isn't exactly glamorous, but if you want to keep those nasty bugs from becoming permanent residents, then you don't want to leave them an inviting feast within the confines of your sink. Plus—on the stress side of the equation—it's pretty dispiriting to come home after school or work only to have to confront two or three days' worth of unwashed dishes piled up in the sink and overflowing onto the kitchen counters. If you're so tired at the end of the day that you know washing the dishes is just not going to happen, at least make a point of spending a minute rinsing them off. This will make them easier to clean the next day and less interesting to any little critters that might be lurking.

Another reason to (at least) rinse off your dishes right away is that some foods, such as eggs, oatmeal, and melted cheese, are famous for being a lot harder to wash off once they've dried on your plates and cookware. Rinse these in cold water because hot water will make them stick to the dish or pan even more—and the sooner you do it, like right after you're done eating, the easier cleanup will be. On the other hand, dishes that are sticky because they've had sugar or oil on them probably need to stand in some hot water for a while. This will dissolve the offending substance and make the dishes a lot easier to clean. Add some dish-washing liquid to the hot water to speed the process.

FYI Sponge or dishcloth? That is the question. There are fans of both and no wrong answer. Plus, there are sponges with a scrubber on one side that may decide the issue for you. There are also handy-dandy sponges attached to a long handle that holds liquid cleaner–great for glasses and cups and for keeping your hands mostly away from the gunk.

Burned-on food is very hard to remove. Put water in the pot or pan that has burned food on it, then add some fabric softener and let it sit for a while. The burned-on substance will come off much easier.

YOUR SINK

If you're lucky, you have two sinks—one which you can use one to soak and wash and the other to rinse. If you have only one sink, it's better to use a small tub or basin that you can place in the sink so that you can rinse the dishes off to the side and not dilute the hot water with cold.

 It's a good idea to have something at the bottom of your sink, either a rubber mat or metal rack, so that if you accidentally drop a dish or glass, it won't fall on the hard sink surface and crack.

Next to the sink you'll need a drying rack with a rubber mat underneath to catch the water dripping off the dishes; keep the rubber mat at edge of the sink so that the water can drain into it. Instead of a rubber mat, you may want to consider getting a microfiber dish-drying mat, which costs about $10. These do a great job soaking up water, avoiding the standing water and stains that you sometimes get with a rubber mat. Plus, they're easy to clean because you can just throw them in the washing machine.

 Stacking the dishes in water in the sink or tub allows the ones on the bottom to soak a bit, thus loosening particles of food.

Your sink may look smooth, but it probably has small cracks where germs can hide away and multiply, which is why you need to clean your sink thoroughly at least once a week with an antibacterial cleaner. If you're going to prepare any food in the sink, such as washing vegetables, clean it thoroughly before doing so.

 Tests have shown that kitchen sinks have more germs than toilets. There are about 500,000 bacteria per square inch in the drain alone. It goes to show that cleaning your sink is serious business!

How to Save Water

Saving water is always a good idea, especially so if it's hot water that costs you money. (And that's not mentioning the environmental impact of heating water.) If you do the dishes under running water, you'll use up a lot more hot water than if you fill the sink, or the small tub or basin that you put in the sink, with hot water to wash with. You can then rinse with cold water.

 The reason you need hot water is that it helps to activate the chemical reaction in the dish-washing liquid, which in turn helps to remove grease from your dishes. Plus, the hotter the water, the faster some items, such as glasses and silver, will dry if left on a rack.

 Don't allow aluminum pans to soak too long or they will darken.

Scrubbing

Since it's more effective to scrub the dishes while they're under water, wear kitchen gloves while submerging your hands into the hot water to preserve your skin. If the water gets too dirty, then change it. If you use the tub or basin method, wash the cleanest items, such as glasses, first, when the water won't have grease in it that will actually make these items dirty.

 If you have "hard" water (meaning it contains more minerals), you'll notice that soap doesn't get as sudsy. Dishwasher detergent is less affected by hard water than soap, so you can add a little in to increase the suds. But don't add too much or rinsing your dishes will require a lot more water.

 Anything made of wood, such as a wooden spoon or cutting board, shouldn't be left in standing water or it will get ruined over time. Dry it with a dish towel right after washing. Never put wooden items in the dishwasher either.

Pans made out of cast iron or steel, such as a wok, needn't be cleaned all that thoroughly. They actually cook better if they've been seasoned; that is to say, if a patina—or dark coating from cooking oils—has developed on their surface. After you've gently washed these items, put them back on the burner and turn it on so that the heat dries them completely; otherwise, they will rust.

You can remove most food from plates or pots with a sponge or cloth, but if food sticks to them, then you'll need to scrub more thoroughly. You should definitely have a dish brush with a long handle as your first line of offense. If that doesn't work, try putting some scouring powder on the stuck food and then brush. And if even that isn't strong enough to do the job, reach for a steel-wool pad, such as Brillo or S.O.S. Just be careful not to scour an item so hard that you will damage it. If you scrape away some nonstick coating from a Teflon pot, for example, further peeling of the nonstick chemicals might then leech them into your food. The best destination for that scraped pot is the garbage.

 CAUTION

Don't scrub plasticware with anything too abrasive or it will quickly become damaged.

 Don't forget to wash the bottoms of pots and pans. If you've gotten any grease on the bottom, it may catch fire the next time you cook.

Taking Care of Your Cleaning Equipment

Even though you're cleaning with hot water and some sort of detergent, the sponge, dishcloth, or brush that you use can still become dirty over time. And since these items end up lying around wet, they become handy places for bacteria to multiply; instead of cleaning your dishes, you could be dangerously infecting them with bacteria.

There are several ways to prevent this from occurring. First, always rinse the sponge, dishcloth, or brush so that no food remains attached to it. Dishcloths can be thrown in the wash, but that's only effective if you do it regularly. Since sponges aren't meant to last forever, throw out your old sponge with some regularity and bring out a fresh one.

CAUTION All the little crevices of a sponge make it a better cleaner, and it also sops up water better than a dishcloth—but those crevices also make good hiding places for microbes to multiply. Every once in a while give a sponge or brush the smell test. If you notice any odor, it's time to either replace it or disinfect it.

WORD TO THE WISE Did you know that most kitchen counters near the sink have more bacteria than the top of a toilet bowl? This is because the sponge or dishcloth you used to wipe the counter down actually infected the counter with these germs. To avoid this, use a separate sponge for countertops and general cleaning. Get packs of different-colored sponges to keep track of which is which.

Taking Care of Your Hands

While doing the dishes, you've had your hands in hot, soapy water, which means they're clean, right? Obviously, to a certain extent this is true, but your hands serve as a gateway to your body whenever you touch your face, so you might want to ensure that they're extra clean by having a dispenser of antibacterial hand sanitizer or liquid soap by the sink. Just before you dowse the kitchen lights, rub some into your hands to be extra certain that you aren't carrying any dangerous bacteria away with you. If you wash your hands with warm water and soap for at least thirty seconds, you'll achieve the same effect, but if you're more likely to use the hand sanitizer, then follow that route.

DISHWASHERS

If you're lucky enough to have a dishwasher, your hands will spend a lot less time in hot water. If your dishwasher is of the newer variety, you probably don't have to rinse the dishes before putting them in, though you still have to scrape off food particles into the trash. If you don't plan on running the machine right after a meal, then you should rinse dishes to keep any leftover food from drying out and caking on, or else have the dishwasher do it by running a rinse cycle. It's always better economically to run the dishwasher when it's full, but the rinse cycle doesn't use much energy and will keep your dishes from becoming food encrusted.

To really get a full dishwasher load (and save even more money and energy), stack like items together: plates of the same size in a row, bowls in a row, glasses in a row, etc. You'll actually stack more dishes in a single load this way, and with everything already organized by type, it will be less of a chore when you unload the dishwasher.

Dishwasher Safe

Not every item in your kitchen is dishwasher safe. Glass items are almost always fine for the dishwasher, although you should verify this for any crystal glasses you may have. You can also dish-wash delicate items such as wine glasses, but position them so that they won't bounce against each other and break. The main category to be wary of is plasticware. Many plastic items may not survive the heat inside a dishwasher. In any event, you should definitely avoid putting anything made of plastic in the bottom basket, where it is closer to the heating element during the drying process.

If you're lucky enough to have inherited your grandmother's silver, be careful not to put any of it next to your stainless-steel flatware in the dishwasher. If they're touching, a chemical reaction could occur that would damage the silver.

If flatware such as forks and spoons nestle together, the water won't penetrate as well and they won't get clean. By placing some up and some down, you'll avoid that potential problem.

If you want to keep your dishwasher smelling fresh, run an empty cycle with a cup of white vinegar thrown into the bottom.

Water Temperature

The water in a dishwasher is supposed to be about 120 degrees. Check the temperature of the hot water coming out of your faucet. If it's much cooler, the dishwasher won't clean as well. However, the dishwasher also won't clean as well if the water is too hot because the water will dry too quickly instead of rolling down the dishes.

If it usually takes awhile for the hot water to make it from your hot-water heater to the faucet, then run the hot water in the sink until it gets hot before starting the dishwasher.

Dishwasher Detergent

Dishwasher detergent comes in three forms: liquid, powder, and tablet. Whichever type you choose, it needs to be fresh for you to get the most from its cleaning properties. Don't buy too much ahead of time or it won't clean as well as it should. A two-month supply is usually about the right amount to purchase. Also, check to see whether the product contains a rinse aid, which can be helpful if you're finding water streaks on your dishes or glassware after washing. If your detergent doesn't include a rinse aid, you can always buy some separately, if needed.

CAUTION If you've run out of dishwasher detergent, don't substitute the dish-washing liquid you use for hand washing. It will create too great a quantity of suds and could cause a leak and damage your machine.

TIME AND ENERGY

If you want to make sure that you do the dishes regularly and that it doesn't take a long time, simply own a limited number of dishes—about four to six regular plates, small plates, bowls, glasses, and coffee cups for one person and around eight of each for two. Running out of items faster forces you to do the dishes regularly. If you have three sets of your family's dishes just for yourself, you'll be tempted to let them stack up and thus create a biohazard. Keep your serving, mixing, and storage bowls to a minimum, as well.

People don't always have the wherewithal to do the dishes immediately after each meal. If you tend to have more energy at night, consider doing your dishes after your evening meal or just before you go to bed. It'll make those occasional rough mornings go more smoothly if your kitchen is organized and ready to go when you rise, bleary-eyed, in search of eggs or cereal.

If you are an early riser, consider rinsing your dishes after each meal and stacking them to soak the night before. Then do your dishes first thing in the morning. Making dish washing a part of your daily routine will keep your kitchen more organized and easy to use.

CHAPTER 8 LAUNDRY

Washers, Dryers, and a Whole Lot More

How to Do Laundry Right

While many people still do dishes by hand, it's rare to find people washing their clothes in the sink, not to mention kneeling by a river to wash them! (The main exception is women who do their underwear and lingerie by hand to protect these items from being damaged by mechanical processes.) So you're going to have a washing machine in your life, either at the laundromat or at home. If you have one at home, you'll find it to be a big time saver, although it will increase your energy costs. Some of the advantages to having your own washing machine include the following:

- It's cheaper than using a laundromat.
- While waiting for the wash to be done, you're home doing other things.
- You can do your wash anytime it suits you.
- Your clothes won't come in contact with someone else's leftover germs.

So if you're still in apartment-hunting mode, you might make having a washer and dryer in your apartment or building a priority. You need only a few basic items to use your washer and dryer: laundry detergent, a clothes hamper or laundry bag, and perhaps a laundry basket. If you want to upgrade your laundry experience, you might get fabric softener (with accompanying fabric softener ball), dryer sheets (to eliminate static cling), stain remover (such as OxiClean or Shout), and a liquid detergent (such as Woolite) for hand-washing delicate items. If you have a washer but no dryer, you'll need a foldable drying rack (usually wooden) and/or a clothesline, assuming you have a place outdoors to string it up.

 If you buy quick-dry underwear, it may be advantageous at times to skip the washing machine and wash it in the sink—especially if you find yourself in an out-of-underwear emergency!

CAUTION Wool garments can be damaged by washing machines and, in particular, by dryers, so to protect them from shrinking, wash these items in the sink with cold water and a product such as Woolite. Items made of wool, such as sweaters, should not be hung to dry as they will stretch out. Instead, to keep their shape, you should lay sweaters flat over a thick towel or two and air-dry them. Never put garments made of wool in a dryer as they'll shrink down to child size.

Separating the Wash

Doing wash is not very complicated, but there is one fundamental question that can stump you: Do you need to wash any garments separately? The answer is that it depends. And mostly it depends on you. Do you feel that your clothes, underwear especially, need to be sterilized in very hot water or are you OK with washing them in warm or even cold water? (You may want to check out the information on germs later in this chapter before deciding.) If you're of the school that says laundry detergent and cold water are fine, then you can pretty much wash all your clothes together and not worry about separating them.

If you have a brightly colored garment (especially red) that's never been washed, you should wash it separately from whites and light-colored clothing—unless you want your whites and pastels to turn a different shade. But if a colored garment has been washed a number of times and you use cold water, then the risk of any dye being released into the wash water is slim. So if you don't want to worry about separating your wash into white and colored, light and dark, use cold water. (Certain delicate clothing should be separated out no matter the water temperature, or else washed in a special bag designed to protect delicate items.)

WORD to THE WISE If by some chance you had a colored garment in your wash that leaked dye, your other clothes may not be ruined if you act right away. Soak the damp clothes in a solution of baking soda and warm water with half a cup of salt and half a cup of detergent. After about thirty minutes, rewash the clothes (minus the offending colored item) in laundry detergent, and hopefully your white clothes will be back to their pristine original noncolor.

The job of separating can be kept basic, as already described, but if you want to focus detailed attention on your laundry, here are a few suggestions:

- You can certainly separate all colored laundry from whites.
- You can wash dark colors (dark blue jeans, black socks) separately.

- You can keep rougher clothing, such as jeans, away from clothing that might be damaged by being knocked about against zippers and tough fabric.
- If you're washing for more than one person, you can wash each person's clothes separately so there won't be any confusion afterward.
- If you separate into piles of similar fabrics—soft cottons with other soft cottons, towels with towels, jeans with jeans—they will dry at the same rate in the dryer. This is because some fabrics absorb more water than others and don't dry as quickly.
- Think about separating out heavily soiled items you want washed thoroughly from those things that need a light or medium wash.

CAUTION Always check the pockets of your clothes before putting them in the wash. Electronics will get ruined, and a single tissue left behind in a random pocket can cover your clothes with lint that's very hard to remove.

FYI Speaking of lint, you may want to separate items that make a lot of lint, such as towels, from "lint magnets," such as corduroy and fleece.

Bras

There are several schools of thought regarding the washing of bras. It is undoubtedly true that machine-washing bras cuts short their life, but whether that merits hand-washing them is up to you. Placing them in a mesh bag when machine-washing them will offer some protection. More damaging to bras are dryers, as the high heat will damage the elastic over time, so you might consider air-drying them if you're concerned about prolonging their life.

PIERRE SAYS I moved my office into my home a few years ago. I was still as busy as ever with work, but spending so much time on the home front meant that I inherited laundry duty. Not a big deal—but my wife's stockings would get all tangled up during the spin cycle and untangling wet stockings made me feel skeevy. Luckily for me, I'd written *Fashion for Dummies* and so knew of the existence of the special bags I refer to above used for women's so-called delicates. I bought one and now her stockings come out of the bag one at a time instead of in a mess of nylon knots. I'm happy, and so is she.

SELECTING THE WATER TEMPERATURE

Whatever machine you use will require that you set a dial or push a button indicating at what water temperature you want the wash to be done: hot, warm, or cold. Hot water disinfects the best, and some of the chemicals in detergents that aren't made to be used in cold water won't become activated unless the water hits a certain temperature. But some garments can be damaged if they're washed in hot water, so you need to read the care instructions on each garment's label.

The disadvantage of a hot-water wash is that it probably will make you do more than one wash, one for clothes and towels that can stand hot water and one for those things that can't. And because colored clothes are more likely to release some of their dye in hot water, you may well have a third wash on your hands. If you have your own machine, more than two loads may not be such a big deal, but using warm or cold water to wash your clothes will simplify your washing experience.

 Warm water helps to prevent wrinkles while cold water is better for clothes with bright colors. The rinse cycle is always done in cold water as that's best for getting rid of the soapy residue.

The Germ Factor

Most of the germs that you would find on your clothes are all around you anyway and won't harm you. However, underwear, as you might expect, can be a different matter, and can be home to germs such as hepatitis A virus, norovirus, rotavirus, salmonella, and E. coli. So when washing underwear, think about using hot water as well as some bleach, even though the likelihood of catching anything from your own clothes is very small. On the other hand, germs can build up in your washing machine, so you might want to run a short wash with bleach and very hot water, without any clothes, every once in a while to disinfect your machine.

Another cleanliness factor is mildew. Leaving clothes in the washer for too long traps the heat, air, and moisture in the washer, and mildew begins to grow. This happens faster in warmer weather. If your laundry has a hint of a "sour" smell to it when you open the lid, you probably need to run the load again to get rid of the mildew. So do your best to start and finish a load in the same day.

WORD TO THE WISE After emptying the washing machine of clothes, make sure to wash your hands. They may have picked up some germs while handling the wet clothes.

Hot water kills germs, but it must be at least 140 degrees. As effective as bleach, however, are the ultraviolet rays in sunlight. So if you hang your clothes out to dry in the sun, you'll be killing any germs that may be left in your freshly laundered clothes.

CHOOSING LAUNDRY DETERGENTS

Laundry detergents come in several forms, including liquid, powder, and sheets. Some machines require a specific type of detergent, so if you have your own machine, read the directions before buying detergent. Laundromats will probably sell you the right detergent or else post instructions. Since you don't want to be the one whose clothes are in a machine that is overflowing with soapy water, read those instructions carefully so that you don't use too much detergent and cause a flood of suds.

Most washers have an automatic dispenser that you put your detergent in. But some older models require that you manually add detergent. If you're dealing with one of those machines, wait for the machine to start to fill with water, add your detergent to the water, watch it dissolve, and then add your clothes. If you add your clothing to the mix before the detergent dissolves, direct contact with the detergent could damage them.

 What's different about Woolite? Fabrics made from animal products, such as wool and silk, require a different pH factor provided by a cleaning product such as Woolite. Both wool and silk do require special laundering skills or they will be ruined, so be certain you know what you're doing or just take them to the dry cleaners.

Detergent and the Environment

Originally designed to help wash clothes better in hard water (which, because of its the minerals, makes soap less effective and harder to rinse off), modern detergents are composed of a whole series of chemicals that have improved their ability to get clothes clean—but at the price of causing problems with our water supply. Some laundry detergents are more ecologically friendly than others, and if this matters to you, then do some research before making your next purchase of laundry detergent.

If your conscience dictates that you use soap, which has been around for thousands of years and does not damage the environment, rather than detergent, you can help your machine to do a better job of rinsing the soap by adding some baking soda during the rinse cycle. A couple of tablespoons should do the trick.

Bleach

Bleach is a very strong cleaner and disinfectant. The most popular brand is probably Clorox, but the generic or dollar store kind is just as good, although it tends to smell stronger. When doing laundry, whether you want to remove a stain or just get your clothes extra clean, bleach will definitely add to the cleaning power of your detergent. But you have to proceed with caution. Bleach is safe on white clothes or white towels, but it can remove the color from fabrics, and any discoloration spots left by bleach can't be removed (it will really do a number on your tie-dyed items!).

Although your laundry detergent will probably get your clothes plenty clean, if you do decide to use bleach and aren't sure whether or not a particular garment will lose its color, perform a simple test. Add one and a half teaspoons of bleach to one-quarter cup of water. Apply a drop of this solution someplace on the garment that can't be seen, like on an inside seam, and then see what happens. If there's no discoloration, you can safely use some bleach when washing the garment, following the instructions on the bleach container with care. In any case, you should never use bleach when washing wool, silk, mohair, leather, or spandex.

CAUTION Some "bleaches," such as Clorox 2, are listed as being safe for colored garments. But these products actually contain hydrogen peroxide, not bleach. However, if you're washing a garment that you really don't want to put at risk, double-check that the Clorox 2 or similar product won't discolor the garment. Test some diluted product on an area hidden from view.

Fabric Softener

Fabric softeners are designed to reduce wrinkles and static, which is a big deal in trousers and skirts. They also keep cottons soft against your skin. And if you want that comforting, at-home-laundry smell, fabric softener is what does it.

Fabric softeners come in two basic varieties: liquids that you add to the wash and sheets that you add to the dryer. If you're going to use liquid fabric softener, you have to put it in the load prior to the rinse cycle for it to be fully effective. Many washers have a special tray that you fill with liquid softener before you begin the load and that will release the liquid at the right time. Some people listen for the washer to finish its first spin and refill with water; then they pour the softener into the washer themselves. The easiest way is to use a fabric softener ball, which you fill with the liquid and toss in with your clothes at the beginning of the load. When the load begins its first spin cycle, the ball opens up and releases the fabric softener just before the rinse cycle begins.

You certainly don't need to use fabric softener, but it has its benefits. It's up to you to decide if fabric softener is a big enough plus to make it worth the expense.

DEALING WITH STAINS

If you dropped food or anything else that's left a stain on your clothes, merely throwing the item in the washing machine a day or two later may not be enough to get the stain out. The first thing to understand is that with some materials, the longer the stain is allowed to set, the more it penetrates the fabric, making it much more difficult to remove. That's why even a basic attempt to remove the offending stain as soon as it happens, by rubbing it with a napkin dipped in seltzer or even plain water, might make complete removal easier later on. It's also why if you wash the garment the moment you get home, the better the results are likely to be.

WORD TO THE WISE

You can buy stain remover wipes that you can carry around. If you spill something that stains your clothes while you're away from home, you can at least make the stain not so obvious. There are also highly portable pen-style stain removers.

But if such measures can't get it all out, then you might need to go the extra mile to fully remove all traces of the stain. A first line of attack, if you're using liquid laundry detergent instead of powder, is to pour some of the detergent directly on the stain and rub the cloth together a bit before starting the machine. You can also soak the garment in some detergent and water in the sink for a while before putting it into the washer.

If you're still not having any luck, then it's time to turn to products specially designed to remove stains, such as the Tide Stainbrush, Resolve Dual Power Laundry Stain Remover, Clorox Bleach Pen, and OxiClean Max-Force Laundry

Stain Remover. From my own experience, OxiClean powder is very economical and, when added to a regular load, goes a long way. You can also use it as a soak for larger stains before washing. The powder is also really good for soaking whites such as socks, T-shirts, cotton gloves, and handkerchiefs. It gets them really clean and white. Even the regular (not maximum-powered) sprayable version of OxiClean is a good spot stain remover. Hydrogen peroxide is also good as a general washing boost in a full load.

Drying Your Laundry

The tried and true method to dry your clothes after washing is to hang them up and let the moisture evaporate. Lots of people still do this, and if you want to save money, then hanging your clothes is an option you should consider. Of course if you do your wash in a laundromat and don't want to lug home a lot of soggy clothes, the clothes dryer option is probably best.

Clothes dryers are pretty simple, but there are a few matters to think about. The first is what not to put into a dryer. As mentioned before, anything made of wool should never be put in the dryer as it will shrink. Items made of silk, such as ties, should be kept out of the dryer as they will lose their smooth texture. Cotton will also shrink in the dryer a bit, but usually not so much that the garment will change size.

As soon as you take your jeans out of the dryer, while they're still hot, stretch them out by pulling the material every which way to keep them from shrinking.

FYI One advantage of front-loading washers is that they spin so quickly that clothes come out a lot dryer. This means the laundry will spend less time in the dryer and may even make air-drying an option.

Items that contain elastic or spandex will also be damaged over time by the heat of a dryer. This may not matter with items such as elastic-banded underwear, which you tend to replace fairly often anyway. But you should be concerned about damaging more valuable pieces of clothing. In addition, setting your dryer to a hot temperature could damage certain other items that are normally perfectly suitable for the dryer. For example, permanent-press clothes do better at a warm rather than hot setting. And if there is a cool-down period, that will help take out wrinkles. Just check the label for drying instructions on any item you're not certain about.

If you accidentally spill anything flammable on your clothes, such as gasoline or kerosene, don't put them in the dryer. You could cause a fire. The thing to do is to wash them first in the washing machine. If after the wash you can still smell flammable material, wash your clothes again until the odor is gone. Only then is it safe to dry them.

An overfilled dryer prevents the hot air from evenly circulating. If you can hang some of the heavy and damper items such as towels on a clothesline, the rest of your wash will dry faster in the dryer. This is why washing and drying like items can be a sanity saver. Tip: When drying a load of towels, put an already dry towel in with the load. The dry towel will soak up some of the steam and moisture created by the wet towels when the dryer heats up, thus helping the heat do its job on the wet towels more quickly.

Lint

All dryers have lint filters, which must be cleaned out regularly. This is best done right after you use the dryer. If you share the dryer with others, it's a good habit to check the filter before you start the machine, in case the previous user didn't clean it. If you don't clean your filter regularly, the lint will not be properly filtered and will gather in the exhaust pipe where it can become a serious fire risk over time. Your machine's lint filter also deals with pet and human hair and will fill up faster when you dry towels, so check it regularly.

Wrinkles

Of course you want your clothes to get clean, but you also want them to look good, which in most cases means being wrinkle free. The traditional method of getting rid of wrinkles is to run a hot iron over the garment to smooth them out. But this is a time-consuming chore. Plus, it takes a certain level of skill to perform the chore properly or you run the risk of ruining clothes by burning them. Listed below are some tactics you can adopt that may reduce the need to drag out the ironing board.

One way to not worry about wrinkles is to give careful consideration to the clothes you buy. Some materials are more likely to wrinkle than others, cotton being an example. However, manufacturers have figured out how to make wrinkle-resistant cotton, though items made of this treated cotton are more expensive. Many artificially made fibers, such as polyester, are very resistant to wrinkling, but they don't feel as good against the skin as cotton. One compromise is to purchase garments made from a cotton-polyester blend, which gives them the feel of cotton along with wrinkle resistance.

How you treat your garments can also add to your wrinkle problems. If you leave your clothes lying in a heap, then the wrinkle gods will have a field day. It may take a bit more effort to hang up your clothes, but this sacrifice will pay off in the long run when it comes to keeping wrinkles from invading your clothes closet and leaving you looking like Jabba the Hutt.

 Steam is an effective wrinkle remover. If wrinkles are only an occasional problem, or if you're on the road in a hotel room, hang the garment up in the bathroom, run the hot water to create lots of steam, and watch most of the wrinkles disappear. If wrinkles are a frequent problem for you, buy a steam wrinkle remover or just a regular iron designed with a steamer setting.

 Hanging up your clothes while they are still warm from the dryer will reduce most wrinkles. Drying items on a hanger, rack, or clothesline is also good for getting rid of wrinkles. Also, you can invest in Downy Wrinkle Releaser, a spray you use when your item is on the hanger—great for tees and soft cotton shirts and blouses.

Ultimately, however, if you want to look your very best, you will need to learn how to iron your shirts and dresses. And if you do accidentally leave scorch marks from the iron on your clothes, try hanging them in sunlight, which will bleach the marks out if they aren't too dark.

Air-Drying Your Laundry

If you have a space for a small clothesline in your mudroom, back porch, or yard, consider putting one up. Hanging items such as sheets, tablecloths, and fine cottons outside helps remove wrinkles without ironing them and gives them that really sweet, fresh scent (not much is better than climbing into a bed with line-dried sheets in summertime). The same can be said for pajamas, nightgowns, and T-shirts, if they've had the advantage of fabric softener.

If an outdoor line isn't in the cards for you, get a foldable drying rack or two. You can still air-dry sheets by folding them a few times and laying them over the rack. A drying rack is also excellent for gently drying sweaters and other items you don't want pulled out of shape. A rack will always be handy for drying those vintage odds and ends you want to handle with kid gloves. And it will save you some drying time and a bit on your energy bill.

TIMING YOUR LAUNDRY

Most people do laundry once or twice a week, often in the evening. But some people let their laundry pile up and devote a full day to washing it. A few times a month they will enjoy a "laundry day," doing load after load of laundry while binge-watching a favorite TV show, ordering pizza, and never getting out of their pajamas. If this is you, no problem. Sure, this approach might make you look like a bit of a slob, but if laundry day works for you, great.

Other people have a hard time fitting a full load of laundry into their busy schedule. If you're like this, the best option may be to put a load of laundry into the washer as soon as you get up, maybe four mornings a week. Then when you come home for lunch or dinner or for a change of clothes before heading out for the evening, just move the load from the washer to the dryer and turn it on. When you return home for the night, remove the single load from the dryer, quickly fold it, and put it away before heading for bed.

However you time your laundry, try to do it regularly and complete the final load before you go to bed—so you don't forget that it is in the washer for days and days!

TIPS FOR USING A SHARED MACHINE OR THE LAUNDROMAT

Not everyone is as careful as you are when using shared equipment, and you don't want to put your wardrobe—which would cost quite a lot to replace—at risk because of something some other careless person did. That's why when using other people's equipment you have to be proactive and check things out before you begin. For example, that puddle on the table where you are about to put your clothes, is it water or bleach? If it's the latter, you could ruin your clothes. So take a few seconds to check surfaces, including those inside the machines. The person before you could have left behind a brightly colored T-shirt that will stain all your clothes when you wash it again in hot water.

It's always better to stick around while the machines are operating, but sometimes that's just not possible. In that case, don't try to pretend you're wearing Harry Potter's Cloak of Invisibility. Make your presence known, smile at the other people, or even talk to them, so that if a laundry thief makes a beeline for your clothes while you're gone, maybe one of these people will speak up or act on your behalf.

When using a communal laundry machine, use your phone to set a reminder so that you get back before your load is finished. This will prevent others eager to use the machine from piling your stuff on a nearby table.

FYI Many laundromats will do your laundry for you. You drop it off in the morning on the way to work and then pick it up, all washed, dried, and folded, on your way back. Of course there's an extra charge for this, but even if you can't afford it on a regular basis, this service could be very useful in a pinch.

Dry Cleaning

The labels on a few of your items of clothing might read "Dry-Clean Only," which means they should be taken to a dry-cleaning establishment to be cleaned. Such places use special chemicals in their machines that are safe for garments that don't mix well with water and detergent. The dry cleaners will do all the work, and they even return your clothes on a hanger and in a nice plastic bag. But this service doesn't come cheap.

The best way to avoid spending a good chunk of your paycheck on dry cleaning is to pay attention to labels when you shop. Stay away from clothing that requires dry cleaning. Of course some items, such as wool suits for men and women, are unavoidable if your job requires them, but these don't have to be cleaned after every use. In fact, if you're careful to wipe away any stains before they have a chance to set, you can wear a suit many, many times before needing to clean it. And if the pants get wrinkled because you got caught in the rain, then either iron them yourself or take them to the cleaners just to be pressed.

CHAPTER 9 HOME MAINTENANCE
How to Keep Your Things from Falling Apart

THINGS WILL BREAK DOWN, SO BE PREPARED

Living on your own means being responsible for everything that goes on in your home. If you want something fixed, it's up to you to get it done. Of course, "getting it done" will mean different things, depending on the situation. Over time, you'll discover that you can handle most maintenance and repair issues by yourself with a bit of practice. But sometimes you will need to call in a professional. Obviously, bringing in help isn't good for tight budgets and is something to avoid, if possible—at least when *you're* the one (rather than your landlord) who has to foot the bill. That's why it's smart to become comfortable with some basic skills, such as hammering nails, screwing screws, and maybe even plastering and painting walls.

If you're the sort of person who's already handy with basic tools, you can probably skim through this chapter. But if you're not, the good news is that most of the skills you'll need aren't difficult to acquire. With a little practice, you too can become a master at putting up a picture, tightening a leaky faucet, lubricating squeaky door hinges, preparing a wall for a fresh coat of paint, and so on. Mastering these basic skills will give you greater control over your life, increase your confidence in your skills, and help you avoid pricey professionals.

BASIC TOOLS

Since you never know when one of these basic home maintenance skills will be required, it's best to have some of the basic equipment at your fingertips. I can guarantee that you'll need at least a hammer or screwdriver at some point, so why wait to purchase these tools until that critical moment arrives?

MONEY SAVER Good tools can last a long time, so you're better off buying the best you can afford. You don't have to buy professional-grade top-of-the-line tools. Just avoid buying the cheapest items, which would probably need to be replaced in the near future.

Hammers: When buying a hammer, don't choose the lightest just because it's the least expensive. Look for the heaviest hammer that you can comfortably wield. Test the hammer's weight, grip, and feel. The heavier the hammer, the more force it has when hitting a nail. But avoid hammers that feel too heavy, as they'll become painful to use if you have a lot of hammering to do (plus, there's the risk that you could lose your grip on the handle during the backswing and let your hammer fly backward, crashing into the opposite wall!). Most people opt for a medium-weight hammer.

At the other end of the head, a hammer has either a round ball, called a peen, or a claw. The claw is most useful as it assists in removing nails, either ones you just put in crookedly or older nails.

CAUTION Hammers are dangerous. Assuming you are holding the nail with your fingers, the chances of the hammer missing the nail head, hitting your fingers, and doing some damage are pretty good. Use less force when hammering. This will slow down your motion, and your aim will be truer.

Screwdrivers: You can't do without the enormously helpful screwdriver in your toolbox. There are two basic types of screwdriver heads: flat and Phillips. Flat screws have only one slot while Phillips screws have an X-shaped slot. Since screws come with different slot sizes, you need at least four heads: a large flat, a small flat, a large Phillips, and a small Phillips. Your best option is to look for a multi-head screwdriver that comes with several heads stored in the handle that you can easily interchange.

Screwdrivers aren't expensive, but if you want to spend a little more money, get a multi-bit ratcheting screwdriver. Ratcheting allows you to leave the screwdriver in place in the screw while you turn the handle back. It makes screwing a lot easier and reduces muscle fatigue on tough jobs. By adjusting the setting, you can both screw and unscrew using the ratcheting procedure, or else turn it off and use it like a regular screwdriver. Note: You might find that this type of screwdriver comes with some less commonly used heads, such as for torx screws. Since you're unlikely to have to deal with these, ignore them, although if you do run into a star-shaped torx screw, you'll be prepared.

The final option is the electric screwdriver. These make dealing with screws even easier as your wrist won't be doing any of the work. Electric screwdrivers often come with rechargeable batteries. They gradually lose their charge, so you'll eventually need to replace the batteries.

Pliers: Pliers are invaluable when it comes to pulling and turning various nails and nuts. Pliers come in different sizes to accommodate the many different situations they are useful for. Pliers that ratchet into several sizes give you more options and increase the odds that you'll have the right equipment for the job at hand. (See Chapter 12 to learn about when you might need larger-size pliers for plumbing repairs.) Adjustable pliers do cost a bit more but wind up being cheaper than having to buy several different ones.

You should also look into getting a pair of needle-nosed pliers. These fit into spaces where normal pliers won't go and so can prove very handy for certain jobs, such as electrical work (they can also be used to cut wires).

 All-metal pliers can be uncomfortable to use, so it might be worth spending a little extra money to get a pair with plastic coating on the handles.

Wrenches: Wrenches are used to tighten and loosen nuts and bolts. While your home may not have many bolts that you need to work on, if you have any wheeled equipment, such as a bike or car, then you'll probably need a wrench from time to time. You can buy either an adjustable crescent wrench or a set of wrenches that come in different sizes. Adjustable wrenches can be a bit finicky to work with, as they often require readjusting during use. But if you don't anticipate needing a wrench very often, it's nice having a single tool available for the job. On the other hand, if you have a particular-size nut that you often deal with—say, the bolt that you tighten to secure the wheel on your bike—nothing beats having a wrench specifically fitted for that size.

An alternative to standard wrenches is a socket wrench set. A socket wrench has a handle that ratchets and many different heads to fit all sizes of nuts. Socket wrenches make certain jobs much easier, but a good set is expensive and might be overkill at this time of your life.

 If you're going to work on a bike or car made abroad, you may need a socket wrench set that is made for the metric system.

Measuring tape: At some point you're going to have to measure something. If you get a longer measuring tape, say 16 or 25 feet, you'll be prepared for most every measuring need that will crop up. The thicker the tape's metal, the less likely it is to twist when fully extended, making the measuring process easier. And the unit should definitely have a brake so that you can pull the tape out to whatever length you want and make it stay there. These features cost a little more, but you'll appreciate having them.

Drills: If you're planning on being a true do-it-yourselfer, then you'll need an electric drill. This drill is mostly used to predrill wood (or some other material) that you plan to place a screw into. If an electric drill doesn't fit your current budget, for a few bucks you can buy a screw starter. It looks like a screwdriver, but it has a drill bit at the end. This bit allows you to make a little starter hole in the wood for the screw. This is much easier than trying to drive a screw directly into the wood without predrilling.

Electric drills can perform many functions. In addition to buying a wide assortment of drill bits, you can purchase other attachments that can turn your electric drill into a screwdriver, sander, grinder, or even a saw. This saves you from having to buy a bunch of separate tools designed specifically for these different functions.

Duct tape: No home should be without a roll of duct tape. This strong material seemingly has a million uses, many of which crop up when you have some sort of problem that requires fashioning a "bandage" for a piece of equipment. Duct tape is typically gray, although you can purchase it in other colors that can make it less unsightly.

Nails, screws, and walls: You now have the equipment to use nails and screws, but do you actually have any? Half of the time you need these items, they come packaged with whatever you need to use them for (think the screws that come with a paper-towel holder kit). But you should still purchase a small box of nails and a supply of basic wood screws, just in case.

If you're nailing or screwing into wood, it's pretty straightforward, but one of the most common places to insert a nail or screw is into a wall, and more often than not, this process is anything but straightforward. This is because of the way walls are built. Old walls were built by creating a lattice of wood onto which plaster was slathered and then smoothed and painted. As plaster gets older it becomes more brittle, which means there's a chance that putting a screw or nail into the plaster will break it apart and leave a gaping hole. The correct technique to avoid this is to locate a stud, one of the wooden slats behind the plaster, and nail or screw into that.

The easiest way to find studs in your walls is to buy a stud finder, an electronic gadget that senses metal and so will tell you exactly where the slats are by detecting the nails that hold them together. If you don't want to spend the money on one of these, you can try tapping the wall. Hopefully, you can detect the difference between the hollow sound of empty plaster and the heavier sound of wood behind the plaster.

Newer walls are usually made of drywall or plasterboard. The frames used to hold these in place are usually made of metal, to which the large slabs of drywall are attached. If you are hanging something light—say, under twenty pounds—you can usually nail right into drywall and the nail will hold. If you buy a picture hook to hang something that has a wire or hook behind it, you'll notice that the nail slants downward when you position it in the hook, with the head of the nail higher than the point. That gives the nail extra holding strength. So be sure that any nail you put in drywall is angled down.

If you need to attach something heavy to your wall, such as a shelf, use a molly (also called a molly bolt). A molly is a plastic sleeve that you put into the wall. First you drill a hole into the wall that is smaller than the molly. You then gently tap the molly through the hole, causing it to become securely lodged. Last, you screw the screw into the molly. Another option for mounting heavy items is butterfly screws. You drill a bigger hole and push the closed butterfly end of the screw through. When the screw gets to the other side, it automatically opens us so that when you fully screw it up against the wall the outer screw has a strong backing within the wall.

WORD TO THE WISE

If you're planning to mount a shelf on your wall to hold breakable items or a valuable flat-screen TV, the smart move might be to call in a pro. Perhaps your landlord's handyman can do the job for you.

SHOULD YOU FIX IT YOURSELF OR GET A PROFESSIONAL?

Many household maintenance and repair jobs are so basic that you'll want to do the job yourself. And as your practical experience grows, the list of things you'll feel comfortable tackling will expand. And don't forget that YouTube and similar sites are great resources for visual tutorials on how to do most anything. Regardless of your skill set, there are going to be those jobs that require outside assistance, which could be somebody you pay or a handy relative.

And keep in mind that in many circumstances, a rental unit will have a maintenance person or company on contract to handle basic repairs that need expertise. You may not have to pay a dime if the repair is due to the normal course of wear and tear (as opposed to your having broken something).

CAUTION Do not try to fix something yourself unless you are confident you can handle the job. Mishandling a job will just cost more money and may jeopardize your relationship with your landlord.

WORD TO THE WISE When someone else is called in to do the job, see if you can make it a learning experience. Make an effort to observe the expert at work. Maybe you'll learn something, so if the problem occurs again, you'll know how to handle it on your own.

When a problem is not the landlord's responsibility and you are forced to hire outside help, you may encounter certain challenges. One is the timing of the service call. Be prepared to be flexible. If you must be gone during the appointment, be sure to arrange things with your landlord or building supervisor, who will have a key to your unit.

A major concern is getting ripped off. Will the expert do a good job? Will he or she overcharge you? Will visiting your home serve as an opportunity to case the place? The best way to help yourself around all these questions is to get a personal recommendation. If someone you trust tells you that a particular plumber, electrician, painter, or handyman is competent and reliable, then you can safely pick up the phone. But if you have to blindly research someone's reputation on your own, the risks increase that you won't be satisfied with the results.

WORD TO THE WISE One way of checking out a business is by contacting your local Better Business Bureau. Although the BBB office can't really tell you how competent a particular service person may be, it can you tell if people have filed complaints about the service person with the BBB office; this way you'll know not to call the business.

CAUTION Don't hire service people who aren't insured. If they are working on your premises and get hurt, they can sue you if they don't carry insurance. Employees of larger firms are usually insured, and you can always ask to see an insurance certificate. But a local guy who paints houses may not be insured; if he falls off a ladder and hurts himself, you could find yourself responsible.

MONEY SAVER Another legal matter to consider is bonding. If a company is bonded, it means that it has met statutory requirements and is covered by insurance so that if something goes wrong, such as if it fails to complete the work, you'll be compensated. Bonding may not be important for small jobs, but it is a must if you're having major work done.

Here's a final consideration about hiring someone to come into your place. In Chapter 2, I discussed the importance of renters' insurance, which protects your possessions from theft and damage. If you have valuable items in your apartment, I recommend that you have this insurance in place before letting a worker into your home. Theft by service people, while rare, does happen. And there's also the chance that during the course of their work they may inadvertently damage an expensive possession.

COMMON MAINTENANCE TASKS

There are many common, easy-to-do maintenance tasks that will help your equipment and your life run more smoothly—and may even earn bonus points from your landlord. Here's a starter list:

- Keep the coils under your refrigerator clean by removing the cover at the bottom and vacuuming or dusting out the accumulated dust bunnies. This makes your fridge more efficient, which saves money, and helps it last longer. Clean the drain pan out while you're down there.
- Keep kitchen drains open and flowing cleanly to prevent clogs—every one or two months, pour a full kettle or medium saucepan of boiling water down the drains to loosen any hardened grease or oil and wash away food particulates. You can then add a half cup of baking soda and a cup of white distilled vinegar down the drain and let it fizz for five minutes. Then flush again with more boiling water.
- Clean the kitchen stove hood and get rid of the oil that builds up on it from your cooking. Use an old rag with some vegetable oil to get the dusty oil residue off first, then clean the surface with regular kitchen spray cleaner. Dust or vacuum out the exhaust fan.
- Clean or replace air filters for your heating and air conditioning unit(s). Dust the vents.
- Vacuum or dust the area behind your washer and dryer—keeping this area lint free will prolong your dryer's life and help prevent fire hazards.

Some toilets are touchier than others, but at some point your toilet will probably overflow. To deal with this, turn off the toilet's water supply valve (the handle is usually located under the tank). If you have a plunger, proceed (otherwise you'll have to call maintenance). With some effort, you'll eventually work away whatever's plugging up the drain. Note: Drain-cleaning products aren't very effective in toilets due to the toilet's watery environment, which dissipates the unclogging solution.

PERSONAL SAFETY ENHANCEMENTS

You want to feel safe in your home, and there are some simple steps you can take that will go a long way to ensuring this. A great place to start is fire safety. Legally, your place of residence must have a fire alarm and probably a carbon monoxide detector as well. When the batteries begin to run down in these devices, they emit a very annoying beeping noise. It's always wise to have a spare battery so that you won't be driven crazy if this beeping starts at 3 A.M. It's even wiser to test these units once a month, using their testing feature.

In the awful event of a fire, stay as low to the ground as possible when making your way out to avoid smoke inhalation (smoke rises toward the ceiling). If possible, cover your mouth with a wet cloth, towel, shirt, or similar item. And before opening a door, check to see whether the handle is hot to the touch. If it is, opening that portal might make your situation worse. Consider finding another way out.

The time-honored best way to protect yourself from crime is to have a good door lock (and to remember to use it!). When you move into a new place, confirm that the locks have been changed. Otherwise, there could be another set of keys to your place floating around. If you're in charge of taking care of a lock change, the cheapest method is to have a locksmith change the cylinder. However, it might be worth asking the locksmith whether he or she believes the locks you have are adequate given the neighborhood. Locksmiths know about crime because after a break-in, they're called in to put in new locks.

 Consider storing valuables and important documents in a well-hidden lockbox or small safe.

Many police departments will make a house call to assess whether or not you are taking the proper precautions. They know what methods of entry the local burglars use and so can offer guidance as to what precautions you should take, such as putting up gates on windows or installing a burglar alarm.

Here's a little story related to the issue of safety. One day I left the house and forgot my key. When I returned, I desperately needed to get back inside, and quickly, as I had a meeting to go to and needed to change. My only hope was the window in the breakfast room, which had an air conditioning unit in it, so I knew it wasn't locked. The problem was that the window was above the cement stairs that led down to the basement, which meant to get to it I'd have to get up on the ledge and inch my way over, risking serious injury if I fell.

So I used an overturned garbage pail to get onto the ledge, and inched over to the window with the A/C unit, giving it a half-hearted push while trying not to fall over backwards in the attempt. That did nothing, so I decided to abandon the mission. But the garbage pail had been pushed away when I climbed up—now I couldn't get back down. Back across the ledge I went and this time I gave the A/C unit a hard shove. I heard a loud snap as the plastic brackets holding it in place gave way, allowing me to push it aside to gain access to my house. I took note that the burglar alarm had not been triggered.

What that incident taught me—in addition to never risking my neck again in a silly stunt like that—is that a thief could break into my house as easily as I did without setting off the alarm. To prevent this, I bought some metal brackets and screwed them into the interior window sill so that now you can't push in the A/C. When I went to remove the unit for winter storage, I was surprised to see that the unit had been pushed in an inch or so—some burglar had tried to imitate what I had done but failed thanks to the sturdy brackets I'd installed.

10 FUNISHINGS AND DÉCOR

You Can Be Stylish on a Budget

MIXING THE NEW WITH THE OLD

Chances are that some of the furniture in your new abode is going to come from your old home or from your relatives. Most people have some odds and ends that they don't need and will gladly pass them on to someone just starting out. But this generosity can create awkwardness. You may not even like what people are offering you. Or you may be saddled with mismatched pieces of furniture. For instance, you could find yourself presented with a dining table from one relative and dining chairs from another—and, naturally enough, the table and the chairs are from different sets and don't match. But you really need that furniture! Should you just accept the generosity and live with a jumbled mix of furnishings?

Regardless of what is gifted to you, at some point you'll probably find yourself looking to acquire your own furniture. If you have a large budget, that'll be a piece of cake, but the premise of this book is that you are (at least somewhat) financially challenged. So read on to learn how to buy appealing furniture that fits your budget and looks good in your home.

ESSENTIAL ELEMENTS OF DECORATING AND FURNISHING

If you have experience decorating living spaces, you'll probably have lots of ideas about how you want your new place to look. But if style is the last thing you care about and you just need a place to crash, you probably won't have to put too much effort into choosing items for your place. Most people are somewhere in between—they would like a nice-looking place that isn't stuffy but gives the impression of being pulled together. The good news is that there are ways you can do that on a budget without a lot of fuss.

Assessing Your Furniture Needs

The first step is to take stock of the furniture items that you already have. Review their various sizes, shapes, and colors. Do you plan to replace any of these things soon? Then create a list of items you'll be searching for in the days and weeks ahead. Measure the spaces where you think they might sit and add the measurements to your list.

Recording measurements and keeping photos of your furniture in your smartphone will help you a lot when you are out and about looking at furniture. Keeping a measuring tape in your bag or car will also help! All of this prep will come in handy and save you time when you're pondering the purchase of an item.

Choosing Colors

Think about the particular colors you'd like to see in your place. A good rule of thumb is to focus on colors that complement your largest furnishings. If you're going to be acquiring wood items, choose woods (or wood stains) with either dark, medium, or light colors, and then keep all your wood furniture within that color group. Don't worry so much about the type of wood. If you stay within the same basic color group, your furniture choices will look more purposeful.

And for pillows, throw blankets, rugs, and curtains, choose a restricted set of fabric colors. Too many colors will overwhelm the place. Then, when you're out hunting for a new couch or a bed comforter, you'll know exactly what colors to look for and can make decisions a lot faster. I recommend that you choose two or three colors that you like and that go together. You can even select shades of just one color. Choosing different shades of green, for example, with white or black can look very smart and modern. A bonus from your restricted color scheme is that you can also choose nearly any pattern or texture for pillows, blankets, or curtains and still make things "go together," even if they don't match. The restricted color scheme will give your whole place a nice "pulled-together" feel without being too obvious.

Taking Your Apartment to the Next Level

You've already assessed the size of the furnishings you have and the spaces you want to fill, so the next step is to keep an eye out for appropriate-size items to complement your space. If your apartment is smallish, think twice about getting a California king-size bed. And if your couch is smallish, you may want to make sure the coffee or end tables are appropriately sized. But once size and color are firmly implanted in your head, you're well on your way to choosing good pieces at any price.

If you want to create a unique space for yourself, but don't want to get a degree in interior design to do it, you can apply a great technique called visual metaphor. If a painting, photograph, comic book, or graphic print inspires you, keep a copy of that item with you (or in your phone). Look for furniture and decorative items that "live in that world." They don't have to literally be in the picture, but if you see a chair or table or vase or rug that looks like it belongs in the picture (and it goes with your color scheme and size needs), consider purchasing it.

For example, let's say you're a big fan of the Batman movie franchise, and you want your place to evoke those films without being silly or over the top. You could build around the films' color motifs of blue, gray, and black, with hard lines. You can subtly build up an impressive look without plastering the walls with Batman posters (although a large Batman carpet might be cool!).

WHERE TO BUY FURNITURE

You can source new or used furniture from a number of different places. The following list is arranged from the typically most expensive venues to the cheapest.

Furniture Stores

If you have a little money to spend on a furniture item, why not start at the top of the list by visiting traditional furniture stores? Though they are the most expensive option, they do offer quality furniture and a helpful, knowledgeable sales staff. If you can't find what you want at the right price, then by all means proceed down the list until you meet with success.

Thrift Stores

Thrift stores should be on your "must-visit" list if you're shopping for furniture on a budget. Many charities run thrift stores, and people like giving these establishments their used belongings—both because they're helping out a charity and because they get a tax deduction for it, which can potentially mean more money in their pocket than selling it outright. Not every thrift store will necessarily carry furniture and home decorations, but many do.

WORD TO THE WISE
Buying from thrift stores is a little bit like a hobby, because you have to keep going back to see what merchandise has come in. You can find some real bargains, but you may have to be persistent. If you make friends with the staffers, they may be willing to keep an eye out for the type of furniture you're looking for and tell you when a new shipment of goods has come in.

Flea Markets

Some flea markets are like a collection of yard sales, as all the sellers are motivated mostly by the desire to rid themselves of items they never use. Others are filled with people who make all or part of their living going from flea market to flea market. In this second type you're less likely to find a real bargain, as the sellers are in it for the profit, not to get rid of clutter. One difference between a yard sale and a flea market is the timing of your arrival. The later you arrive at a flea market, the better your chance of bargaining with the seller as he or she will not be eager to pack up whatever is left and drag it back home again.

If something is a hundred or more years old, it's considered an antique, giving the seller an excuse to jack up the price. If you're just starting out, you're probably better off staying away from antiques.

Yard and Garage Sales

While the goods sold at yard or garage sales bear a price, it's usually quite low and therefore affordable—and quite possibly even negotiable. There's likely to be stiff competition for the better goods, so the earlier you hit the yard sales, the better the merchandise you're likely to find. By the end of the day, whatever is left probably belongs in the garbage, not in your place. As always, it pays to inspect carefully items you are considering purchasing, as yard sale items can harbor hidden problems. At least the owners should be on hand to answer questions you may have about the age and condition of the item you're interested in.

If a yard or garage sale is being run by the children of a deceased parent, you need to be a bit more careful than usual. It's possible the house was neglected for many years, and the children may not know much about the history or condition of the item you're interested in.

"Street Shopping"

Most communities schedule periodic neighborhood garbage pickup for large items such as furniture. If you go out on the day when people are tossing out unwanted clutter, you may find worthwhile items at no cost. Just be sure to get an early start, as other people will be doing the same thing. And remember to take a vehicle that can hold whatever salvage you think may work in your home.

If you live in a college town, you can "street-shop" at the end of the semester, as students heading for home will sometimes leave large belongings on the curb. Also, if you're not too proud and are looking for a specific object, ask friends and relatives to keep an eye out for you where they live. The greater your search area, the more likely you are to find what you're looking for.

PIERRE SAYS Never pick up any bedding off the street, whether a mattress or sofa bed. If bedbugs are in it, they could put all your other belongings in jeopardy. Once my wife and I once bought a piece of used furniture from a store and a few days later found our house infested with fleas. Trust me, that is not fun—and it's a heck of a lot of work to get rid of them. So watch out for sketchy items that might have unwholesome critters hiding in them.

The Internet

Near certain availability is the big advantage of getting what you need on the Internet (from sites such as Freecycle, Kashless Krew, or Craigslist). Rather than *hoping* that you'll find a suitable coffee table on a given shopping expedition, you're pretty much guaranteed of finding one close to what you're searching for somewhere on the Internet. Tip: If people have put their belongings up on Craigslist (or any similar website) because they're moving, their desire to get rid of said merchandise will increase as their moving day approaches and so will their willingness to accept lower offers. Check to see if there is a specific date by which the object must be sold, and act accordingly. Of course if you wait too long, the object may not be there when you do act.

CAUTION Shopping on Craigslist is not risk free. Unwary people have been lured into robberies, carrying a lot of cash with them to purchase an item from the "seller." Make sure that you're meeting someplace public and safe so that you don't wind up the victim of an armed robbery.

FYI You have to be a member of Freecycle (mentioned above) to participate. Since each group has its own rules, make sure to check how Freecycle in your neighborhood operates.

If you need a vehicle to pick up your purchase and don't have one or a friend who does, companies like Zipcar may provide an affordable solution.

Buying New

While new furniture certainly can be expensive, that doesn't mean there aren't plenty of opportunities to buy new furniture at an affordable price. It just takes some research and effort on your part to find a good deal. One thing to keep in mind is that while a lot of furniture looks like it's made out of pricey solid wood, today most furniture is not. It may have the appearance of solid wood, but if it doesn't cost a fortune, it's most likely made of pressed wood. Pressed wood is made from wood chips that are compressed and glued together. It's not as durable as solid wood, but it still looks good and will be less expensive.

 Another advantage of pressed wood is its comparative lightness. If you live in a five-story walk-up and aren't using a moving company or elevator, then pressed wood furniture will be easier to lug up to your apartment than traditional solid wood furniture.

 Be careful not to overload shelves made from pressed wood with heavy objects like books because they can sag in the middle after a while. Also of concern, furniture made from pressed wood has only a thin wood veneer and won't stand up very well to being sanded down. This might be an argument in favor of old, used furniture, which is more likely to be made from real wood and therefore can be sanded and polished to look almost new.

Another way to save money is to buy do-it-yourself furniture, the sort made famous by Ikea. Since you're the one putting it together, the price goes down. And since the furniture is already in pieces, you can use even a Prius as a moving van to easily transport your Ikea purchase. Assembling Ikea furniture isn't always all that simple, and you will need special tools, which the company provides. But if you're in a do-it-yourself mood, by all means don't hesitate to tackle an Ikea project. After exerting a little effort, you'll have a stylish new piece of furniture to show off in your apartment.

As with used furniture, when investing in new furniture you also need to make certain that the color will be right. Better to bring a sample home and be sure you love it than to regret having chosen the wrong color wood for decades. Or keep photos on your phone to help you make color assessments while you're out shopping.

You also need to consider your lifestyle when buying new furniture. For example, if you love cats, then you don't want to spend a lot of money on a fancy couch that will likely be ripped to shreds. Or if you have a lot of ex-football players as friends, then you don't want to buy delicate furniture. So think about *how* you will use your new furniture before plunking down a lot of money.

 Sofas and chairs upholstered with microfiber cloth are more resistant to cat claws because there are no loops in microfiber for their claws to catch. The material is also easy to clean and isn't a hair or fur magnet.

SPACE-SAVING FURNITURE

There's a good chance that space will be at a premium in your new home, so think about furniture that doubles as something else. The most common example of this would be the sofa bed. Although great space savers, sofa beds do have drawbacks: The mattresses are often less than ideal, especially in a cheap sofa bed, and they're heavy to move as you have the weight of both the sofa and the bed frame, plus the mattress.

Futons offer a similar, typically more lightweight option. And futons offer a greater variety of mattress choices, so you can find one that is comfortable to sleep on. And then there are Murphy beds, which fold up against the wall and offer decent-quality mattresses. They can, however, be on the costly side.

You can also find tables that fold in assorted ways. You can keep them in a small configuration when you're eating alone and expand them when you're entertaining guests—which is certainly better than everyone sitting around the room with their plates in their laps.

 Retail places like Target and Cost Plus World Market sell furnishings specifically tailored to small apartments.

FURNITURE SETS

You can buy sets of furniture for your bedroom, living room, and dining room. Sets have the advantage of giving you a uniform look rather than a potentially jarring mix of styles in one room. But sets can also lock you in. If you've bought a furniture set and later find a new piece of furniture you just love, it could clash with the pieces in the matched set. On the other hand, once you've bought a furniture set you can say "Done" and not have to worry about the furniture in that room anymore.

ESTABLISHING YOUR PERSONAL DÉCOR

Filling your new home with cheap furniture may be unavoidable at this stage of your life, and that's just fine. But this doesn't mean that your décor has to suffer. As mentioned previously in this chapter, if you figure out a basic design scheme—selecting a basic wood color and restricting the color palette—before you furnish your apartment, you can enjoy both practicality and a bit of flair and style.

Purchasing accessories that fit your decorating plan (and budget) makes your place look purposely designed and eclectic. If you're worried about breaking the bank, then pick a number for your budget and stick with it. The rest of this chapter will advise you on how to acquire the items you need to complete your desired look.

If you need to purchase a major piece of furniture, you might decide to do without it for a while until you can save up to buy something of quality. Well-made furniture can literally last a lifetime. On the other hand, if you're the type who enjoys implementing a new look every few years, then there's probably no need to bide your time.

If you don't feel confident in putting a decorating plan together, don't be afraid to ask for help. People who fancy themselves decorating doyens are usually willing to lend their talent out. Just make sure you ask people whose judgment and taste you respect. See how they decorated their own homes. Avoid someone whose place overwhelms you with countless knickknacks when you walk through the door. And always make your "consultants" understand that you're on a limited budget.

If you place a large piece of furniture, such as a couch, catty-corner, you can store items behind it that you don't want in plain sight.

Walls and Windows

Your walls take up a lot of space, don't they? That's why some people consider them to be the highest priority when it comes to accessorizing. First, make sure the walls have a fresh coat of paint. (Wallpaper is another option, but it's messy and often difficult to deal with and may not be worth the trouble.) Paint comes in a wide variety of shades, and there are plenty of mixing and matching options. If you're not quite sure what you want, consult with someone in the paint department at your local home improvement store.

Before you start painting the walls or putting up wallpaper, talk to your landlord to get his or her approval. And ask the landlord about the ramifications of your plans. When you move out, will you be expected to repaint the walls a neutral color or take down the wallpaper you put up? Remember, you have your security deposit at stake and don't want to diminish the amount you'll get back.

Your windows are another large feature in your abode, so try to pick window accessories—drapes, swags, blinds—that complement your walls, keeping your chosen color scheme in mind! Then throw some pillows in that same color scheme on your couch and select a couple of wall hangings.

Rugs

Another large space begging for some attention is your floor. Rugs are a good way to decorate floors because they feel good to walk on in bare feet and make a room warmer. Plus, if you have downstairs neighbors, they will appreciate a rug's sound-proofing qualities. It's for this reason that in some buildings rugs are mandatory; if that surprises you, then you've probably never lived anywhere with someone overhead clomping around on rugless floors in the middle of the night.

In addition to color, rugs lend texture to a room. Bare wood floors and wood furniture give a very uniform look, so having a rug will break that up. Plus, rugs can make sitting on the floor more comfortable, which is helpful when you have a lot of friends over.

If you're buying a used rug, it's probably more worn in some places than in others. Sometimes you can get lucky and find a rug whose worn parts will fit nicely under some of your furniture so that they will remain unseen.

Cloth Coverings

If your acquisitions are in need of some TLC but you don't have either the skills or desire to refinish or refurbish them, cloth covering can do wonders, both for masking the appearance of these pieces and for improving the overall look of the room. Tablecloths, the most common such accessory, represent a wide variety of styles and colors. But you can also put runners on dresser tops and occasional tables that will cover scratches and burn marks and brighten up your place at once. Check vintage markets for old-fashioned tablecloths and runners, or shop on Etsy.com. Don't forget that what you put on top of the cloth is also decoration. A bowl of fruit not only adds color and depth, but it also frees up more storage space in your kitchen.

MONEY SAVER If your dining room chairs suffer from threadbare seats, see if you can remove and cover them with stapled cloth. This simple treatment will make them almost as good as new—or at least a lot better than they were.

Lighting

Did you know that lighting is more than just another way to decorate? It also plays a role in your health. Having too little light, which happens in winter, can make you feel sad and rundown. So you want your living space to offer you as much light as possible. Start with the place where you most like to sit. If you do a lot reading there, make sure that whatever you'll be reading will be well illuminated. If you spend a lot of time on a laptop, then you'll want light that won't create a glare on your screen. Floor lamps with a three-way bulb are great for additional lighting in corners or next to desks. And spotlights can be a fun way to draw attention to a favorite piece of artwork.

Plants

Plants are actually good for you as they soak up excess carbon dioxide and give off oxygen. They're also colorful, especially flowering plants, and they quite literally add life to your home. Do a web search for low-maintenance indoor plants at affordable prices. Japanese peace lilies, for example, can be expensive but are very easy to care for. Some ferns are less expensive but require more attention. If you're concerned that you might forget to water your plants, think about getting drought-tolerant plants such as cacti. They'll forgive you if you neglect them for a few days.

CHAPTER **11 ELECTRICITY**

Circuits, Wiring, Breakers and More

ELECTRICITY POWERS YOUR LIFE

Have you ever thought about just how dependent you are on electricity? Probably not too much, right? But sometimes we're forced to, like when the power goes out for a few hours. Then it really hits home that we're more dependent on electricity today than ever. Even if half our gadgets don't plug directly into the wall because they're portable, they still need to be recharged by electricity. So it doesn't hurt to develop a basic understanding of how electricity works, and how you can become more efficient using it and save money. Electricity can of course be dangerous, but with the proper precautions you can safely tackle a number of minor electrical problems yourself before needing to call in an electrician.

WHAT TO DO IF THE POWER GOES OFF

Whether because of a bad storm, someone accidentally crashing into a power line down the street, or reasons wholly mysterious, from time to time you'll find yourself without electrical power. It's not fun and it can be a bit scary, but it will happen and it pays to be prepared.

If you find yourself without power, the first thing you should do is look out the window. If it seems that everyone in your neighborhood is in the same predicament, then there's nothing you can do about it but wait.

CAUTION A power outage may strike without notice, so now's the time to prepare a power outage kit. A flashlight is certainly useful, especially if it's the kind that can be charged by turning a crank—then you won't have to worry about working batteries. It's also wise to have a few candles to place about the house, along with matches or a lighter to light them. And a portable radio that runs on batteries will allow you to stay tuned to the news. You may catch word of what caused the blackout.

However, if it appears that the problem is localized to your home, you may be able to fix the problem yourself. First, consider the devices and appliances that were running when the power went out. If you were using something that consumes a lot of power, such as a hair dryer or microwave oven, or if you had many lights on and gadgets going, then your first step should be to unplug whatever may have caused your personal power grid to flatline. The reason is that when power is restored, it won't immediately go out again because the power-hungry electricity gobblers you had turned on won't resume sucking all your juice.

A localized power outage is caused by a circuit (an electrical pathway) within your home getting too hot. Electricity is caused by a flow of electrons, which generate heat as they move through the wires of your home to your devices. If too many of them are moving too fast, then that heat becomes dangerous. The heat could cause a wire to melt and spark an electrical fire. To prevent that from happening, either the circuit breakers or fuses in your home will shut the power off if one section of your wiring is drawing current at a dangerous level.

CAUTION Did you know that the handy power strips everyone depends on can themselves potentially overload? Check your power strips from time to time; if one often becomes very hot, it could suffer a meltdown and cause a fire. The solution is to buy a power strip that come equipped with its own circuit breaker. If the power strip becomes overloaded, it will shut down.

Somewhere in your home is a metal box with a hinged cover in or on the wall (often near the kitchen and high enough that children can't reach it) that contains either circuit breakers or fuses. If you're renting a room in a house, the box might be in the basement or on the side of the building.

Circuit Breakers

If your building was built in the last four or five decades, or if its electrical system has been upgraded, you'll see a series of switches in the metal box. These are called circuit breakers. If one circuit got too hot, that switch will automatically go to the off position. All you have to do is switch it back to the on position to restore power. (As mentioned earlier, hopefully, you'll have unplugged whatever caused the circuit breaker to blow so that it won't immediately switch back to the off position.)

Circuit breaker panels often also have a larger main power switch, usually at the top or bottom of the panel, that will cut power to every circuit. If you have an electrical problem that could be dangerous (see below), it may be best to turn off that switch so that all power is cut rather than trying to guess which particular circuit switch you need to shut off.

Fuses

Fuses are the old-fashioned way of preventing an electrical overload from burning down your place of residence. Though quite effective, fuses are more trouble to maintain than circuit breakers because they must be replaced when they blow out from an overload. Fuses have little glass windows, and when a fuse blows you can see that the inside of the fuse will be black, telling you it needs to be replaced. Assuming you have spare fuses, you unscrew the one that blew out and screw in a new one. Then go check that the electricity is back on in the part of the house where it went out.

Because they have to be replaced, it's a good idea to keep some spare fuses on hand. Fuses are marked with their type and amperage (how much electricity can flow through them before they cut off the electricity). Fuses usually unscrew, so if you're not sure exactly what type of spare fuses you need to buy, you can remove one (which will cause a blackout in part of your domain) and take it to the hardware store. You could also just take a picture with your cell phone and bring that. Either way, staff at the hardware store will tell you what type you need to buy.

 If you're lucky, someone before you will have labeled each fuse or circuit breaker so that you can easily tell which room or part of the house that the fuse or circuit breaker controls. The labels would read something like "living room" or "bathroom." An appliance that uses a lot of electricity, such as an electric stove, might well be on its own circuit and will be labeled as such.

DEALING WITH ELECTRICAL PROBLEMS

Short Circuits

If one fuse or circuit breaker is always cutting off, you should assess whether too many devices and/or appliances are plugged into that circuit, including big-power consumers such as electric dryers. If you can't find anything obvious that is causing continual power outages, then you could have what is called a short circuit. In this case, something is wrong in the wiring, which means you or your landlord should call an electrician. Short circuits are potentially dangerous, even if there is a mechanism to cut off the power such as a fuse or circuit breaker, so you need a professional to handle this problem.

Smells

If you detect a burning (or otherwise unusual) smell coming from an electrical device, immediately unplug it. If that doesn't stop the smell, then there could be a problem with the wiring in your walls. The safest recourse would be to turn off the main power switch. A wire burning inside your walls could cause a major fire, and you can't risk trying to guess which particular fuse or circuit breaker is the one to turn off. Such a delay would allow the danger to worsen. You or your landlord will need to *immediately* call an electrician to check things out.

Power Surges

Normally, electricity flows at a fairly constant rate, but spikes in electrical power, called power surges, may occur from time to time. Various things can cause a power surge, from something that goes awry at the power company to a bolt of lightning that strikes miles away. There's nothing you can do about power surges, but you can take steps to protect sensitive equipment that might be damaged by such surges.

Computers, in particular, are vulnerable to power surges, which is why it's advisable to plug your computer into a surge protector. The more you pay for one of these, the better protected you are—to the point that some surge protector manufacturers even offer guarantees to reimburse you if your computer gets damaged while plugged into their top-of-the-line protector. (Keep in mind that while this sort of guarantee might get you a new computer, it won't restore your fried data—which you've hopefully been backing up on a regular basis!)

WORD TO THE WISE Although it's impractical to unplug sensitive equipment regularly, if you're going away for an extended period, it may be worthwhile to unplug your computer to prevent a power surge from damaging it. The same goes for any other costly electronic equipment you might have, such as a large-screen TV.

Brownouts

The opposite of a power surge is a brownout. These occur most often in summer during hot weather when air conditioners are turned on at full blast. The electric company may not be able to meet the demand for all this juice, so to compensate it reduces the amount of electricity flowing through everyone's wires. One immediate effect you'll notice is that any lights you have on will seem dimmer than normal. Brownouts can damage sensitive equipment such as computers, so it would be wise to shut yours down and switch to using a battery-powered laptop or tablet.

During a brownout, try to avoid opening the fridge so that it remains cool inside and its motor doesn't go on and off too much. And assuming you want to run your AC during a brownout, try not to use too much other electricity in the house. This way the limited power coming in should be sufficient to run the AC unit without causing its motor to strain too much from a lack of power.

CAUTION Brownouts can damage electric motors, such as those used by elevators, so you may want to take the stairs to avoid getting caught in a stuck elevator during a heat wave.

DOING YOUR OWN ELECTRICAL WORK

CAUTION WARNING! You should be extremely cautious when working on wiring. If you're not 100% certain that you can do a wiring job, then you should leave it to an electrician.

Once you understand how to operate your apartment's system of fuses or circuit breakers and have mapped out the various circuits, you can safely do some electrical work in your home since you can shut off the electricity to the spot you're working on. Let's say that you want to replace a simple on-and-off light switch with a dimmer switch. This is a safe and easy job, assuming you flip the correct circuit breaker or unscrew the right fuse before you begin. (If you have *any* uncertainty about this, seek assistance before proceeding.) Once you've cut the power, all you then have to do is follow the directions on the dimmer switch package, which are generally straightforward.

WORD TO THE WISE When doing electrical work, always read the directions first before taking things apart. And it's a good idea either to take some pictures of the original wiring or to jot down some notes describing it, so that if you can't get the new equipment to work, you can at least properly restore the old wiring.

DOWNLOADS There are hundreds of helpful instructional resources on the web about basic electrical repair and installation jobs. Just search for the task you have in mind—for example, "how to wire a three-way switch"—and you'll find videos or detailed instructions on websites such as YouTube, wikiHow, and so on.

SAVING ELECTRICITY

Being smart about your use of electricity saves you money, but it also reduces environmental damage. How? The electricity that comes into your home was generated at a power plant, which could be powered by burning coal or some other fuel. These emissions can be harmful to the atmosphere and to air quality.

The easiest way to save electricity is to turn off anything that consumes electricity that you're not using, such as lights when you're not in the room. Most homes are filled with consumer electronics, which together can add significantly to your power bill. Keep them turned off or in a low-power state when you're not actively using them. On a similar note, take advantage of your programmable thermostat, if you have one.

Purchasing energy-efficient electrical equipment, such as compact fluorescent lightbulbs, is another way to reduce your consumption of electricity. Look for the Energy Star label to get the most energy-efficient products. When you use appliances, be smart about the cycles you select. With your washing machine, try to use cold water whenever possible. And make sure that your clothes dryer isn't running for ten or fifteen minutes longer than it really needs to.

 If you've done everything you can to reduce your electricity usage and your bill doesn't go down, call your electric company to make sure it has been actually checking your meter. If for some reason the electric company can't access your meter, it will continue to charge you based on estimates derived from past usage, rather than bill you for your actual consumption.

 Anything that uses electricity to generate heat—to heat your home, heat water, or dry clothes—can be more expensive than gas or oil. Since rates for electricity, gas, and oil change regularly, if you use electricity as a form of heating, it may be worth checking to see whether changing equipment could save you money over time. On the other hand, electric space heaters, which heat only one room, can save you money by allowing you to keep your thermostat turned low and providing extra heat only in the room you are currently occupying.

CHAPTER 12 PLUMBING

Everything from Unclogging Toilets to Fixing Leaky Faucets

LEARNING ABOUT PLUMBING

There are two types of plumbing issues you're likely to encounter, the mundane and the urgent (hopefully, you will have read this chapter before you're standing knee deep in murky water!). You can probably learn to handle the sorts of plumbing jobs covered in this chapter yourself. But there will be others that require a plumber's assistance, because water flowing onto the floor faster than you can mop it up is a very bad thing. So if you have family, friends, or coworkers in the neighborhood, ask them to recommend a good plumber and keep his number handy.

SHUTOFF VALVES

Whether you need to do a bit of minor plumbing maintenance or prevent a domestic disaster, you must first be aware of your home's water shutoff valves. Shutoff valves are knobs that you turn to shut off the water to the faucet in a sink or to the toilet. The two shutoff valves to a sink (one for cold water and one for hot) will probably be in the cabinet beneath the sink's basin, whereas a toilet's single valve (it uses only cold water) is typically found on the wall behind the toilet. Since it's likely that the valve you want to shut will be in the on position, you turn the valve clockwise to shut it.

 Finding the shutoff valve for a tub or shower can be trickier, as it may be located behind a panel in the wall. If you can't access it, you'll need to turn off the main shutoff valve (discussed below).

Because shutoff valves aren't used very much, minerals from the water can accumulate inside their mechanism and they can become stuck, making them difficult to turn. Since you don't want to break the valve, don't try forcing it with a wrench or pliers. First you might try applying a lubricant such as WD-40 and waiting a few minutes for it to sink in. Machine oil or even vegetable oil might also work. If that doesn't help, try loosening the nut at the base of the stem and then try turning the handle.

If you want to make sure you can turn your shutoff valves when needed, make a practice of turning each of them on and off a couple of times a year to prevent minerals from building up. This will also help to familiarize you about where they're located.

The Main Shutoff Valve

Every residence has a main valve to shut off the water coming in from outside. In a house, this valve is often located in the basement or out in the yard, typically near a wall. If you live in an apartment, you likely won't have access to the main shutoff valve and will need to ask the landlord or building manager to shut it.

It's fairly common for the main valve to not completely shut off the water but rather to only slow the flow down. If that's the case, if you turn on another faucet that isn't being worked on, optimally one between the main valve and the one on which you're working, the excess water will flow out and not reach the area you need to stay dry.

BURST PIPES

A burst pipe—usually caused by old age or freezing—is probably the worst household plumbing disaster, and with water spilling out at a fast clip, things can get messy fast. Hopefully, the nearest shutoff valve will stop the flow until professional help arrives. If it doesn't, turn off the main valve, or get someone else to do it if you can't access it. Fixing water pipes is probably best left to professionals, so your next step after shutting off the water supply is to call a plumber.

Wrapping some duct tape around the area of broken pipe can slow down the flow of water, but such a remedy won't stop it. Local hardware stores usually carry patch kits, assuming you can find a hardware store easier than a plumber. Patches are relatively easy to install. They won't stop the water from flowing for very long (or may only reduce a full blast of water to a slow leak), but they can get you through an emergency.

How to Unclog Your Toilet

While burst pipes are rare, toilet clogs are . . . well, as they say, s**t happens. You want to be prepared for this common problem, so buy a toilet plunger at the earliest opportunity. Plunging a stopped-up toilet isn't a pleasant task, but not having a plunger when confronted with a stopped-up toilet is far worse.

WORD TO THE WISE Pay attention to the kind of plunger you buy. A toilet plunger has a flange or a funnel-cup shape attached to the bottom of the stick. A regular plunger has a cup shape that looks like a ball cut in half. A regular plunger is good for sinks, showers, and bathtubs, but toilets require the flange to apply pressure to their awkwardly shaped drains.

The concept is to push down vigorously on the plunger, which will force the water down through the drain, along with anything that is clogging it. Plunging is a two-step process, the down and the up, so make sure that you work at both. Sometimes the clog will clear with only a few plunges and sometimes with several. There must be enough water for the plunger to have an effect, so add water to the toilet bowl if the water level is too low.

FYI If you're having trouble clearing a toilet clog, try adding *hot* water to the mix, along with a bit of dish-washing liquid. This will warm the rubber in the plunger and help it make a better seal; the dish-washing liquid may also help to dissolve the clog.

If all your plunging efforts lead to naught, you have two choices. The first is to call a plumber and just deal with the expense (if it's a middle-of-the-night call, a plumber's service can be quite pricey). Your other option is to use an auger or plumber's snake, a long cable that you force down the drain by turning. It will push even solid clogs through the drain. If pushing won't work, try using it to pull out whatever is causing the clog.

FYI Don't have an auger? Try unbending a wire clothes hanger. It won't be as effective as an auger, but in a pinch it may break up the clog.

Preventing Toilet Clogs

There are many causes for toilet clogs, but the good news is that the three major causes are all mostly preventable *by you*. Probably the most common source of trouble is simply using too much toilet paper. Another big problem is flushing things down the toilet that really should instead be tossed into the trash. If you have a "sensitive" toilet, avoid flushing products labeled "flushable" for a while and see if the situation improves. And a third source of trouble can be clogged water jets. If the outlets for the water are clogged, then the water won't come out from the tank with sufficient force to push down what's in the bowl. When cleaning your toilet, make sure to use the brush to wipe under the rim of the bowl so that you clean out the jets.

WORD TO THE WISE A common issue in today's world isn't just too much TP going down the drain, but also wet wipes and feminine hygiene products. Some are "flushable," meaning they are supposed to disintegrate in water (although sometimes they don't dissolve immediately, which can cause trouble), but many (such as common baby wipes) are not flushable and should go in a lined wastebasket.

Toilet Tanks

Toilets can clog at the bottom, but they can also mess up at the other end, inside the tank. The mechanism inside a tank is fairly simple, but rather than describe it I advise you to watch a how-to video on the web if you want to learn more. What you'll learn is that these mechanisms are fairly easy to repair or replace.

TIME SAVER You can find toilet repair kits with handy instructions in most any hardware store.

PIPES AND DRAINS

A Note about How Pipes Work

You probably never think about where water and other stuff that goes down a drain flows to, but the answer is simple: Eventually, it winds up in a sewer. Since sewers carry a nasty combination of fluids, including those that get flushed from toilets, I think you'd agree that the less contact you have with sewers the better.

You might be curious about why the sewer gas emitted from these waste products never seems to come up through the waste pipe system and into your kitchen and bathroom. The reason that doesn't happen is that the pipes running under drains are U shaped. These U-shaped pipes are called traps. The water that remains at the bottom of the U creates a barrier that keeps the smells from entering where you live and breathe. However, there is a downside to this clever solution: Things that go down the drain can get caught in this trap and eventually cause a clog.

 There's an additional benefit to the U shape. If something valuable and sufficiently heavy, such as a diamond ring, falls into the drain, it would likely get caught in the trap and thus be retrievable. While this lost-and-found feature isn't why traps are U shaped, many a careless person has been delighted with it.

 If you have a drain that is seldom used, the water in the U could dry out, allowing unpleasant odors to waft in. If your nose suddenly takes offense at the air in your home, the simple solution may be to pour some water down that rarely used drain.

How to Unclog a Drain

The main item that clogs bathroom sink drains is hair (or hair combined with soap or shaving cream residue). And the longer the hair of the residents, the more likely you are to encounter clogs. Grease is the likely culprit in a kitchen drain, though various food particles will also play a part.

 If you notice that a drain is starting to drain water slowly, don't wait for it to clog completely, which would make unclogging the drain a much bigger job. Work on unclogging the drain right away, before it stops up completely.

If you believe the advertisements, the only way to clear a clogged drain is by using some commercial product. Those products can be very useful when you are faced with certain tough clogs, but simply pouring a pot full of hot water down a drain may do the trick, so you should think about trying that first. (Note: Don't pour *boiling* water down the drain, as it might melt pipe sealants.) Some people prepare their own concoction of baking soda (put down the drain first) and vinegar (put down the drain second). The two will chemically react and fizz and in many cases clear the clog, if you follow up after half an hour or so with very hot water. If your homemade fixes don't work, the next step would be to consider commercial products such as Drāno. But even those will sometimes fail. What then?

If a chemical product won't dissolve the clog, then it's likely that a hard object needs to be removed from the drain. You could try using a regular plunger designed for everything other than the toilet.

 If you attempt to use a plunger on a sink or tub that has an overflow hole, block it before plunging to make the plunger more effective.

Hardware stores sell inexpensive drain-cleaning tools with little claws on them that are designed to reach down into drains and pull up clumps of hair and soap. In a pinch, you could unbend a wire clothes hanger and make a small hook at the end. An auger is probably strong enough to push through the clog, unless there is something hard down the drain that won't budge.

If you're still having trouble—or if your goal is not to unclog the drain but to remove something that went down it—then it's possible to remove the U-shaped pipe (discussed earlier), though you'll need the proper tools (which vary, depending on your system) and some arm strength to get this done. At this point, it might be a good idea to consult with someone at a hardware store.

As you probably know, complex plumbing jobs can be difficult and messy. Unless you're mechanically inclined, it's probably wise to contact the building manager to bring in assistance.

How to Fix a Constantly Running Toilet

If the water in your toilet continues to gurgle long after you've flushed, the fix might be as simple as jiggling the lever a few times. If that trick works, it probably means that the rubber flap at the bottom of the toilet tank somehow got stuck in the up position and that water is leaking into the bowl and not reaching the right level, which would normally shut the water off. If this happens only once in a great while, no big deal. But if it happens a lot, remove the toilet tank cover and look inside. Here are the steps to take:

Step 1. Check the flushing process. After you have removed the tank cover, the first thing you should do is flush and observe what happens—there's a good chance you'll spot the problem, which is often quite simple to solve, such as untangling the chain that attaches the lever to the flap. If it's something you can fix, turn off the toilet's shutoff valve and flush again so that you can operate in a dry tank.

Step 2. Check the chain tension. One possible reason for your problem could be that the chain connecting the handle to the flap is either tangled or broken. You can easily check this out by simply pushing on the handle and seeing if the flap does what it's supposed to do, which is to go up and down. Tip: The chain could also need some adjustment in terms of length. Try shortening or lengthening it and see if that helps the flap fall more effectively into position.

Step 3. Check the flap. If that's not the problem, take a look at the flap itself. Perhaps it's become corroded and is no longer making a tight seal. If it looks like it's rotten, then you'll need to change it. (If you look at the assembly, you'll see that this is not a terribly complicated job.)

Step 4. Check the ball or float. If the chain and the flap aren't the problem, it might have something to do with the ball that goes up and down with the water level (or the concentric float value in newer toilet mechanisms). Check to see whether the ball looks to be intact or whether any water is inside it. Tip: If there's water in the ball, it will be too heavy to float all the way to the level it's supposed to reach to shut the water. To remove the water, unscrew the ball and empty it out. Also check to see if there are any cracks in the ball, in which case it will need to be replaced. If your toilet tank has a concentric float valve installed rather than the older style ballcock assembly, it may well be simpler to just replace the entire float valve rather than trying to figure out what's wrong with it.

Step 5. Check the ball arm. If the ball looks OK, it could be that the ball-arm may not be moving into the correct position to stop the water from running. You might be able to fix the problem by bending the arm slightly. First try lifting the ball with your fingers when the tank is full and see how much you have to move it to get the water to stop. If the ball arm lifts up only a fraction of an inch, then try to bend it in the middle with the ball going downward and see if that fixes the problem. The same idea, bending the ball arm, holds true if it seems that the ball is hitting the side of the tank, impeding its movement.

Step 6. Check the ballcock assembly. The last place that could be causing the trouble is the ballcock assembly, which is the mechanism that allows the water to flow in. This equipment might look intimidating, but in actuality it's not that complicated because you can remove and replace the entire thing fairly inexpensively. Just remove it and take it to a hardware store; a salesperson will help you find a replacement that fits.

The steps I've listed above are, of course, viewable in any number of how-to videos on YouTube and other sites. Check them out and see for yourself how simple this process is. Of course, it's perfectly understandable if you prefer to skip the do-it-yourself approach and call your building supervisor, particularly if the landlord will cover the repair costs.

PIERRE SAYS

I'm not the Mr. Fix-It type, but I've discovered over time that many plumbing issues are actually pretty straightforward. So, every once in a while I dive in to make plumbing repairs, and more often than not I'm successful. But I could be more efficient about it! My local hardware store is about five blocks away. It seems I've never made a repair that hasn't meant *at least* two trips to this store, and sometimes it's three or four. In part, this is because I'm impulsive and think I know what I'm doing when I actually don't. Sometimes I need a different part than what I thought I needed, and sometimes it ends up that I don't have the right tool for the job. When I start one of these projects an hour or so before the hardware store closes, I sometimes find myself sprinting there to buy what I need to complete the task. So what's the lesson here? If the place you buy hardware requires a bit of a commute, be extra careful before heading out so that your shopping list is as accurate and complete as possible. Or else always begin your work first thing in the morning!

FIXING DRIPS

A dripping faucet doesn't exactly qualify as a plumbing emergency, and in fact many people are quite content to live with them. But the amount of water that you can lose from a drip can be staggering—especially if you're paying for it! And that's doubly true if it's hot water, in which case you're paying for both the water and the heating of it.

Drips are often caused by a worn-out washer or O-ring, the rubber seal that keeps the water from the pipes, which is under pressure, from coming out of your faucet. Eventually, this rubber wears away and causes a drip. Washers themselves are cheap and replacing them, at least in most faucets, is not that complicated. It's basically an unscrewing and rescrewing job. The tricky part might be locating what it is you have to unscrew. Very often there's a decorative cap on the faucet that covers the screw. Once you pry that off with a flat screwdriver or knife edge, the rest is relatively easy.

There are four basic varieties of faucets: compression, disc, cartridge, and ball. Most faucets that have two separate handles, one for hot and one for cold, are compression, though some are disc. The single-handled faucets are called washerless, but there are still parts that can wear out and need to be replaced. Compression faucets drip from the faucet into the sink. The other three varieties are more likely to leak water from the base of the faucet.

The goal is to gently take apart the faucet, examining for wear and tear, and replacing any washer or other part that looks like it's the cause of the drip or leak. Access how-to videos on the web to help you through the process, and to help you identify the type of faucet you have.

Once you've removed the old parts, bring them to a hardware store so that you can make sure you're getting the exact replacement. If any of the screws look at all damaged, bring them in for replacement, too.

Another source of drips can be poorly fitting or worn out faucet attachments, such as aerators. In areas with hard water, minerals build up in aerators, and water starts dripping or spraying from the air inlets. Fortunately, aerators are easy to remove and replace.

CAUTION The best piece of advice you can get with regard to changing washers is "Don't do any more damage." If you run into a problem, don't force anything. For example, you wouldn't want to accidentally strip the groove (where a screwdriver fits into) of the screw you're trying to remove, or getting it off will be much more difficult. So never use too much force, but try other methods of removing a tough screw, including using WD-40 or some other lubricant to loosen it first.

WORD TO THE WISE If you're having trouble removing a screw, try inserting a thick rubber band into the groove to give the screwdriver a bit more grip. By pushing as hard as you can into the screw and turning it slowly, you'll have a better chance of unscrewing it, though it will most certainly have to be replaced once it's been removed. Another option is to get a screw extractor, which is a special blade made to fit into a screw with a stripped head (making it impossible for a normal screwdriver to grip). They're not terribly expensive—under $20—and may save the day.

PART THREE:

HOW TO TAKE CARE OF YOURSELF

13 HEALTH

How to Take Care of Yourself and Work with Your Doctor

ORGANIZING YOUR MEDICAL HISTORY

If you have a chronic health problem such as asthma, I'm going to assume you know how to deal with it. If that's not the case, then find out—quick. This chapter covers the everyday health issues that can crop up and how to be prepared for them—as well as what to do if these health issues are something for which you need medical attention.

The first thing to do is to compile a basic medical history of your life. This information can be critical in the case of a medical emergency, but it also makes preparation for visits to doctors or other medical professionals much easier. You can easily email your medical history to your doctor's office in advance of an appointment (more and more doctors are asking for such things). If you have certain diagnoses or allergies, you can write them down correctly once and remember them when filling out forms or answering questions. Add some information about your family's medical history. If close members of your family have certain diseases, such as diabetes, you're more likely to get them, too.

If your emergency contact (usually a friend or family member) has a copy of your medical history, he or she will be able to provide the information to medical providers if you are unable to answer questions yourself. Your medical history doesn't have to be elaborate or fancy, but it should be very clear.

CAUTION You probably already know this, but if you've ever had an allergic reaction to any type of medication, whether prescription or over the counter, you should make note of that. For example, you need to be aware if you're allergic to aspirin, or a simple medical issue could turn into a life-threatening one if you are given aspirin. Your parents probably know about any medication allergies that you may have, so ask them if you're unsure. Get the information from them now. You don't want to call your parents at 2 A.M. to inquire about which medication to take for a splitting headache.

Medical History Essentials

As you create your medical history, be sure to do the following:

- State your legal name and date of birth.
- Indicate your contact information and the names and phone numbers of two emergency contacts.
- List your drug allergies (prescription and over the counter), food allergies, and other allergies (to wool, latex, or other substances). If you do not have allergies, be sure to write "Allergies: none."
- Record the medications you are currently taking, including medicine names, doses, and dosage schedule. Include inhalers and over-the-counter medications such as ibuprofen. If you use them only occasionally, write "As needed" beside them.
- List all your ongoing diseases or conditions, whether chronic (always present) or recurring (from time to time). List any treatments that you are undergoing. Also provide the reasons for any hospitalizations, such as for long-term illness or major surgery.
- List all shots and immunizations you may have had and still need. You can lump your childhood shots together as "childhood immunizations," but specify such things as tetanus shots and immunizations you may have received before traveling abroad. Be sure to indicate the year you received your shots.
- Describe your family's medical history. List any major illnesses that your parents, grandparents, or siblings may have suffered, such as cancer, respiratory problems, heart disease, and so on.
- Provide the contact information of your primary care physician. This is particularly important for emergency responders or medical staff, who can send updates on your health to your physician. Your primary care physician should have the most complete record of your medical history.

DOWNLOADS The My Medical app for Android and iPhone (**www.mymedicalapp.com**) allows for a comprehensive medical history to be stored on your phone and computer. It also provides areas for keeping track of appointments and for emergency info in case you're in an accident (even on a password-protected phone).

About.com has a good, one-sheet emergency form that you can fill out and keep folded in your wallet for emergencies. Keep a copy on file at home and another with your primary emergency contact. Visit **firstaid.about.com/ library/PDF_files/Medical_Info_Sheet.pdf**.

WORD TO THE WISE Be certain to update your medical history every time it changes. Surgeries, new medicines, accidents, and new shots can all change the picture of your overall health.

TAKING CARE OF MINOR HEALTH PROBLEMS

Medicine Cabinet Basics

You may be one of those hardy souls who never gets a cold, but that doesn't mean some piece of soot won't fly into your eye and make you miserable. So you have to be prepared for a variety of medical issues, not just for yourself but potentially for guests who may need a painkiller for a headache or a bandage for a minor cut.

Here's a basic medicine cabinet checklist. **Essentials:** painkillers and fever reducers such as ibuprofen or aspirin, a thermometer, cold and flu medicine, eyedrops, bandages, antibiotic ointment, and cough drops. **As needed:** allergy medicine, itch-soothing lotion (such as calamine or hydrocortizone cream), antacids, aloe-vera gel for burns, sunblock, and antidiarrheal medicine.

MONEY SAVER One simple way to acquire many of your basic medicine cabinet needs is to buy a first-aid kit from a drugstore. A first-aid kit contains antiseptic wipes, bandages, gauze pads, an instruction booklet, and a whole lot more. These kits come in all manner of complexity (and cost), so you don't necessarily need to go for the top-of-the-line version. Just get what you feel is suitable for your needs.

Cuts, Scrapes, and Burns

It's kind of scary to think about how fragile our skin actually is. It really doesn't take much to cause damage to it, which can be both painful and even potentially dangerous—because once you damage your skin's protective seal, germs can creep in.

You need at least two items in your medicine cabinet to deal with a cut, scrape, or burn: an antiseptic to kill any germs that are poised to infect your body and a bandage to cover the wound and prevent germs of all sorts from entering your system. A box of assorted bandages and triple antibiotic ointment should be OK for most wounds, though larger ones will need gauze and tape. A pleasant side effect of most antiseptic creams is that they also soothe.

 CAUTION You may have heard that alcohol is an antiseptic. It's true that pouring something from the liquor cabinet onto a cut will probably kill any germs that are lurking. But be advised that the pain that alcohol will cause coming into contact with an open wound will instantly convince you to invest in a proper disinfectant!

The human body of course has a lot of built-in safety features, and the bleeding from most small cuts will stop within moments because of clotting (also called coagulation). If you find a basic cut bleeds for a long time, it may be because you had taken some aspirin or ibuprofen earlier. These medicines are anticoagulants, which means they have properties that thin the blood and keep it from clotting too quickly. This is why people with heart conditions often take low doses of aspirin every day. It thins the blood so it doesn't clog the heart. If a wound is severe enough that the bleeding won't stop on its own, then you'll need stitches. For this, you're likely to find yourself in the emergency room.

 FYI If you're bleeding badly, hold a clean cloth to the wound and put as much pressure on the wound as possible. Even if you can't stop the flow, you can slow it down until you get medical attention.

Feeling Faint

Seeing blood, particularly your own, can make you feel light-headed or may even cause you to black out entirely. Faintness often starts with feeling a little unfocused and dazed and then typically leads to a lack of balance, dizziness, and a darkening in the peripheral vision. The darkness often starts to creep over the rest of your vision and a ringing in the ears begins. These are a message from your body, and if you heed them, you can often recover from faintness before your body *forces* you to lie down.

Quickly find a place to lie down flat on your back with your legs elevated above your heart and head. This helps the blood flow back to the heart and brain faster. After putting your feet up for a while and getting ahold of yourself, make certain to slowly drink some room-temperature water and nibble on something with protein, such as cheese or peanut butter. When you feel a little better, take a break for a healthy meal.

There are many reasons you might feel dizzy or light-headed from time to time. Dehydration, lack of protein, or too much sugar in your diet can have adverse effects on people's day-to-day functioning. Several underlying medical conditions may be at the root of recurring fainting spells. If the light-headedness continues for long stretches or recurs regularly for several weeks, see a physician. The cause could be as simple as low blood pressure or as complicated as a heart condition.

Splinters

Even if a splinter is visible, pulling one out with your fingernails may not mean that you got all of it. And leaving a little piece of wood—which potentially is covered with germs—inside your flesh is never a good idea. So to remove splinters you need a pair of tweezers. To make sure the tweezers themselves are germ free, either dip them in rubbing alcohol or heat them over a flame (then let them cool) before trying to latch onto the splinter. If removing the splinter proves impossible, seek professional help to prevent infection.

Motes in Your Eye

You're walking down the street, minding your own business, and suddenly something gets in your eye, causing you more discomfort that you can bear. You pull on your eyelid to get some tears going, but the irritant won't wash out. Now what do you do?

The first thing to know is what *not* to do: Don't rub your eyes! If you do, whatever it is could become embedded, making it much harder to get out. Or if it's a piece of metal on the surface, it could scratch your cornea.

The best approach is to wash your eye out with a fluid. Fill an eyecup with water, preferably water that's been either distilled or boiled (and then cooled), although plain old tap water probably won't harm you. After you fill the cup, tilt your head back, put the cup over your eye so that there's a bit of a seal, and roll your eye around until you wash the particle out. It's a simple and effective operation.

If you don't have an eyecup, other options that work just as well include a saline solution, eyewash, and eyedrops. In most circumstances, squeezing some saline solution in your eye helps remove the offending mote.

Taking Painkillers

Oft-overlooked aspirin is truly a miracle drug, even though no one is 100% sure how it works. It's good for subduing headaches, relieving cold symptoms, and reducing fevers. In fact, if you ever think you're having a heart attack, take two aspirin before you call for an ambulance. So having a bottle of aspirin around is a must (unless, of course, you're allergic to it).

Although aspirin is clearly effective, over time it has lost market share to other types of painkillers. The main reason for this is that aspirin is known to irritate the stomach, although you can purchase aspirin with a stomach buffer included, such as Bufferin. The nonaspirin competitors described below don't have this side effect.

CAUTION Aspirin, as mentioned earlier, thins the blood. If you have an injury that may have caused internal bleeding, don't take aspirin. Or if you have been taking a lot of aspirin and are injured—for example, from falling off a bike—watch out for any swelling as it could indicate that internal bleeding is occurring. Inform your doctor of your aspirin intake. Never take more than the recommended dosage of aspirin, as the extra aspirin won't increase its ability to lessen your pain and could produce unwanted side effects.

The most common alternatives to aspirin painkillers are acetaminophen (Tylenol) and ibuprofen (Advil, Motrin). Aspirin and ibuprofen treat both pain and inflammation. Acetaminophen treats only pain. Ibuprofen, like aspirin, can damage the lining of your stomach, but it does have a stomach buffer to reduce this side effect. Both acetaminophen and ibuprofen are best taken with a bit of food, perhaps a few crackers, for example, to give the lining of your stomach some protection. Acetaminophen, on the other hand, does not cause the same type of damage to your stomach and so it is tolerated by more people.

Knowing the generic names for your preferred brand of painkiller is very helpful. For example, ibuprofen, acetaminophen, and naprosyn are generic for Advil, Tylenol, and Aleve, respectively. Many stores, such as Costco and Target, have their own generic versions for less money. The generics typically work just as well as the brand name—they just don't have the fancy, shiny coatings!

WORD TO THE WISE If you know that you're going to be sore—for example, you haven't played tennis in years and you're going to play the next day—take a painkiller such as ibuprofen a little bit before the start of the game. That way it will have kicked in by the time you're done and you'll have less pain to deal with.

SIGNING UP FOR HEALTH INSURANCE

If you're twenty-six or under and your parents have health insurance, through the Affordable Care Act (Obamacare) you can continue your health insurance coverage on their plan. It doesn't matter whether you live with your parents or not and whether you are single or married. However, if you are employed and covered by your employer's plan, then you will be dropped from your parents' plan.

If you are not covered, because your parents either don't have coverage or are no longer alive, or because your work or school doesn't provide insurance, then you must make your own arrangements. The Affordable Care Act will give you access to either your state's health insurance exchange or, if your state doesn't provide one, the federal government's exchange. Go to **www.healthcare.gov** to learn more. Another option is to research group coverage options, particularly if you're self-employed. There are, for example, group coverage possibilities available to freelancers.

The cost of health insurance is high and so many young people do without. They may feel that they are relatively healthy and the risks are worth taking. A discussion on the merits of such a belief does not fall within the scope of this book. But if you're feeling invincible about your health, keep in mind that people without health insurance often don't receive preventive care, which can assist in the early detection of disease. Preventive care can mean a lot of things, from eating properly to not smoking to wearing a helmet while bike riding, but what it really comes down to is regularly visiting your doctor for checkups. Also, remember that unexpected accidents can happen to people of *any* age: car accidents, sports injuries, falls, slipping on ice, etc.

FINDING A DOCTOR

If your move out into the wide world didn't involve a lot of miles, you may be able to continue seeing your old doctor. Otherwise, you'll need a new primary care physician, and the time to look for one isn't when you have a fever of 103 degrees but right now. Be aware that finding a good doctor may take some research. Even if several people recommend a local doctor to you, that doesn't mean that you'll like the doctor.

Your health insurance policy, if you have one, may make your search easier. If you have insurance, odds are that not every doctor in your new neighborhood will accept it. So you have to find a doctor who is on your plan. If you are getting your insurance through school or work, talk to the human resources people (or equivalent) to learn about your options. If you're still on your parents' plan, ask them for information to help you get started with your search.

CAUTION As mentioned earlier in this chapter, you'll want to update your medical history before you start searching for a doctor. One important reason to have your own copy of your medical history is that your old doctor could retire or die, and then your records could be difficult to obtain. If your new doctor doesn't ask you about your medical and family history, don't say to yourself, "Whew, I just got away with something," but instead ask yourself whether this physician is careful enough to watch over your health.

 All women should have a gynecologist, and some gynecologists can also act as primary care physicians. Since you know you'll need to find a gynecologist, you might look for one who could fill both roles.

Is Bedside Manner Important?

Does it really matter if you like your doctor? Yes, it does, because if you don't, you'll stay away. You'll tough out certain symptoms rather than go to see your doctor. Bedside manner isn't necessarily as important in a specialist. If you have a medical issue and need a certain type of doctor, then you want the one with the best medical skills and should be more willing to put up with a gruff demeanor. But for your primary care physician, who you'll be seeing the most often, you want someone with whom you feel comfortable.

PREPARING FOR A VISIT TO THE DOCTOR

Bedside manner is waning in importance these days because insurance company policies are forcing doctors to spend less time with their patients. If a doctor can spend only a few minutes with each patient, that doesn't leave much time for small talk, and yet that small talk can be very important in eliciting helpful health information. Given the limited time that medical professionals have nowadays, you should prepare carefully each time you have an appointment to see your doctor.

The first thing to do is to put together a list of questions. Let's say you have a cold but you also have this pain in your side that you want to ask about. During the course of the examination, with the breathing, coughing, temperature taking, and so on, you forget to ask the doctor about your side pain. Then, while your hand is on the doorknob as you exit, you suddenly think about the pain, but by that time the next patient is on his way to the examination room and it's too late.

So prepare a list of questions and don't hesitate to give it to the physician. That way you'll get answers.

WORD TO THE WISE

If you have a serious medical issue, a trip to the doctor's office can be difficult and stressful. You may forget to ask all your questions, and there's a good chance you'll also forget a lot of what the doctor says, especially if you're at all upset. That's why it's better not to go alone. If your parents live too far away and you're not in a relationship, bring along a friend. Many medical offices will permit a friend to be present in the examination room. But even if your friend is left in the waiting room, he or she can debrief you once you're outside and before you've had a chance to forget what the doctor said.

Your Role in Maintaining Your Health

Perhaps up until now you always had a parent with you when you went to the doctor and you may have relied on that parent to take charge, so to speak. But if you're in complete control of your health these days, then you also have to take control of doctor visits. Even a very considerate doctor doesn't have quite the same stake in your health as you do and so you have to retain as much control as you can. Hopefully, you won't be dealing with anything serious, but use any doctor visit as a learning experience. Learn to describe symptoms, get over shyness, and ask questions. Tip: Dress up a bit when going to the doctor. If you're wearing ripped jeans and a T-shirt in the doctor's office, it's possible that you won't be taken as seriously as you would've if you had dressed more formally.

PIERRE SAYS

A while back I had a medical problem, not super serious, but very painful. I started out going to local doctors, but I wasn't satisfied with the results so I started moving up the ladder to specialists. Eventually I had surgery, which helped but didn't solve the problem. I then got hit with another problem, went to a specialist who spotted the source of my original problem, and I had surgery once again that fixed it. The moral of this tale—and I've seen it again and again—is that today you have to manage your own health care. Generalists don't have enough time and specialists are too narrowly focused, so it's very easy to fall between the cracks. The science of medicine can perform miracles, but your personal miracle is unlikely to happen unless you or someone who is personally concerned for your welfare is supervising the process. Take nothing for granted when it comes to your health.

Did you know that different brands of the same medication may produce different side effects? So if a doctor gives you a prescription that makes you feel uncomfortable in some way, speak up as there may be a substitute that will work better for you.

VISITING EMERGENCY ROOMS

Whether or not you have a doctor, you still may find yourself in an emergency room someday—if not for you, then for a friend. The one thing about emergency rooms is that you never know what to expect. You could go in with something minor and be out of there in half an hour, or you could go in with a broken bone and be kept waiting for hours. The case load at emergency rooms ebbs and flows, though longer waits often occur on weekend nights.

ERs don't necessarily work on a first-come, first-served basis. They practice what's known as triage, which means the most serious cases get first priority. Even if only a few people are waiting when you arrive there, the ten who follow you may end up seeing a doctor before you do.

 Visits to the emergency room can be pricey! That's why it pays to be very familiar with your health insurance policy, so you'll understand what your own expenses will be when you visit the ER.

 Urgent-care facilities are viable options for people who don't have a primary care physician, don't need an emergency room (yet), or need to see a doctor quickly after regular business hours. They can be pricey, but most areas have ones that are open on the weekends or until midnight. Some are even open 24/7. Most take insurance, but they also offer a cash option if you aren't covered. You may want to call ahead to learn how much your visit might cost you.

UNDERSTANDING NUTRITION

Being careful about what goes into your stomach is perhaps the single most important aspect of preventive health care. If you want to live to a ripe old age and enjoy a meaningful life as you get older, and not one restricted to a hospital bed, pay attention to what you eat and how much you eat. Both factors are important. Maintaining *perfect* nutrition isn't realistic, but eating only what tastes good in unlimited quantities is certainly not the way to go. Moderation is key.

This isn't a book about nutrition—which is obviously a huge topic—but here are some basics that may give you the incentive to try to improve your diet. Improving your diet does take effort, but the long-term benefits make it a worthwhile endeavor.

Eat fresh as often as possible. Keeping fresh fruits and a few veggies for snacking helps you get a variety of nutrients and fills you with fewer calories.

 Farmers' markets are actually fun to attend, so why not drop by one and see what it's like? You may find a live band and gourmet food trucks. Going with a friend or two to pick up some inexpensive produce and having a yummy bite to eat could be a relaxing way to spend a morning or afternoon. And you'll be inspired to cook!

Cook for yourself frequently. Use as many whole ingredients as possible to up your "healthy" factor a lot, even if what you're cooking doesn't seem that healthy. A homemade pizza with store-bought dough is still healthier than takeout. A soup combining canned whole beans and diced tomatoes is still healthier than the brand-name alternative. Attempt to cook your own meals (beyond heating up canned ravioli or frozen entrées) several times a week. Invite some friends over to share the meal (eating with other people is inherently healthier as well).

 If cooking for yourself is brand new to you, there are many great books and websites that can get you on your way. *Cooking Basics for Dummies* is a helpful book to have on hand. Or google "recipes for beginners" for tasty items to start with.

Watch your portion size. Try eating a variety of foods in smaller portions. Remember that restaurant portions are larger than you really need. So go with smaller portions, refrigerate leftovers, and save a little money and a lot of calories.

Try to eat vegetarian a few times a week. Cutting down on your consumption of red meat will limit your weekly calories and help your heart in the long run.

Plan your meals for the week. It can actually be a fun exercise to plan a week's worth of healthy meal options. And it will help keep your grocery bill down. Review your calendar and determine which days of the week will be best for cooking and which will be best for eating leftovers (for example, on busier days when you'll be returning home late and tired). Choose the recipes that appeal to you. Then make a list of groceries you'll need for those meals and for breakfast and lunch. Planning what kind of snacks you may want is also helpful. If you make a list of just the necessary items, you won't spend money on extra groceries that will sour on you, you'll make fewer trips to the grocery store, and you'll be more likely to eat what you have on hand because you've planned for it.

CAUTION The Centers for Disease Control and Prevention, the government institution that looks over the nation's health, has a good, basic website that you should check out. It won't take up a lot of your time but will get you started on developing an understanding of the basics of healthy eating. Go to **www. cdc.gov/nutrition/everyone/basics/index.html**.

DEALING WITH PSYCHOLOGICAL ISSUES

It sure would be nice if our brains were always in a cooperative mood, but that's often not the case, is it? We all suffer bouts of being "down in the dumps," and young people are just as likely to be stricken as older people. Sometimes it seems that our society doesn't treat psychological problems as seriously as physical ones, but the bottom line is that if you're suffering from a psychological problem, it's as real and damaging to your overall health as a broken leg or stomachache.

If you're living on your own for the first time, you may experience loneliness, or perhaps may feel sad and gloomy. There's a lot you can do to handle these feelings on your own. Schedule enjoyable activities outside the house after work or school a few times a week, invite a friend or acquaintance over to hang out, or focus on a favorite project or hobby. In other words, engage your mind in social or pleasurable activities. It's not always easy, but you'll find that you are usually able to maintain an emotional equilibrium and carry on with your life.

But if you find that your feelings of loneliness worsen, or if your loneliness progresses to depression, it's time to see your primary care physician. He or she can help you find a cure, be it a referral for therapy or a prescription for a mild antidepressant.

If you are in the grips of a major depression, or if you have suicidal thoughts, I strongly recommend that you immediately call one of the hotlines below. They are accredited and staffed with people who can help you. (Source: http://psychcentral.com/lib/telephone-hotlines-and-help-lines/000173):

National Suicide Prevention Lifeline: 1-800-273-8255
National Suicide Prevention Lifeline: 1-800-273-8255
National Addiction Hotline (24 hour): 1-866-701-0102
National Depression Hotline: 1-800-826-3632
The Crisis Help Line (for any kind of crisis or trauma): 1-800-233-4357

Addictions

Cigarettes, alcohol, and drugs are the first things that come to mind when you think of an addiction, but there have been cases of young Koreans dying while sitting in a video game emporium for days at a time, hopelessly lost in the game they were playing. Humans are prone to addictive behavior, and you need to be aware of that potential in yourself. If you have habits that may indicate that you're either addicted to something or closing in on that status, then immediately take steps to get treatment.

Some addictions, such as those to certain hard drugs, seem to occur so rapidly that it's really impossible to prevent them (although to a degree this seems to depend on the individual). But other addictions, the ones you're more likely to run into, such as to gambling, alcohol, porn, or video games, take time to develop.

Once you're addicted to something, whatever it may be, you will need a lot of professional counseling to kick the habit. So the real trick is not to become addicted at all—and the first step toward prevention is recognizing that something you are doing has the possibility of turning into addictive behavior. If you are overindulging in anything, force yourself to stop for a while. The more difficult it seems for you to stop, the more concerned you should be that you are trending toward addiction. Addictions can definitely be overcome, but rarely without a lot of effort, so halfhearted attempts are sure to fail.

If you're not sure whether something you are doing is a sign of addiction, ask some friends what they think. If the universal response is "You're doing that way too much," then accept the fact that you have a problem and start to deal with it. Some people are better off going cold turkey while others do better with the slow withdrawal method.

PREVENTING CRIME AROUND THE HOUSE AND OUT AND ABOUT

Just as important as taking care of your physical and mental health is the need to protect your safety when living on your own. It's never wise to fully let your guard down or become complacent. Being aware of potential dangers and deterring them goes a long way toward protecting your health and your peace of mind. While no one can guarantee that nothing bad will ever happen, being confident in your ability to avoid and prevent most crime keeps you happy and able to enjoy your new life. Here are the safety precautions I recommend you take. They pertain to any neighborhood, whether you live in a seemingly safe area or in a sketchier part of town.

In Your Place

- Always lock your doors and windows when you're away. Locking your doors when at home is a good habit, too. Nearly half of all burglaries occur through an unlocked window or door.
- Install adequate lighting for the front and back doors. Consider using lighting that is activated by a motion detector or that comes on at dusk and goes off at dawn. Lighting calls attention to people passing through an area.
- Use timers on lights or lamps inside your home. Set lamps to different times for going on and off. Petty thieves are less likely to break into a home with lights on inside.
- Always keep your garage or storage rooms locked with high-quality padlocks.
- Don't let mail pile up in your mailbox. Uncollected mail suggests to intruders that you are on vacation. If you're going away for a few days, ask the Post Office to put a vacation hold on your mail service.

- Don't leave a spare key anywhere outside your place. But do ask a trusted friend to keep it in case you are locked out.
- When someone knocks, ask who it is and look through the peephole. Many burglars knock first and walk away if they hear someone inside.
- Keep curtains drawn or blinds closed when away. Keep valuables away from window views, if possible.
- To avoid identity theft, shred all personal information before putting it in the recycling bin.

Vehicle Safety

- Keep car doors and windows closed and locked when parked.
- Don't leave any valuables—or anything—visible in the car. Lock items up for a short time in the trunk. Otherwise, take items into your home or workplace and put them away. Keep your car clean so that it isn't a temptation.
- Keep only essentials in the glove compartment.
- Park in a well-lit lot or street if you cannot park in a garage.
- If you cannot afford a car alarm, consider an antitheft device such as a steering-wheel lock.
- Generally, a modest car doesn't attract the attention of thieves. But if you love your fantastic sports car, put as much care into securing it as it is worth!

Personal Safety

- Use common sense when walking alone, after dark, or in unfamiliar places. Be aware of people in your vicinity and of dark areas or corners to avoid. Most people don't mean any harm, but being aware of them makes you less of a target in general.
- Stay on well-lit streets and parking lots. Consider keeping with you a whistle or a small flashlight.
- Walk to cars or around the neighborhood with another person when fewer people are around, such as late at night or in the earliest hours of the morning.
- Keep your phone at the ready when you're out alone—in a pocket, not in a bag or purse.

- Wear bags cross-shouldered or under your jacket to make them harder to steal.
- If you feel insecure in your neighborhood, consider adding pepper spray to your key ring. But first be sure to check any legal restrictions that your state may impose on this form of self-defense. Also learn about its physical effects.

In Your Neighborhood

It may sound counterintuitive, but consider being outdoors in front of your place or on your porch regularly throughout the weekends or evenings. Take walks with a friend or neighbor. Water lawns or plants, clean your car, sweep patios or sidewalks. A neighborhood that comes to life with people outside equals an active, aware, and *watching* neighborhood, and that can cut down on suspicious activity in your immediate area. And you may get to know and trust a few of your neighbors.

Numbers to Know

Keep a card with the following numbers on your refrigerator and in your car: police nonemergency line (to report suspicious activity, a break-in, or vandalism), the local gang tip line, the graffiti cleanup line, and a neighbor's phone number.

Being actively involved in your neighborhood goes a long way toward keeping it a great neighborhood.

CHAPTER 14 COOKING
You Are What You Eat—and Cook!

LEARNING TO COOK

Today Show host Savannah Guthrie once admitted on the air that when she first moved out she had to call her mother to learn how to boil water. That's a low bar to set for this chapter, but perhaps not too low because if you never paid attention to how the food was prepared in your parents' home, then the workings of a kitchen could be pretty much of a mystery. This chapter won't show you how to cook a gourmet meal à la Julia Child, but it will show you around the kitchen so that you can turn to cookbooks or the web to dig deeper.

WORD TO THE WISE

When you do look at a recipe, make sure to read the whole thing. You wouldn't want to discover right at the final step that you need an ingredient or piece of equipment you don't have.

BASIC COOKING EQUIPMENT

Just as with home maintenance, the joys and successes of cooking depend heavily on your equipment. The good news is that it's possible to cook a wide variety of simple, tasty meals using just basic equipment. It all hinges on how much you care about what you eat (keeping in mind that good nutrition isn't to be found in an all-ramen noodle diet).

Assuming you have taken care of other kitchen basics such as the coffeepot, toaster, and microwave oven, you'll need to get the following items to cook for yourself:

- saucepan—1 quart
- pasta pot—5 quart
- large frying pan with lid
- cookie sheet
- colander or strainer
- potholders
- pasta server

- spatula
- knives
- cutting board
- can and bottle opener
- cooking spoon
- tongs
- measuring spoons
- measuring cups

 Some frying pans aare "nonstick," which means they have a coating that prevents food from sticking to them. If this material starts to come off, the pans can become dangerous, so you have to protect them. Be sure to store and clean nonstick pans properly. Never scour them or use metal cooking utensils on them. Wooden and plastic cooking utensils are safe to use.

Here is an annotated list of other handy cooking items:

- Pyrex baking dishes are great for baking casseroles, roasting chicken, and storing leftovers.
- An electric hand mixer is handy if you like mashed potatoes (or the healthier versions: mashed parsnips and mashed cauliflower). A hand mixer is also indispensable for blending cake mix or making a pumpkin pie.
- A steamer basket is great for steaming fresh vegetables and doesn't cost a lot of money. But if you don't have one, you can buy steamable vegetables in the freezer section and cook them in the microwave. Ziploc bags are designed especially for steaming vegetables in the microwave.
- A corkscrew or other type of wine bottle opener is a must-have if you are cooking with wine or serving it to oenophiles.
- A stovetop or electric kettle makes boiling and pouring hot water far easier. A teapot is useful if you're the type of tea drinker who likes to brew a whole pot of tea.

 Microwave safety: Not every plate or dish can safely go into a microwave. Anything made with metal will create a shower of sparks, and other types of cookware can be damaged or give off harmful chemicals. So check the labeling on your cookware to make sure it is microwave safe.

FOOD SAFETY

However the food you prepare winds up tasting, you absolutely don't want to sicken yourself in the process. Here's a list of a few dangers to watch out for:

Bloated cans: Whether you just bought that can of beans or whether it's been in your kitchen cabinet for a few years, if it's bloated throw it out! Something is growing inside with the beans that will either sicken you or, if it's botulism, possibly kill you. If you kept the receipt, you can take the bloated can back to the store, but whatever you do, don't eat the beans.

Mold: While some cheeses, such as Roquefort, are made to have mold in them, mold is not something that you should ingest in any other form. So if there's something greenish or white growing on your bread, veggies, or anything else, toss it out.

Milk: Open a fresh container of milk and smell it. If you ever purchase milk that doesn't have the same smell you just inhaled, empty it down the drain, particularly if it's cheesy.

Salmonella: If you've ever survived food poisoning, odds are the culprit was the bacterium *Salmonella*. To avoid inflicting this nasty bug on yourself or your guests, cook your food thoroughly and wash up carefully after preparing a meal. Carefully clean areas where you were cutting raw vegetables and meats.

Fresh chicken: The source of most *Salmonella* infections in the United States is either chickens or eggs. Sorry, but you have to treat a fresh chicken as if it were toxic—because most likely it is. So, when cooking it, be *absolutely sure* that the inside reaches 165 degrees, which means that any organisms growing inside have been killed. You also have to scrub anything you used to handle the chicken before cooking—such as a kitchen counter that came in contact with any part of the uncooked chicken—with hot water and detergent, or better yet some sanitizing liquid containing bleach. And don't forget to wash your hands after handling raw chicken.

Storing leftovers: Research has shown that plastics—all plastics, even those that are BPA free—leech a variety of chemicals into any food that is stored in them. That's especially true if you place hot food into a plastic container. So if you must use plastic for food storage, at least let the food cool first. Try to assemble a collection of glass containers, which are safe for food storage. One cheap way to do this is to save glass jars you've purchased from the market and just repurpose them as storage containers once you've consumed the food they originally contained.

WORD to
THE WISE

How do you tell if the chicken you're cooking has reached the right temperature? The easiest way is to use a meat thermometer. (Some chickens are packaged with a built-in one that pops up when it is done.) Otherwise, cut into the chicken to make sure the meat isn't still pink and that any juice is clear. If you want to know at what temperature other foods need to be cooked at, consult this chart: **www.foodsafety.gov/keep/charts/mintemp.html**.

Stocking Your Pantry

You'll want to have certain food items on hand most of the time so that you'll always be able to throw together a decent meal. If you try to keep the following items "in stock," your cooking life will be much easier:

- whole-wheat sandwich bread
- flour tortillas or pita bread
- 1 lb of spaghetti
- 1 jar or can of spaghetti sauce
- shredded or crumbled cheese such as cheddar, feta, or parmesan
- milk
- yogurt
- fruit—apples, bananas, and oranges as basics, but also seasonal fruits
- fresh or frozen vegetables such as corn, green beans, peas, or mixed vegetables
- leafy-green vegetables such as green-leaf lettuce or baby spinach
- canned beans—black and pinto
- canned corn, whole kernel
- canned diced tomatoes
- canned chicken or vegetable broth
- rice
- 1–2 lbs of sugar
- small box of Bisquick or other baking mix
- garlic, powdered or minced (in a jar)
- Italian seasoning
- taco or chili seasoning
- assorted nuts such as peanuts, walnuts, or almonds
- nut spreads such as peanut or almond butter
- eggs
- olive or canola oil for cooking

- 1 lb of lean ground beef
- 2 boneless chicken breasts
- 1 lb of precooked chicken breast pieces

With just this list, you will discover a variety of simple ways to make pasta, a quick soup, an egg scrambler, sandwiches, burritos, tacos, and snacks. You only have to take a chance, throw some items in a saucepan or skillet, and go where your culinary imagination leads you.

Food Shopping

Do you ever think of food shopping as a battle? You should because there's an army of people trying to sell you food and they're willing to use every trick in the book to deprive you of your hard-earned dollars. So if you want to get the most bang for your buck when it comes to food shopping, you have to craft a battle plan.

Rule 1. Plan your meals ahead of time. While you're home, plan breakfast, lunch, and dinner for every day of the week. Take a look at what you already have in the fridge that you can build menus on. Is some chicken sitting in the freezer? Plan to bake it this week. Are chili seasoning and a can of beans languishing in the cupboard? Pick up one more can of beans and some diced tomatoes and make a chili. Also look at your calendar to see when you'll actually be home to cook. If you're not going to be home, you don't want to spend the extra money on food you won't use. If you know you'll have leftovers from a certain night, you can build those into your plan as well. If you put together a menu before heading to the store, then you can figure out what you will actually need to buy.

 MONEY SAVER Planning ahead doesn't mean you can't change shopping gears when you get to the store. For instance, if you spot a sale on scallops, which you adore, then go ahead and buy some. But if you never plan what you're going to fix for your meals, you will end up spending more money than you would if you had followed a thoughtful plan.

Rule 2. Always shop with a list. A grocery list helps you to make sure that you end up buying everything you need so you don't have to go back to the store to pick up an essential ingredient you forgot. If you learn to shop from a list and stick to it, you'll purchase just what you need and be less prone to potentially pricey impulse buying.

If you're familiar with the store you'll be shopping at, try to assemble the list according to the layout of the store so that you can be as efficient as possible. See rule 4.

Rule 3. Never go food shopping hungry. If you're hungry while browsing the supermarket aisles, *everything* will look tempting. Tame your stomach before you leave your home if you want to avoid returning with an unplanned bag of snacks.

Rule 4. Time your shopping trips. Why do you never see a clock in supermarkets? They want you to linger because the slower you go up and down the aisles, the more you'll end up buying. If you have a list and make a race out of it, I guarantee you'll spend less money.

Rule 5. Don't assume items at the end of the aisle are on sale. Sometimes they are, and sometimes they're not. If you don't see a sign that reads "Sale," then assume they are not. Food manufacturers usually have to pay for an "endcap" display, and so the price you pay may actually be higher to make up for that special placement cost.

Buying larger sizes appears to cost you less if you compare the unit costs. But research has shown that when you have more of something, you use more of it, so that unless you're very disciplined, larger-size packages can actually make you spend more money. That's why manufacturers are so eager to sell them.

Rule 6. Shop fresh. If you want to save money and lower your calorie intake, buy fresh foods and avoid prepared foods. Why? If a food item has been prepared, you're paying for that preparation. Sometimes that's fine because time is money and the time you save not preparing could be more valuable to you than the added cost. But if you want the highest value, then try as much as possible to make your meals yourself.

Fresh food is usually also healthier since it doesn't contain preservatives and other additives, and in most cases offers more vitamins and other nutrients.

Rule 7. Be smart about using coupons. If you're going to use coupons, use them only on items you were intending to buy anyway. Think about it: If you buy something you don't really want or need, just because you have a coupon for it and will save money, why not save the *entire* retail price by not buying it at all?

Rule 8. Keep a running shopping list on your fridge and add items to it as needed. Then, when you sit down to plan your meals for the week, you can add those items to the rest of your shopping list (that you planned for the week) and not forget about them.

There are plenty of meal-planning and grocery list templates are on the Internet. Do a Google image search for "meal-planning grocery list template" to find some free printables. Then print them out and put them on your fridge for planning and list making. Also, there are a lot of great apps for keeping shopping lists on your phone. Grocery iQ is free, has a web interface that syncs with your phone, and allows you to keep a list of favorites that you buy every week. It also has a feature where you can share lists with a roommate so that you both know when the other has purchased something for your place, helping you avoid duplicate purchases.

If you're on a tight budget, you may be able to get help in supplementing your food budget. What used to be the Food Stamp Program is now called the Supplemental Nutrition Assistance Program (SNAP). Whether your financial situation qualifies depends on where you live, as each state sets its own rules. If you want to know more, go to **www.fns.usda.gov/snap/eligibility**.

BASIC FOOD PREPARATION TECHNIQUES

While knowing how to boil water, open cans, and microwave food is probably all you need to exist, at some point you're going to want to expand, at least a little bit, into the wonderful world of cooking. You'll want to try recipes, perhaps develop a few tasty go-to dishes, and in general experiment with your food preparation to learn what you really enjoy. To start, here are some basic preparation techniques that should help you to add some variety to your diet.

Pasta cooking: This is the easiest kind of food to make on your own. Typically you boil the pasta in a large pot while throwing together a sauce (with or without meat) in a large saucepan or skillet. Then you combine the two. Ready-made sauces help a lot, but lighter sauces can be made from oil, garlic, vegetables, and shredded cheeses from your pantry. Quick, easy, and great for leftovers!

One-pot meals: These are great because you typically use only one large skillet or saucepan on the stove, so there is less cleanup. Usually, you cook one part of the meal first (such as the meat) and then add other items (such as the vegetables) as you go along. These fast, simple, and hearty meals tend to be very healthy, too. Great for when you have a few close friends over.

Baking: This cooking method isn't just for cakes anymore. Anything that you usually like fried—such as chicken, fish, or pork chops—is healthier and more flavorful if it is baked. Baking meats and potatoes is also less fussy than heating up and monitoring the oil from frying. So look up a great baked chicken recipe to really impress a date, or just have a lot of prepared chicken in the fridge to last throughout your busy week.

Crockpot meals: The crockpot is the best friend of busy working types and people who live where summers are hot. This appliance will slow-cook a delicious meal without heating up the kitchen with high oven temperatures. The crockpot itself is worth the small investment (usually $30–$50). In the morning throw some chicken thighs, water, onions, and Italian seasoning into it and in the evening return home to a slow-cooked dinner that is ready and waiting for you!

George Foreman Grill: Possibly the greatest innovation for apartment dwellers since the hibachi (who has a hibachi anymore?), this convenient grill makes anything you would want to BBQ in a no-fuss, no-muss way—and fast. It is also great for making panini-like sandwiches.

 A lot of terrific cookbooks are out there for each of these styles of cooking. Hit up the bargain section of your local bookstore and you're sure to find some. But you can also get them for free on the Internet, where lots of sites dedicate entire articles and categories to recipes. Google "cheap," "easy," or "beginner" with "crockpot," "slow cooker," "one-pot meal," or "George Foreman Grill." You'll find many sites and suggestions to choose from.

Basic Recipes

OK, you've stocked your pantry, you know a bit about different cooking techniques—you're probably pretty hungry by now, aren't you? This section will provide instructions on preparing a basic selection of nutritious, easy-to-make dishes. And keep in mind, you can explore almost endless variations for each of these dishes.

Preheating ovens is actually pretty important to cooking. Most ovens take five to seven minutes to fully heat to high temperatures, and that is time that your food isn't cooking completely. Try to remember to turn your oven on before you begin prepping your food so that it is already preheated when you put your dish in to cook.

Pasta

One of the easiest ingredients out of which to make a meal is pasta, be it spaghetti, elbows, penne, flat noodles, or bows. To make pasta, all you do is:

- Boil enough water in a saucepan to cover the pasta; add a pinch of salt or olive oil if you want.
- Throw some dried pasta into the water and stir a time or two (to keep it from sticking together).
- Wait for the pasta to get soft (see package for cooking time) and pour it into a colander to drain the water.
- Transfer to a plate and add whatever you want on top to make it palatable.

Here are some basic toppings and sauces for pasta:

Butter: The fastest and easiest, butter melts right into the hot, drained pasta on your plate. Add a little shredded cheese to the top and some peas steamed in the microwave, and you've got a fast snack. Oil-based sauces are generally better for your health, though.

Garlic and oil: Put a couple of tablespoons of olive oil in a small saucepan and heat it over low to medium heat. Throw in 1 teaspoon or so of chopped garlic and heat it up for about 5 minutes. Stir a few times (sautée). Watch it turn golden, but don't burn it. You can adjust the amount of garlic to suit your taste. Pour the garlic-oil sauce over your plated pasta and toss.

> **Variations:** Add chopped red onion, sliced mushrooms, fresh baby spinach, sliced olives, and/or precooked chicken breast pieces to the sautée. Drizzle the pasta with a bit more oil. Add crumbled feta or shredded parmesan. This is a great Greek-style pasta.

 Once you are comfortable with the sautée technique, a whole world of recipes will open up to you!

Adding frozen vegetables: To both the butter and oil-based sauces, you can add frozen vegetables to give your meal a little nutritional boost. Broccoli or blends such as California or Italian style work great.

Steaming in the microwave: Place vegetables in a microwave-safe bowl and add 1 inch of water (or so). Cover the bowl with plastic wrap, leaving one corner open to vent. Microwave for 5 minutes. Drain water. Add to pasta after draining.

Boiling with the pasta: During the last 3 minutes of cooking your pasta, add the package of frozen vegetables. Drain with the pasta when the pasta is finished cooking.

Basic spaghetti: Cook 1 lb spaghetti in a pasta pot. In a frying pan, brown 1 lb of ground beef, ground turkey, or ground chicken until completely browned. Pour a full jar of spaghetti sauce into the meat and stir. Drain pasta and combine in pan with sauce. Toss to coat and then plate.

Baked variation: Replace spaghetti with 1 lb penne. Cook as above. Spread the penne mix into an oiled or sprayed 8x13 baking dish. Cover with 2–4 cups of shredded cheese of your choice. Cover with aluminum foil. Bake at 350 degrees for 25 minutes. The pasta will get a richer flavor from the baking.

 Cooking spray is the fastest and easiest way to oil a baking dish. But you can take olive or vegetable oil, pour a tablespoon into a paper towel or napkin, and spread the oil onto the baking dish. Be sure to coat the sides as well as the bottom!

Tuna Noodle Casserole

Here's a simple but tasty tuna noodle casserole that you can prepare in less than half an hour.

- Boil some water and then add a 12 or 16 oz bag of wide egg noodles. Drain when the noodles are soft.
- While the noodles are cooking, cut up some cheddar and Swiss cheese into small pieces, about a cup (or handful) of each. (Shredded cheese will work, too.) Heat a can of cream of mushroom soup with a splash of milk in a saucepan, stirring with a cooking spoon. When it gets hot, slowly add the cheese a little at a time so that it melts.

- When the cheese is melted in the soup, add one can of tuna (drained of water or oil) so it too heats up. When your sauce is done, combine it with the noodles in the pot and stir.
- Add a can or package of steamed peas and stir the whole thing some more.

Baked tuna noodle casserole: The basic dish described above is quite enjoyable, but many people like the baked version. Pour the whole mixture into an 8x13 baking dish, add some more shredded or sliced cheese to the top, and bake at 400 degrees for 20 minutes, checking to make sure the cheese has melted but not burned. And then, voilà, the casserole is ready to be enjoyed.

 If you make more than you can eat at one sitting, don't worry. Pastas and casseroles often taste better the next day, reheated. The sauces have had a chance to soak into the noodles.

Boiling Potatoes and Rice

Two other basic side dishes that are normally boiled are potatoes and rice.

Boiled Potatoes

- Peel the potatoes, usually 1 or 2 per person, depending on size. Cut them up into chunks (quarters for small potatoes or eighths for large ones), and put them into a saucepan, covering them with an inch or so of water. Bring them to a boil, then set the timer for 15 minutes.
- Test them with a knife or fork to see if they are soft. The utensil should slide through the potato chunks easily, with no resistance in the middle. Once they're soft, drain them in a strainer and you're done. Basic boiled potatoes are fast and easy with butter or oil.

Mashed potato variations: Follow the directions above, then put the potatoes back in the empty pot, add a splash (¼ cup or so) of milk and some butter, and using a potato masher, mash away. Instead of milk, you can use sour cream or cream cheese if you want a richer mashed potato. Plain yogurt will make a rich but healthier mash.

 Using an electric hand mixer to mash potatoes will be easier, and you can make them as smooth as you like them. You can also add sour cream, garlic, or a packet of ranch or Italian dressing seasoning to give them some kick.

Rice: Rice requires much less water, 2 cups of water for 1 cup of white rice. (Check the package for cooking recommendations for brown or wild rice.)

- Put both the rice (1 cup) and water (2 cups) in the saucepan. Heat on high.
- When the water comes to a full, rolling boil (larger bubbles), turn the heat to low, and cover the saucepan with a tight lid. Set the timer for 20 minutes. Do not lift the lid during the first 20 minutes.
- Check when the timer goes off to see if the water has been absorbed. The rice should be moist but not swimming in water. Turn off the heat immediately when the rice is finished. Be careful not to let it burn, which can happen quickly once there's no more water in the bottom of the saucepan.

WORD TO THE WISE

Don't lift the lid too often to see how the rice is doing, as that will let out too much steam. The lid helps to pressure-cook the rice, and the steam is part of that pressure. If you let the pressure out, it doesn't cook as well. Once you think it's done, then you can check.

Baking Dinner

You may think the word *baking* applies only to desserts, but pretty much anything you can fry you can bake. Baking takes less oil, and so the result is less greasy and more healthy, and there's no risk of getting splattered with hot oil.

Baking fish fillets or steaks: Let's say you wanted to bake some fish fillets (or steaks) such as flounder or salmon.

- Spray, oil, or butter a cookie sheet or baking dish and lay your fillets on it.
- Calculate the thickness of the fillets. Often they are ½ inch to an inch. Cook the fish for 5 or 6 minutes per ½ an inch at 425 degrees.
- Test the fish at the minimum cooking time (test 1-inch fillets after 10 minutes). Jab a fillet with a fork and twist. If the meat flakes and the juices are a milky white, it is done. If it doesn't flake, test it again in 3 or 4 minutes.

Dress up your fish: Dab some butter on your fillets and then sprinkle them with some Italian-seasoned breadcrumbs before baking.

Baking dishes are extremely handy for giving you options in cooking. Pyrex is the brand name everyone knows, but other brands are out there. The standard size for baking dishes is 8x13, but they also come in smaller sizes that are great for smaller casseroles and baking things such as fish fillets and chicken breasts. Many also come with lids, which are great for storing leftovers.

Baked Potatoes: Potatoes work great for baking. Give them a good scrub with the rough side of a sponge and put them in the oven. You can bake them directly on the rack or on a cookie sheet. They can take some time to get soft, about an hour, but they don't take any more effort than cutting them in half and adding butter and/or sour cream. Remember to remove them with tongs!

Cooking times for a standard-size "baking potato" (the higher the temperature, the dryer the potato will be):

- 45 minutes at 400 degrees
- 60 minutes at 350 degrees
- 90 minutes at 325 degrees

Sweet potato variation: You can do the same with super-healthy yams and sweet potatoes. For a sweet treat, pour a little maple syrup or brown sugar after you've cut and buttered them, and they're delicious.

 For crispy-skinned baked potatoes, bake them directly on the rack without wrapping them in foil. For soft-skinned potatoes, wrap each potato in aluminum foil. This actually steams the potato.

Baked Chicken Drumsticks: Chicken drumsticks are one of the cheapest parts of the chicken, and they usually come in a large package. You can bake half and freeze half for later. Or bake them all and have leftovers and quick snacks all week long. This is a healthier alternative to fried chicken.

- Rinse your package of drumsticks with water. On a large plate, place 1 cup of flour or baking mix (such as Bisquick). Sprinkle into the flour some seasonings you like (garlic, Italian seasoning, taco seasoning, anything). Mix it up with a fork.
- Roll the drumsticks in the flour mixture. Place on a greased or sprayed cookie sheet. (You can put aluminum foil on the sheet and

spray and grease that. It will make cleaning up the cookie sheet a lot easier!)

- Bake in oven at 400 degrees for 35 minutes. Remove the sheet and turn each drumstick over with a pair of tongs. Bake for another 15 minutes. Remove. Let them cool 10 minutes or so before eating! They're hot!

Eggs

Eggs are easy to make and give you protein. And nobody said you can eat them only at breakfast.

Scrambled eggs: The easiest to get right and the most versatile are scrambled eggs, one or two eggs per person.

- Crack your egg(s) into a bowl and add a splash of milk (optional). Beat them using a fork or whisk until the yokes break and blend a little with the whites.
- Melt some butter in the frying pan on medium heat. Spread the butter around the pan. Pour in your eggs.
- As they heat up, the bottom of the egg mix will begin to solidify. When the bottom seems to have cooked, mix the eggs up a little with a spatula or spoon. Let the juicier sections get a little more cooked. Stir again. At this point, you should have some distinct mounds of scramble. If there are still some juicy spots, go ahead and flip them with a spatula for a third time. When they're fluffy, dish them out and you're done.

Scrambler variation: You can also add leftover bits from your fridge to create a "Scrambler." Just add them to the egg mix in the bowl or in the frying pan. Things such as the last bit of cream cheese from the tub, the last bit of shredded cheese from your baked potato night, half of an onion chopped up, some leftover baby spinach, tomato and mushrooms from a salad, the last of the salsa from your party, or that last piece of bacon in the package. Anything that you think would taste good mixed together will usually go well in scrambled eggs. It will also up the nutrition and satisfaction factor!

 The fewer times you stir scrambled eggs, the fluffier they will be—stir them only two or three times and let them cook a bit in between and they'll come together well.

Easy Soup

Soups are easy and fun to play around with. If you have a can of broth (any kind), some canned beans, tomatoes, and veggies, you can experiment with soup possibilities by adding other leftovers such as ground meat, salsas, or fresh veggies. A go-to soup for every occasion is this easy taco soup you can make in less than 20 minutes. Great for cold nights, when you're sick, or when you're having people over. Keep these ingredients in your pantry, and you'll never lack for a great soup.

Easy-Peasy Taco Soup: Mix all ingredients together in a large pot. Heat until warm, stirring occasionally. Serve with tortilla chips and sour cream.

- 1 can black beans, drained and rinsed
- 1 can pinto beans, drained and rinsed
- 1 can petite diced tomatoes, drained
- 1 can sweet corn, drained
- 1 can white chicken breast, drained
- 1 can cream of chicken soup
- 1 can green enchilada sauce or salsa verde
- 1 can chicken broth
- 1 packet taco seasoning

Vegetarian variation: Omit the canned chicken breast. Substitute vegetable broth for the chicken broth and cream of mushroom soup for the cream of chicken.

Gluten-free variation: Use a gluten-free taco seasoning (such as from Trader Joe's), and substitute ½ can of evaporated milk for the cream of chicken soup (there's usually flour in creamed soups). Make sure you use gluten-free tortilla chips like Frito Lay/Tostitos or Mission tortilla chips.

15 **LIVING ARRANGEMENTS**

How to Get Along with Roommates and Neighbors

ALL ABOUT LIVING WITH ROOMMATES

In prior chapters we've covered much of what you'll need to know about coping with your new environment after your move out. In this chapter, we're going to cover how to get along with the people who may be sharing your new surroundings with you. More often than not, young people living on their own for the first time will, because of financial necessity, have one or more roommates. But even if you're living by yourself, you may still wish to skim this chapter for any possible helpful nuggets of wisdom.

HOUSE RULES

In college you're usually assigned a roommate and the two of you just have to figure out how to live with each other. But when you're choosing roommates and picking a place to live together, it's often wise to set down some rules, perhaps even before you start the process of looking. (Of course, if you're moving into a place that already has tenants, you'll probably have to adapt to their rules.)

While you can't plan for every problem you and your roommates will encounter, thinking ahead may help to avoid some of them. Having moved from home where your parents set the rules, you may dislike the idea of needing to set your own—but the big difference is that these new rules will be chosen by you and your roommates.

Agreeing on a set of rules can go a long way toward smoothing over the inevitable bumps in the road that roommates encounter, but if two personalities are completely mismatched, rules may not be enough to help. For instance, if one roommate is pushy and bossy while the other is meek and mild, then the relationship can actually become abusive. So if you have a weakness of some sort, make sure that you don't pair up with somebody who might take advantage of it. This can be hard to predict, but since you'd rather be safe than sorry, just walk away if you notice any signs of a significant personality mismatch.

Sharing

In drawing up rules, you need to first assess possible sources of conflict. The types most likely to come up have to do with money, even if money itself isn't in the forefront. For example, sharing food can be a problem if one roommate is on a tight budget and the other isn't. Using up your roommate's peanut butter may not seem like a big deal, but it can cause inconvenience and, over time, create resentment. So it's better to talk about how you're going to handle such situations.

For the health of your relationship, it's often better to discuss ahead of time such steps as putting labels on each other's food containers rather than to be forced into adopting such a tactic after a fight. Another set of expenses that can trigger problems concerns heating and cooling, which can be expensive. For example, one roommate prefers to stay warm and doesn't care how high the heating bill is, but the added cost is killing the other roommate's budget. In that case, an acceptable solution may be an electric heater for the chilly roommate, particularly if that roommate agrees to pay extra.

WORD TO THE WISE Whatever anyone's attitude is about sharing expenses, it's easy to be generous once or twice. But if you're the one being mooched on constantly, then that quickly gets old.

CAUTION Two people could have the same income and still have problems with sharing, so it's certainly something to discuss no matter what. But if the differences in income are known right from the start, then having an early discussion about sharing is a key to keeping the atmosphere as pleasant as possible.

Cleanliness

While a slob doesn't pay enough attention to his or her environment to notice the habits of roommates, an untidy roommate can drive a neat freak crazy. So deciding where you fit on the slob-to-neat-freak scale is an important first step. Whatever you do, don't assume your roommates will have the same habits regarding cleanliness that you do.

Here's one example of how this type of difference may impact you. Let's say that you're in the habit of cleaning up right after a meal, but your roommate often hasn't washed the dishes he piled up after his previous meals. When you say something about it, the response is "I'll get to it," but you've come to realize that could mean hours or even days. So even if you use separate dishes, you're going to be stuck. And since a sink full of dirty dishes could attract bugs, this situation poses an even bigger problem.

If you and your roommate had discussed this ahead of time, perhaps you could have compromised. For example, the slovenly person would eat only on paper plates that can be thrown away. The reality is that you two perhaps weren't meant to be roommates, but once you are, separating will not be easy.

While husbands and wives sometimes have to cope with these sorts of conflicts, remember that in marriages there are bonds of love that give a couple added incentive to compromise. Love can also make it easier to make up after a fight. With a roommate, it's better to avoid such conflicts in the first place.

The hours you keep can also be a problem, particularly if one roommate's activities interfere with the other's sleep. Again, this is something that you really should discuss ahead of time. It's the sort of issue that could turn into a deal breaker, particularly if you two have highly incompatible schedules.

Privacy

Many issues, ranging from looking at one another's computers to inviting guests over, fall under the banner of privacy. Certain highly sensitive privacy issues—for example, asking a roommate to leave the premises so that the other can share some intimate moments with a boyfriend or girlfriend—probably won't present a problem, simply because they're implicitly understood by everyone. But it's the smaller irritations that develop into the bigger problems, especially if there are no social norms to smooth things out.

Understanding each other's background can give you some clues about what obstacles to look out for. Someone who has brothers and sisters will likely have fewer privacy issues than an only child. Different cultural backgrounds can also be a source of friction. For example, people from some cultures stand at a certain distance when talking to others. Such small differences in behavior can be problematic when it comes to sharing a common living space.

If you and your roommates are single at the beginning of your living arrangements, it's possible that at some point someone in the household will change his or her relationship status. While you can't plan for every situation (and after all, *you* may be the one who first gets a boyfriend or girlfriend), you could spell out in the beginning that if one roommate becomes a couple during the terms of the lease, there will be limitations on how frequently the significant other gets to visit or spend time at the apartment. Having weekend visitors is one thing, but a full-time arrangement is quite another. And if you can't agree on a time limit, then you should at least agree on a financial adjustment so that this added roommate contributes to rent and expenses.

In truth, imposing financial penalties may not be what you are really looking for, but psychologically they're easier to bring up than telling your roommate he or she has to kick the loved one out the door. Of course if you both change status from single to double, then it might just be a matter of accommodating each other. But the more people there are to deal with in a living space, the greater the potential for personality conflicts.

ARE YOU FRIENDS OR JUST ROOMMATES?

Moving in with friends can make things both easier and more complicated. If a friend is acting in an annoying way, it's going to be easier for you to honestly confront him or her because you have an existing relationship. On the other hand, being roommates with a friend can also make things claustrophobic if you want to have your own life, particularly if you're looking to develop a new set of friends. If your roommate thinks that the two of you will always be doing everything together, conflicts can arise. So if expanding your horizons is one of your goals in living on your own, then it may be better not to room with a friend in the first place. At the very least, it's something to think about.

The other side of this coin can occur if your friend/roommate refuses to accept whatever changes in behavior you've requested. If you just can't stand the situation, you may have to lose or damage the friendship in order to get your sanity back. That's why having a roommate who isn't also a friend has its benefits. If you don't get along, moving on has a much less traumatic downside.

 You may be in a situation where you wish to ask for a potential roommate's references. If you get references, use them. Obviously, people who are listed as references won't say anything very bad, but by reading between the lines you can perhaps find out some useful tidbits that will help you to judge how well you and the potential roommate will mesh. If you sense any hesitancy or lack of candor in the reference, be a bit pushy and see if you can't get the reference to spill the beans.

When meeting and evaluating potential roommates, don't look at them as a potential friend. If a friendship develops, that's fine, but your evaluation should focus on their suitability as a roommate. Do they seem to have a compatible personality? Are they responsible? What is their school or work schedule? The answers to these questions will help you figure out whether a candidate is a good fit as a roommate. The person may have some negatives–everyone does–but as long as those negatives aren't grating bad habits, then the potential is there for you two to live together harmoniously.

College Roommates after College

If you're looking for a place to live after college, and your college roommate is too, think carefully about rooming again with him or her. Don't jump into this scenario because of your familiarity with each other. Yes, you may have gotten along quite well while in college, but sharing permanent living quarters is different. When living in a dorm or other college setting, everyone has to make compromises and you're not together for 365 days a year. But if you're moving into your own apartment, you may want to have some privacy and personal space. Your college roommate may still be the ideal person to move in with—that depends on a lot of factors—just don't assume that to be the case, or be pushed into it. You first need to think carefully about what a future with the two of you sharing the same space outside the college environment might look like.

NOISE

Too much noise in the living space can really be a source of discord. For example, a student who needs quiet to study may not mix well with an employed roommate who needs to unwind with his or her favorite music blasting.

When conflicts arise, it is important to remember that not everyone shares your view of how to live. Just because you do something your way doesn't make their way wrong, just different. A good first step to resolving a noise problem is to ask yourself *why* doing things a certain way is so important to you. This will help you be clear in your own mind what your needs are. Then try to understand things from your roommate's perspective. This will help both of you negotiate a peaceful living arrangement. If you ask your roommate, "How does this help you out?" or say, "This helps me out because . . . ," a productive conversation can take place. If you help out on things that are important to your roommate, he or she will be far more likely to respect what is important to you.

College dorms are universally noisy, and most college students manage to adapt. But sharing an apartment is much different. You can't just head to the library across campus to get some peace and quiet. And while everybody usually buckles down during exam time at college, if you are working and need to bring work home regularly, then needing quiet could be a year-round requirement.

LIVING WITH YOUR NEIGHBORS

The first thing to remember about your neighbors is that you're *their* neighbor, too. Being a good neighbor is a two-way street: Both sides need to behave in a neighborly fashion and help out when there's an obvious need, such as checking in on an elderly neighbor or keeping an eye out for troublemakers.

Still, neighbors can intrude on your life in a myriad of different ways, the most common being excessive noise, noxious smells, which often seem to waft in when you're trying to eat, and the harboring of various bugs, which then find their way into your place. Neighbors may also inflict on you their rambunctious children, barking dogs, snooping eyes, and cold stares, all of which can make life in your abode unpleasant.

Usually, the best way to politely ask neighbors to keep an annoying behavior under control is in person. If you need to knock on their door when you know they are home, brave up and do so. Keeping your voice light and your approach nonthreatening and kind will go a long way toward taking the sting out. Most people don't know they are being a nuisance and will be embarrassed and apologetic. If knocking in person is not an option, write a nice note and include your email address.

The worst thing you can do with an annoying neighbor is escalate matters by returning the favor. Why? Because some people like to pick fights, and so your responses will give them more incentive to be obnoxious. You neighbor may take you more seriously if you try to do the right thing and behave like a solid, level-headed adult. Complaining to your landlord should be your last option, not your first. But if your polite attempts to resolve the situation on your own don't succeed, then you may finally be forced to contact the landlord (assuming the neighbor is a tenant who lives in your apartment complex, not in the private residence next door).

Take a look at your lease to see what clauses there might be that the landlord could enforce. If there's a "peace, quiet, and enjoyment" clause that affects you, doubtless it's also in the tenant-from-hell's lease, and you can remind the landlord of that.

 If you have the ability to record whatever obnoxious activity is taking place, then do so. It's hard to prove awful smells, but noise and other activities can be taped, either through an audio recording or a video. If the activity, whatever it is, rises to the level where the authorities might have to be called in, then it's even more important to have this type of documentation on hand.

There's a good chance that a neighbor who is bothering you is also bothering others. If you're planning to put pressure on your landlord to take some action, gather the support of other tenants. By acting together, you're more likely to achieve a satisfying result.

 There are many reasons to always pay your rent on time, but being a tenant in good standing can be important when making complaints against other tenants. If you're a good tenant, your landlord won't want to lose you and will put in more effort to make you happy.

Of course landlords don't have complete freedom to act. Many would love to throw out tenants who cause them trouble, but evicting a tenant is a costly procedure and most landlords will avoid doing so. Dealing with such problematic tenants is what makes landlords charge as much rent as they can get because they know a landlord's duties include dealing with unpleasant tenants.

BUILDING STAFF

While this won't apply everywhere, your new home may have an assortment of staff, including a building supervisor, handyman, and doorman. Since there will be times when you need them, you have to make sure that you stay on their good side. Be polite and friendly with them and, if appropriate, tip them. Staff members traditionally get a tip at the end of the year during the holidays. How much to tip is always a big question and depends on several factors, including your rent (the more you pay, the more you should tip) and how often you use their services. You can't go wrong asking your neighbors what they tip so that you won't fall out of line. Of course if you need a particular service that is out of the ordinary, you should also tip at that time.

 It's a good idea to keep some small bills around for tip money so that if you need the super or handyman to come up and do something for you quickly, you won't be stuck with having only twenties when all you want to tip is $2 or $5. Plus, this small change could come in handy for the pizza delivery guy as well.

If there is a staff member who's not doing his or her job, ask other tenants if they've noticed the same thing. If not, then perhaps it's personal and you can try to gently correct whatever is going on or just learn to live with it. But if others say they've noticed the same as you, then maybe you can circulate a letter of complaint to the landlord that all of you can sign. A letter with several signatures will be more effective than a letter with only yours.

CHAPTER 16 DORM LIFE

Becoming Familiar with a New Environment

IF YOU'RE COLLEGE-BOUND...

While this book isn't especially geared toward the college-bound, moving away from your parents' home to a college dormitory is still one of life's bigger changes, and some thoughtful, objective advice can be a big help. That's exactly what I hope to provide in this chapter.

WORD TO THE WISE Remember, your move represents a big change for your parents, too, so it may be a good idea to discuss with them some of the tips and ideas in this chapter.

LIVING WITH ROOMMATES

The process of being squeezed into a small space with one or more complete strangers has understandably always been a source of anxiety for young people living on their own for the first time. So, what can you do to improve your odds of getting compatible roommates?

The first line of defense is to pay attention to the forms your school sends you regarding dormitory life. Most schools will send you a survey on your roommate preferences, your temperament, and your interests. They also often ask if you have a particular roommate in mind, perhaps a friend who is also attending your college. If you fill these forms out honestly and specifically, the school will do its best to find a situation that suits you. If you are a very social, talkative person who likes to have friends around a lot, you'll want a roommate who shares that level of sociability. If you are taciturn and studious, you'll want a roommate who respects your need for quiet.

Most colleges offer several dorm room options. Look at them carefully and make your preferences clear. Some dormitories will be classic style, with long hallways full of two-person rooms, all of which share a single large bathroom, a large common room, and a kitchen—a highly social setup. Other dormitories will be "pod style," clustering three or four double rooms together around a common area, a small kitchen, and a bathroom. Yet other dormitories may even offer single-occupancy rooms that cost a little extra for the privacy. Reading about your options in advance and filling out the forms will help your school place you in a dorm situation you can live with.

PIERRE SAYS At some point, either before or after you meet them in person, you're probably going to check out your roommates on Facebook and other social media sites to learn more about them. Just keep in mind that they'll do the same thing to learn more about you! It's probably already been drilled into your head that whatever you post on the web will stay with you forever, but having your new roommates check you out on Facebook is probably the first time you will have to face the consequences of your postings in real life. I'm not saying you shouldn't be proud of who you are—but at least take a few moments to review your profiles to see if there are any sharp edges that you may wish to soften.

Early communication between you and your roommates will include various types of information. You'll open with the practical—such as, who's already got a fridge or microwave to contribute, assuming such items are permitted. And of course you'll bring up more personal matters in terms of social scene, musical likes and dislikes, and so on. But keep in mind that it's the entire package that counts, so no matter what information you exchange, you should try to keep an open mind. If you're truly concerned about compatibility with a potential roommate, contact your school. But in general it's best to give your roommates a chance. If, after a week or two, things are clearly not working out, then look for a change.

You Don't Have to Be Best Friends

You of course want to get along with your roommates—after all, you'll be sharing a small living space with them. But that doesn't necessarily mean you'll become friends with them. A college campus is an amazing constellation of thousands of different people, a good number of whom will share some of your interests. These are the people whom you'll want to hang out with and who may develop into friends. It's great if you share interests with your roommates, but all that's really important is that you can live together in harmony. So make that your goal, and if it turns out you're not going to be friends, you won't be disappointed.

It's possible that your roommate will want to be friends with you, but you're not that interested in reciprocating. It may be wise to let your roommate know this ahead of time so that he or she won't be disappointed. And, as the semester moves along, you just might find your attitude toward your roommate changing. If so, then you'll be more comfortable integrating him or her into your other set of friends.

Five Sample Rules to Set with Your Roommates

Ultimately, to achieve harmony with a dorm roommate, you simply need to be courteous, communicate kindly, and understand that living in such close quarters will require a lot of flexibility on everyone's part. Consider creating a set of five etiquette rules for you and your roommate to follow. It will go a long way toward keeping things tolerable.

Cleanliness: Keeping your place clean should be a shared responsibility. Set up one day each week to tidy things up, especially food and laundry. Letting things get out of hand on the tidiness front will drive one or both of you nuts.

Study hours/Quiet hours: While the library or study rooms may be an option most of the time, there will be days or evenings when studying in your dorm room is necessary. Also, one of you may need quiet space for sleep or relaxation. Setting specific hours when the room will remain quiet for study or sleep, say, 11 p.m. to 7 a.m., will simplify things.

Guests: Most roommates will have friends in and out of their room during the day or weekend, which normally isn't a problem so long as they don't overstay their welcome. Set a rule with your roommates about how long friends can hang out before asking permission to stay longer. After all, there are usually plenty of common rooms or other places on campus to congregate and socialize.

Sleepovers: The policy I recommend for sleepovers may seem simplistic, but it's that way because overnight stays are a sensitive subject. The rule is that sleeping in your dorm room should be reserved only for the roommates who live there and no one else. If you want to set up an exception, that's your choice, but all roommates need to be comfortable with it and agree to it. This applies to any guest who might stay over, whether a boyfriend or girlfriend, or just a regular platonic friend.

Privacy: Privacy concerns also extend to matters of personal information and the personal lives of you and your roommate. If you find out your roommate failed a class, it stays between you two. If your roommate finds out your significant other cheated on you, it stays between you two. Set a rule that personal details are to stay private and will not be used for gossip with friends. Mutual confidentiality also includes the use of digital cameras, cell phones, and social media. Respecting your roommate's privacy in close quarters will go a long way toward easing tensions that may arise between the two of you.

If rule breaking becomes a problem for you and your roommate, ask for help from a resident advisor (RA). Sometimes an RA can help roommates work things out in ways they hadn't thought of.

MOVING-IN DAY

Moving-in day is usually pandemonium. You're going to need help, so make arrangements to bring a family member or friend along with you to help. Say your good-byes at home to those who aren't traveling with you, and make definite plans to see your family at the first available weekend. That will help nervous parents process their feelings. Whoever you choose to go with you should be the most sensible and even-keeled friend or family member you can find, someone who will help keep your own nerves steady.

WORD TO THE WISE Should you have your parents go with you on move-in day? In some ways, it might be emotionally simpler to have a single, dependable friend help you rather than your parents. But what if one or both your parents want to go? That may increase the emotional trauma a bit (probably more so for them than you), but it might be a good idea. Beyond helping you move your stuff and get your things set up, there's a good chance they'll have some great suggestions for *how* to set things up, particularly given the typically cramped nature of most dorm rooms. And they might well buy you a thing or two that same day, after assessing your situation. But here's something else to consider: Your going off to school will be a bittersweet experience for your parents—if they both go with you, they'll be able to console each other on their trip back home.

If you are moving to a university far away and cannot take a helping hand with you, keep your packing light so you can move the most essential items on your own. If you're of a sociable bent, helping someone else carry his or her stuff into the dorm will probably get you help in return.

Because there's so much activity on moving-in day, colleges often set times when they want you to perform your move so that elevators and stairwells aren't jammed. But of course everyone wants to get started as soon as possible, so have a game plan in mind and a checklist of things to do in the order they should be done.

What You'll Need at the Start

The easiest way to move into a dorm is to take only the barest essentials at first and then use a certain amount of budgeted cash to purchase other items when you arrive. The essential items you'll need for your first few days on campus are:

- bedsheets
- blankets
- comforter
- mattress pad or egg crate (Those mattresses can be stiff!)
- pillowcases
- pillows
- computer or laptop
- printer
- USB flash drive
- alarm clock
- cell phone
- cell phone charger
- extension cords
- backpack with basic desk supplies
- hot pot or electric kettle
- one serving spoon
- small hard-plastic bowls and plates
- bath towels
- bathrobe
- shower caddy (to hold your toiletries)
- shower flip-flops
- washcloths
- everyday toiletries
- personal documents: a file with your school, dorm, and room information; your student ID or enrollment info; your personal medical file

Of course it's tempting to want to buy and gather everything you think you'll need ahead of time and bring it with you, but until you actually see your dorm room and can measure how much space you have, some things are better left unpurchased until after you arrive. And you'll also want to check to see if your roommates will be providing certain items that everyone can share, such as a television. Once you've moved your essentials in and taken stock of the room, you can begin to see how you can arrange it for maximum space value. Also, you can begin a list of items you can shop for locally.

Two items that are almost guaranteed to be of use are duct tape, which is handy for all sorts of purposes, and bed risers, which you put under the legs of the bed to raise it, providing you with additional storage space. Many students go to the local garden supply department and purchase cinder blocks to raise their beds. Check with your RA to see if cinder blocks are allowed; if they are, you can use them to cheaply create under-the-bed storage space. Since you probably won't be allowed to hammer nails into your walls, you'll find that duct tape or double-sided tape can serve as a way to attach things. Most schools recommend Blu-Tack or other reusable adhesive gum to put up posters and light decorations.

 The college bookstore probably carries everything you need in the way of office and school supplies, but at a premium price. Before you leave for college, check out where the discount stores nearest to your dorm are—places such as Target or Walmart. In a college town, these stores will stock the same items as the college bookstore but at much lower prices. Just make sure to visit these stores as early as possible because the most popular items do sell out.

 As mentioned in Chapter 6 (repeated here in case you missed it!), many college dorms have extra-long single beds, meaning you have to purchase special sheets that won't ever fit on any other bed. If you plan on bringing sheets that you purchased ahead of time, don't assume your bed will be a standard single. Make sure that you know the exact size of your bed or the sheets you bring may not come close to fitting.

ARRIVING AND SETTLING IN

The first day or two on a new campus can be overwhelming, so feel free to take it slow. Once you have set up the basics in your room so you can comfortably sleep and find the things you need, take a break. Relax with a walk around your campus and become acquainted with your new surroundings. Find the places you'll need to visit, such as the dining hall, the student union, the bookstore, and the library. Keep an eye open for pleasant places where you may be able to study.

Universities will also schedule certain orientation activities for new students during their first few days on campus. Even if you aren't the "joiner" type, consider participating in one or two of these activities. You'll meet a wider variety of people than just in your dorm. And if you're the introverted type, you'll be able to spot the other introverts pretty quickly and team up. But the activities are designed to help you get comfortable on campus and blow off some steam. So take advantage.

If you're going into town to, for example, buy something for your room, ask the others in your dorm hall if they would like to go with you. Or see if you can get a ride with someone else. Going with other people new to campus will help break the ice and probably make the shopping more fun.

Bathrooms

For most students, getting used to dorm bathrooms is one of the biggest immediate adjustments they must make. Most students will share their bathroom with a minimum of four to six people. Many dorms have one large bathroom for upwards of twenty people on a hall. The bathroom is one of the places where you will quickly learn about your dorm mates' odd quirks!

First, try to figure out the "protocol" in your bathroom. If you share it with only a couple of people, you can probably leave a few of your regular toiletries in the shower or on shelves in the bathroom. In larger bathrooms, people "helping themselves" to others' toiletries may be a problem. Either way, it is a good idea to get a shower caddy.

 A shower caddy is a light plastic bucket or bag into which you can put your shampoo, shower gel, washcloth, deodorant, razors, and so on, making it easy to carry your items with you to the shower each day. **Dormco.com** has a variety of shower caddies, shower shoes, and towel sets for sale. The site also carries a wide selection of other dorm-friendly products such as footlockers, dorm safes, bed risers, and storage containers.

You'll also want an awesome set of large towels (four or so)—the larger the better. Bath sheets (extra large towels) are very popular in dorms. Shower flip-flops are helpful as dorm showers can be rife with fungus that can take to your feet very quickly. A robe also comes in handy. When finished showering, take your towels back with you to your dorm room. There are usually hooks where you can hang them to dry. If there aren't, grab a few stick-on hooks on your next shopping run. Over-the-door hanging racks are also good for dorm towel storage.

Finally, you'll need to get used to competing for shower spots during the high traffic times, such as 7 to 9 a.m., when many students are getting ready for their first class of the day. If you really need your bathroom privacy, consider getting up early to use the bathroom first thing before your dorm mates.

Kitchens and Cooking

Most dorms have a kitchen attached to a common area with a full-size oven and stove, cabinets, refrigerator, microwave, and sometimes cookware and utensils. If you plan on doing any type of real cooking, you'll want to check out the supplies and condition of the kitchen to see what else you need.

If you keep any food items in the refrigerator or cabinets, be sure to mark them as yours with address labels or a marker. You may have to deal with people helping themselves to your food from time to time, so be certain you're willing to deal with that. Otherwise, keep it in the mini-fridge in your room.

WORD TO THE WISE People are less likely to mess with items that are in paper bags or grocery sacks kept in kitchen cabinets. Try labeling everything and tying it up in a bag before storing it in a cupboard.

The microwave will get the most use for the rounds of popcorn, Hot Pockets, and takeout leftovers that need to be heated up. The rest of the kitchen, though, is often up for grabs if you want to cook your mom's mushroom-chicken or peach cobbler recipes. Be certain to clean up immediately after you cook in the kitchen. You may find that others are not so considerate and you'll be left to clean up before you can cook. If you know who is leaving dirty items out, politely ask him or her to clean up so that others (and you) can use the kitchen readily. If the problem persists, discuss it with your RA. It is a health hazard that has to be addressed. Ultimately, though, deciding that *you* will take responsibility for the cleanliness of the kitchen you want to use will go a long way toward cutting down your stress and annoyance. Just be willing to clean it up from time to time, and you'll have a good space in which to cook a decent meal.

Another option for dorm dwellers is in-room cooking. With a mini-fridge and a hot pot or electric kettle, you can make a lot of simple, easy foods. A few plastic bowls and plates, a colander, some utensils, and a mug or two are really all you need. Milk and butter can be kept in the mini-fridge along with condiments and things such as hot dogs.

Top Ramen, Cup Noodles, and Kraft Macaroni & Cheese are the most popular items for dorm cooking because they are cheap and can all be cooked in a hot pot or with water heated by an electric kettle. Not to mention canned ravioli or chili beans or canned soup. Even basic spaghetti with pasta sauce can be done in a hot pot.

While it is great to be able to cook a late-night snack or some soup when you've got a cold, don't overdo it with the kettle cooking! You'll find yourself feeling run down after a while if everything you eat comes out of a can. Limit the number of meals you eat on your own in your room. Go to the dining hall or student union to grab a bite, or cook something in the kitchen for yourself and a few others in your dorm. Remember to make mealtimes social, and your body and your mind will thank you.

Common Areas

Every dorm will usually have a variety of common areas. Pod dorms will provide a shared living room–like common area for a handful of people. Larger, traditional dorms will have one large common room for each wing, intended to hold a few dozen people. Many times dorm activities are planned in the common room, as well as social functions such as movies or game nights. Some common rooms have pool or ping-pong tables or a television. Sometimes these rooms will be deserted, which makes them a good place to escape to if you want to hang with a friend or read a book for pleasure. At other times, the common room will be a hotbed of activity. If you're socially inclined, making this your "living room" of sorts means that you'll see a lot of people come through at different times and you'll meet a lot of new people in your building. If you're introverted, the common areas are great places for people watching, so don't write them off.

If you want to plan an event yourself (such as a birthday party or a movie night), you can usually book the exclusive use of a dorm common room with your RA or dorm activities leader.

RESIDENT ADVISORS

Some college students make a ton of friends quickly and, if they're not mindful, may end up working on their social life a lot harder than their studies. But other students can become depressed because they have no social life, which also can make it more difficult for them to focus on their studies. So the key is to find a balance. This is when a good resident advisor (RA)—or whatever they're called at your particular college—can be useful.

RAs are paid to help students, and most people who become RAs are drawn to this type of work because they want to be helpful. So never feel like you're bothering your RA with a problem, because it's very unlikely that they'll feel bothered. That's not to say that every RA will be able to solve every student's problem, but it does mean that it's worth going to your RA if you're troubled by something that you can't handle by yourself or just need some quick answers or advice.

But is feeling lonely a problem an RA can handle? Absolutely. In fact, making sure that every student gets properly integrated into college life is what they're there for. College administrators understand that not every one of their students is good at making friends and so they make sure that there's a system in place to help them out. Part of the money you're paying to live on campus is going toward the salary of your RA. So don't hesitate to go to your RA when you're faced with any situation that you need help with.

STUDYING

When you were in middle school, your teachers warned you that you'd better improve your study habits because high school would be much harder. And then when you were in high school, your teachers said the same thing about college. Whether or not these predictions came true for you back then, there are some major differences about studying in college.

The first is that you won't have your parents watching over you to bug you about it. Whether or not that will be a good or bad thing for you depends on how self-motivated you are. As early as you can, take a look at your class and work schedule, then schedule time dedicated to studying. Most students find that studying in shorter bursts (up to one hour) in their room or outdoors to be helpful. For the added focus factor, longer, dedicated study sessions are usually best done in a library or a designated study room.

Don't be afraid to utilize study rooms. Many dorms have special rooms in each wing dedicated for study or quiet time—for exactly those times when your dorm hall is offering too many distractions. Use them when you find yourself tempted by the comforts of your dorm room or your friends having fun. Book time in them when you need to study late at night and don't want to disturb your roommates or be distracted.

As you get to know certain people in your classes, consider arranging time with a study partner. It can be motivating to just sit with someone else who's serious about their studies. And often, if you have a question about something, the two of your can work it out together.

Going to the library to study offers several advantages. First, there's quiet. And seeing all those other students studying will make it easier for you to study without distraction. You may notice people from your classes there, which could lead to forming study groups and comparing notes.

Whatever your musical tastes, putting some classical music in your phone or iPod may be a good study aid. Classical music can help you block out other distracting sounds without being too distracting in and of itself.

STAYING HEALTHY

Living in a dorm means you'll be in close quarters with many other people, so you can be exposed to all kinds of illnesses. Be on guard against them! Watch your nutrition and your cleaning habits carefully. Get plenty of rest and keep up your physical activity. The dining hall is a great source of free food, but be careful about your portion sizes. The foods you crave when you're stressed out may be high in fat or sugar, which will pack on the pounds and won't help your immune system. Hit the salad bar and fresh fruit as often as possible. Become a regular at the student gym or aquatic center. And consider participating in enjoyable recreational sports, such as ultimate Frisbee, racquetball, soccer, or basketball.

One of the advantages of being a student on campus is the immediate access you have to health care. You probably paid a student health fee upon enrollment, so you should use those services without embarrassment. If you're coming down with the flu, the health center can get you medication. Some universities offer flu shots for students. If you injure yourself, the health center can look at your injury. If you're sexually active, you can get contraceptive care there. The health center should be your first stop if you're feeling unwell at any time. And if you have any preexisting conditions, the center can help you keep an eye on them when you're under the stress of midterms and finals!

PIERRE SAYS Peer pressure is one of the main reasons why binge drinking is a problem on many college campuses. I know how powerful peer pressure can be, because like everyone I've experienced it myself plenty of times. But that still doesn't change my very simple recommendation about binge drinking: Don't do it. It's not worth it. Your best bet is to *avoid* situations where drinking may get out of hand. And let's be frank here, because this is a touchy subject for some: If you have close relations who are alcoholics, you're at greater risk of becoming one yourself. If you're in an uncomfortable social situation where people are pressuring you to drink, an effective strategy to get them off your back is to lie. Say that you have hepatitis C or some other liver disease and your doctor has ordered you not to have more than two beers at a time, or whatever amount you deem safe. Always remember that doctor's orders, real or fake, can be really effective when it comes to fighting peer pressure.

LEAVING YOUR DORM

Leaving your dorm is a subject you don't really think about until you to have to deal with it. Most dorms require you to vacate your room entirely for the summer. Even if you are staying on campus for summer school, you will probably have to move to a designated dorm for summer students. Many universities use their empty dorms in summertime for weeklong conferences or retreats for corporations, churches, or organizations, and people may be staying in your former room. The university will set ground rules for the date and time you have to completely vacate your room to avoid being fined—and that time is often the day after finals end. So you're busy, stressed out, and exhausted and you have to move!

It is best to keep your dorm room hoarding instincts to a minimum during the school year. Of course, you will acquire many new things during the months of your residence there. But in the weeks leading up to finals, try to book a few hours a week to pruning your dorm room stash. Here's a list of things you can do to prepare yourself:

- Donate or throw away items you no longer have any use for: clothes, term papers you got Cs on, notebooks from that class you hated last semester, canned food items you know you won't eat, items you bought when you first arrived but didn't need. Be ruthless.

- List items that will stay with you throughout the summer, whether you're spending it at home, traveling, or working out of town.. Try to lighten your load by taking only your must-haves, like laptops, go-to items of clothing, etc.
- Get a friend or two to go in with you on a rented mini storage unit for the summer. Pay it all up front through the end of September, if you can. That'll give you enough time in fall to move back into your dorm (or your first apartment) and clear out the unit. The smallest units are usually sufficient to stack two people's items for a few months. If you're coming back in fall and staying in a dorm a second year, your stuff will be in storage waiting for you when you arrive. If you're moving into a new apartment in fall, you can set up your apartment basics first and then go get the items you want from storage as you need them.
- Pack up and label items to go to storage: winter clothes, mini-fridge, kitchen stuff, the cinder blocks you put your bed on, bedding, books, and so on. Take as many items to storage as possible in the week or two before finals. It'll help clear out your room and keep you focused on finals.
- The day you vacate, get up early (no matter how much you want to sleep), take the rest of your items to storage, then pack your car with the remaining items. Then you can hit up the bookstore to sell back books or run the errands you need to run.

WORD TO THE WISE

If you are moving from your dorm directly to an apartment, consider getting a storage unit anyway. In a new apartment, you may find you don't need every single dorm item with you right away, and having a month or two to decide what you will keep and what can be tossed from your dorm will take the pressure off you for a while.

CHAPTER 17 SEX AND RELATIONSHIPS

Understanding the Physical and Emotional Aspects of Relationships

IT'S A BIG SUBJECT

While no subject can be covered comprehensively in only one chapter, the chapters in this book offer you enough information for your basic needs. But that's going to be harder to accomplish in this chapter, because the topics of sex and relationships lend themselves to entire books (I should know—I've written some with Dr. Ruth Westheimer). But the information I offer in this chapter is universal and will hopefully be of some value to you.

RELATIONSHIPS

While there is a moral and religious component to being against premarital sex or having many sexual partners, there is also a practical side to it. The more sexual partners a person encounters, the greater the odds of either becoming infected by a sexually transmitted disease (STD) or causing an unintended pregnancy. But there's also another danger to being promiscuous: suffering emotional damage.

It may appear easy to have sex with someone without any emotional attachments, but so often those emotional attachments develop anyway, either in one or both partners. Your goal should be to protect yourself from this sort of emotional turmoil, and to try not to cause anyone else to experience it. Yes, people are free to say no to sex, but there are myriad pressures that cause people to say yes when they really shouldn't. This book isn't here to tell you what to do in these situations, but to convey the message that there are important consequences you must take into account and absorb.

Dating is supposedly passé, but is that a good thing? Before the dating era, parents arranged marriages, a custom that is still the norm in many parts of the world. That people would choose a partner for themselves is a somewhat recent development, but is even having a partner out of date? That's something you have to decide for yourself. If you don't want to get married and have children, then today's hookup culture may suit you.

But if marriage and a family is your goal, you need to think carefully about the actions you take. Keep in mind that the process of looking for a marriage partner can take time, and the earlier you start the better—otherwise, you could let Mr. or Ms. Right slip by while you were busy hooking up with people who weren't worth the effort. You have to recognize that you don't have an unlimited amount of time, so you need to actively pursue your goal, whatever it is, rather than just drift.

WORD TO THE WISE Traditional dating may be out of style, but if you're looking for an adult, long-term relationship with a partner you can love and respect (and who will love and respect you), a little traditional romance goes a long way. Taking the time to get to know a romantic partner before hopping into bed can increase your happiness with that partner down the road.

Making a Commitment

It seems many young people today are reluctant to make a long-term commitment in a relationship. Now that societal pressures have pretty much evaporated and two people can be in a relationship without marriage, taking that big step to commit has become much harder to do. Of course, many couples today do make that commitment. There is no right or wrong answer. But if you're looking for a commitment and realize that the person you're seeing isn't, then it's time to move on. Don't delay such a move, hoping for the best, but make it as soon as you see that a long-term relationship is probably not in the cards. And if you're the one who isn't looking for a long-term commitment, be up front about that as soon as the issue comes up. Be honest and fair with your romantic partners from the beginning. You will save everyone from wasting time and pinning hopes on the wrong person.

Ending a Bad Relationship

It can take time for a relationship to mature. At the start, there's that "love is blind" thing, and until those rose-colored glasses come off, you may not be able to realize that you're in a bad relationship. Sometimes it just takes a few weeks for the "new" to wear off, but other times the hormones in a relationship don't calm down for six months or a year. But at a certain point the evidence starts to pile up and you ignore it at great risk.

Psychology Today says that a happy relationship will have five positive interactions for every one negative interaction. Not that you should keep score, but if your happy and actively encouraging moments far outweigh the fights and the put-downs, you're probably on the right track! To learn more, go to **psychologytoday.com/articles/200403/marriage-math**.

The future may seem vast at this point in your life, but sooner than you think you're going to wonder where the time went. Wasting years in a lousy relationship is just not something you should tolerate, especially if a breakup is inevitable. There's no good time to break up, so the rule should be the soonest possible moment once you're certain that the relationship has to end.

Breaking up is hard to do—there's no getting around that. It's what makes not breaking up so tempting. Staying in a bad relationship is often the path of least resistance. There's an old saying that applies here: The coward dies a thousand deaths while the brave man dies only once. Either you face the single pain of a breakup or you live with the day-to-day pain of being unhappy. Yes, breaking up is difficult, but you just have to bite the bullet and get it over with as soon as you know it's the right thing to do. Your life will be so much better.

Some people also fear being alone and so will wait until they have a new relationship on the line before leaving their current relationship. If this route seems tempting, get out of the old relationship as soon as possible. If you keep your current partner on the line while trying to hook another, you are dangerously close to cheating—in fact, you may just *be* cheating. If your goal is to live an adult life on your own, take responsibility and commit to one person at a time. Or commit to no one but yourself.

 WORD TO THE WISE Not having to face this dilemma is why many people don't get into relationships in the first place. But you also can't win at the game of love if you're not a player.

SEXUAL RELATIONSHIPS

Sexual activity is one of life's bigger choices. Are you *ready* for sex, emotionally, physically, and in terms of personal confidence? There's no requirement or specified time line for becoming sexually active. You can wait a long time before you start, and you can stop if you're not jazzed about it for some reason. Having a satisfying sex life begins with being satisfied with yourself and with your partner.

Sexual Satisfaction

Figuring out how to get the most pleasure from sexual activity is a complex topic, but there are a few important points to make that are not as well known as they should be.

The most important point is that it sometimes takes young people a while to learn how to become fully sexual. Young men tend to be concerned about sexual performance and how to be a good sexual partner. A man in his twenties may simply not feel he is prepared for sex or for pursuing partners sexually. Young women sometimes need to learn how to give themselves permission to enjoy sex and have orgasms. This is certainly not true of every young woman, but it is true of some. These women feel that something is wrong with them because they are unable to completely enjoy an activity that everyone else seems to be doing with ease. That the partners of these young women are also usually inexperienced doesn't help matters.

 PIERRE SAYS You shouldn't feel pressured or required to engage in sex just because you are living on your own. Being comfortable with the choice to have sex and being comfortable with your partner are integral to a fulfilling sex life. There's no need to rush it, and the only timetable that counts is your own.

Another important point has to do with the media's distortion of sexual relations. When heterosexual intercourse is depicted in movies or on TV, more often than not the couple is embraced in the missionary position and the woman is enjoying orgasmic ecstasy. The truth is that a majority of women cannot experience an orgasm while the male is in the superior position. The female orgasm requires clitoral stimulation, and most women don't get enough of it in this position. Figuring out how to make sure the woman is sexually satisfied from lovemaking is vital yet often neglected.

Many young men don't have the control they want over their orgasms during intercourse; in other words, they climax too quickly. It's called premature ejaculation. Developing this control is something that every man should learn if for no other reason than it will give him greater self-confidence. But when you connect the dots to the fact that most women can't climax from the stimulation they receive from intercourse alone, it's clear that male control isn't the most important skill when it comes to female satisfaction. What is important is good communication so that both partners can let each other know what is most pleasing to them. In particular, the female should teach the male how to please her. If the two of you are sufficiently intimate to be having sex, then you should also be able to discuss your sex life.

 Though we are all born sexual creatures—male babies have erections and female babies can lubricate in the womb—there is still a learning curve when it comes to having sex with others. More patience and less panic will go a long way toward helping you to get better at it.

Safe Sex

If you are having sex, there remains the issue of safety. It's almost impossible to guarantee that sex will be perfectly safe. You can use condoms, the other person can show you test results, you can even keep your underpants on, but there's still some element of risk. For example, a person with the sexually transmitted disease herpes can be shedding viruses from a patch they have on their thigh or buttocks. Taking every precaution can certainly help reduce the risk involved in sexual activity, but there is no real risk-free sex. It is imperative, then, that you take responsibility for your protection.

CAUTION Think a lie detector would help you remain safe? Some STDs don't cause any symptoms or cause only mild unrecognizable symptoms, but they can still be transmitted to another person, possibly causing a full-blown case. So someone can tell you with complete honesty that they are disease free—but the truth is that they may be harboring a disease and are completely unaware of it.

 CAUTION Sadly, certain STDs may cause no symptoms that a woman can sense and yet they still may do serious damage over time to her reproductive system, perhaps even causing infertility. And these STDs have infected tens of millions of people in the United States. So while one doesn't want to be an alarmist, the dangers of STDs are very real.

Does this lack of a safety guarantee prevent most people from having sex? Of course not, because the urge to have sex is strong and can overpower concerns about safety. The only course of action is to do everything possible to lower the odds of getting an STD to as close to zero as possible. And the first step toward that end is to always be prepared. Yes, having condoms on hand is the most common precaution and a very good step, but the most basic safeguard is to make sure you know as much about sex and sexually transmitted diseases as possible. When it comes to sex, knowledge is power.

 A word about tests for STDs. If people say they've recently been tested and do not have any STDs, does that mean that you can't catch a disease from them? The answer is no, and for several reasons. First, they could be lying. It happens. Second, not every test is thorough, and some tests may not be able to detect certain diseases. Most important is the fact that HIV has a long incubation period. Someone could be recently infected with HIV, get tested, and not show any antibodies against HIV (what the tests look for), yet the virus may still be present and infect a partner.

PREVENTING AN UNINTENDED PREGNANCY

Using condoms is the most common method to prevent an unintended pregnancy. Condoms offer an added value—they help to reduce the spread of sexually transmitted diseases. But condoms aren't always used properly. They can fall off or break during intercourse or are accidentally left inside the vagina. Knowing how to use condoms is very important if you want to benefit from the protection they offer.

 I recommend that you read "How to Use a Condom Correctly" on **health. com/health/condition-article/0,,20195422,0.html**. For other related articles, DOWNLOADS type "condom" in the website's search box.

 If you're a woman, as soon as you are considering becoming sexually active, WORD TO THE WISE make an appointment with a doctor to thoroughly educate yourself about your contraceptive options.

Another way of preventing pregnancy is to use hormones, most commonly taken in the form of a birth control pill. They can also be injected or given to women in other forms. This method is very effective but doesn't provide protection against STDs and so should be used in conjunction with condoms if you are not certain that your partner is disease free.

Birth control pills are available as a prescription from your doctor. You can also see a doctor at a women's health clinic (such as Planned Parenthood or another nonprofit clinic) and get a low-cost prescription. The pill's effectiveness in preventing pregnancy is highest when taken every day at the same time, without fail. If you miss days or take the pill at different times, its effectiveness goes down. (Note: If you have the 21-day pack form of the pill, then your schedule will be different.) Also, be certain to ask your doctor about other things that may decrease the pill's effectiveness, such as other prescriptions you may be taking (antibiotics, for example, can sometimes be a hindrance).

CAUTION There's a cost to taking the pill. Some women negatively react to it, gaining weight or in some cases losing their sex drive. So while the pill is taken by millions of women and is very effective, it's not perfect. But the pill can also have some positive health side effects, such as clearer skin and reduced discomfort during menstruation. Different brands of prescriptions have different side effects, so don't be afraid to try a few over several months to see which ones suit you the best.

An IUD (intrauterine device) is placed inside the woman's cervix by a gynecologist. It is very effective at preventing pregnancy and doesn't really have any side effects. If the pill isn't right for you, ask your doctor about this option. Technology has made these devices more comfortable, and many brands are safer than they once were.

The withdrawal, or pullout, method can also be used to prevent pregnancies. With this method the man withdraws his penis from the woman's vagina before he ejaculates. There are two serious problems with this method. The first is probably obvious: Sometimes the man fails to pull out in time and ejaculates inside an unprotected vagina. The second is less so. When a man is excited, his Cowper's gland secretes a fluid that acts as a lubricant for the ejaculate when he has an orgasm. You may notice that a man's erect penis has a droplet of fluid coming from it before he has an orgasm. That's the Cowper's fluid. While the fluid coming out of the gland doesn't contain sperm, it can pick up stray sperm in the man's urethra and deposit them in the woman's vagina long before he's ejaculated. It's not very likely that the few sperm that are picked up can cause a pregnancy, but it's still a possibility. So relying on the withdrawal, or pullout, method to protect you against pregnancy means you are taking some big risks.

The best method of birth control, whether male or female, is the kind you control yourself. If you're a woman, don't depend entirely on a man "pulling out" in time. If you're a man, don't depend entirely on a woman taking her pill regularly. If both men and women take responsibility for their own precautions, an unplanned pregnancy is far less likely to happen.

Finally, some people rely on the rhythm method. Normally, a woman is fertile for only a short time every month, and it is possible to predict when that time is and avoid unprotected sex. The problem is the word *normally*. Even women whose periods are as regular as clockwork sometimes experience a month when they're irregular, and that's how they can find themselves pregnant when they don't want to be. So relying on this method is a crapshoot. There are ways of increasing the odds in your favor, but most take a lot of effort.

DOWNLOADS Several iPhone and Android apps (such as iPeriod) help women monitor their menstrual cycles, fertile periods, and ovulation days. Keeping track of these things will help when using family planning or contraception of any kind.

A number of over-the-counter contraceptive aids are on the market for women to use, such as spermicidal films, inserts, and sponges. They can be messy, and you usually have to use them within an hour before intercourse. These methods are best used in conjunction with another contraceptive such as condoms or the pill to help ensure 100% effectiveness. But they are inexpensive and readily available at your local pharmacy.

The Morning-After Pill

Millions of times a year, women who did not want to be pregnant wind up pregnant. But if you think there's a possibility this might happen—you notice a broken condom, the man ejaculates before pulling out—all is not lost. A doctor can give you a prescription for what's been called the morning-after pill, though they're just regular birth control pills and you actually take more than one. These pills can prevent a pregnancy. So if something that could cause an unintended pregnancy happens to you, don't wait (the window of opportunity is seventy-two hours). You have emergency contraception on hand.

For a true emergency, when the sex and the accident were completely unplanned, you can get Plan B One-Step, a brand of emergency contraception, available over the counter without a prescription at a drugstore, a Planned

Parenthood health center, or a family-planning clinic. The cost is usually somewhere between $30 and $70.

> **CAUTION** If you have been raped, you should always go immediately to a hospital emergency room and be checked out, whether you're worried about pregnancy or not. The ER will help you with a dose of Plan B, examine you for any other health issues, and assist with filing a report with the police. Emergency workers are trained to help you.

Abortion

A pregnancy can be terminated by an abortion. For many people, this isn't a consideration for moral or religious reasons. For most others, abortions are a last resort, when an unplanned pregnancy or childrearing isn't possible for financial or personal reasons. Ultimately, abortion is an intensely personal matter because the woman is facing a life-changing event. Consulting with her partner, her family, and her most trusted friends can give added insight and support throughout the process.

Before making a decision, schedule an appointment with the doctor or a women's health clinic as soon as possible in order to get as much information as you can about the procedure. Then think the decision over carefully and conscientiously. With care, consideration, and support, a woman will likely come to the best decision.

Also, abortion is *never* intended to be regular form of birth control. First, it can be an expensive procedure. Second, repeated abortions may cause long-term fertility issues, a major concern if a woman wants to have children later. Therefore, it is better to take as many precautions against unplanned pregnancies as possible rather than rely on abortion.

GETTING HELP

When you're sick, you see a doctor. When you have a toothache, you visit a dentist. But when faced with a sexual or relationship problem, seeking out a professional isn't always the choice people make. One reason for this is that such problems are embarrassing. Bear in mind that professionals who handle such issues all day long don't find them embarrassing, so once you're seated in their office, they'll put you at ease. Yes, it's harder to make an appointment with a therapist than an optician, but your sexual health is just as important as any other aspect of your health.

Can the advice of friends be helpful? Yes, it can. But it can also be harmful. Therapists, on the other hand, have undergone specialized training. They have listened to the feedback of hundreds of patients and have come to learn what works and what doesn't. A friend who gives you advice based on just his or her own life experience could be way off the mark when it comes to your situation.

FAQs

Q. I'm a female who's never had an orgasm. Is there any help for me?

A. Some women can be very individualistic when it comes to having orgasms, and no partner is going to be able to guess what will trigger an orgasm for them. So you first have to find this out for yourself through masturbation and then teach your partner.

Q. I'm a male who can masturbate without difficulty, but when I'm with a female I can't maintain an erection.

A. The more a man worries about his erections, the harder they are to obtain or maintain. One trick that might work is to concentrate on a sexual fantasy. That will arouse you and hopefully will stop any worries from causing erectile failure.

Q. Is there anything I can do to make my penis bigger?

A. If you're seriously overweight, losing weight would help since some of the exposed portion of the penis gets buried under layers of fat. For anyone else, the answer is no.

Q. Does penis size matter?

A. Since most women don't receive sufficient clitoral stimulation through intercourse, the size of the man's penis is often irrelevant. The fact is that men with large penises cause many women to experience pain.

Q. How frequently should a couple have sex?

A. It's different with every couple. Couples should talk about this. And if one-half of a couple feels a need for more orgasms, masturbation is a good alternative.

Q. We used to have sex all the time and now we almost never have sex. What's wrong?

A. Often it's a relationship issue. Even minor resentments or irritations will affect a couple's sex life. It could also be something outside the relationship, such as job stress, or just a lack of time. While many people prefer spontaneous sex, if you're having difficulty connecting, for whatever reasons, planned sex will keep your overall relationship healthy.

Body Issues

Body issues can play a role in sexual difficulties. For example, some men worry about the size of their penis. If they've seen a lot of pornography, that doesn't help matters, because porn stars are chosen for the size of their equipment. But since most women can't have an orgasm from intercourse no matter the size of the man's penis, men should just push such worries aside.

And while both sexes worry about their overall appearance, women have more societal pressures that contribute to a poor body image. Not feeling good about your body can lead to low self-esteem, and low self-esteem can lead to an assortment of sex-related problems. Instead of feeling that you deserve a partner who treats you with respect and love, you may wind up with partners who are bullies and abusive. So, what can you do about this? Try thinking about your wonderful body in terms of its whole being, its amazing physical capabilities, and your positive attributes, both physical and mental. Such positive thinking can go a long way toward shutting off those negative attitudes and help you feel better—and sexier!

CAUTION Body image problems can range from mild to extreme, the latter including conditions such as anorexia and bulimia that can even be deadly. If you feel overwhelmed by a poor body image, know that you can seek help from a professional who can treat the issue.

All these issues can be overcome with sufficient knowledge. Sometimes a person needs professional help, but if you don't even recognize the true nature of a problem, how can you possibly get help? Readers of this book who are not fully satisfied with the way their personal or sex life is going should consult one or more books that explore this topic in greater depth.

Pornography

Porn can cause people of both sexes to have body image issues. It can also cause a myriad of relationship issues. There are many couples whose sex life has gone down the drain, because one partner (the male more often than the female) can't stop masturbating while looking at porn and so has no sexual energy left for his or her partner.

Most people can have a drink or two of alcohol without any negative consequences, but people predisposed to alcoholism can't have even one drink without risk. It seems porn has similar qualities. Some people can't stop themselves once they start relying on porn for sexual arousal, and it prevents them from being able to maintain a serious relationship. If you find yourself in such a situation, the only solution is to go cold turkey. Just as an alcoholic cannot have even one drink, the only way to prevent porn from taking a serious toll on your love life is to stay away from it completely.

WORD TO THE WISE When considering porn, think about your values and how you respect your partner. Porn is often the fastest way to make sex with a real, live human being you love and respect less satisfying. So consider curbing or eliminating porn in your life if you want a fulfilling sex life with a valued partner.

PART FOUR:

HOW TO TAKE CARE OF YOUR MONEY

18 BANKING

Checking Accounts, Saving Accounts, Credit Cards, and More

REASONS TO USE A BANK

If you pay any attention to the news, then you know that banks have had their problems recently. So let's start with this critical piece of information: Money you put into a bank is 100% safe. That's because there's a government insurance program called the Federal Deposit Insurance Corporation (FDIC) that insures your money for up to $250,000. If the entire banking system were to collapse, then, yes, your bank account would be in peril because there wouldn't be enough money in the insurance fund to cover every possible account. But the odds of that happening are much lower than a thief reaching under your mattress and making off with your stash of cash.

But security isn't the only reason you should keep your money in a bank. First, the only thing the money under your mattress will collect is dust—but if you put your money into a savings account or certain checking accounts at the bank, it could collect interest. Online bill paying is another great convenience of the modern banking system. Living on your own, you're going to have bills coming in every month from a variety of sources. But you can quickly and easily pay these bills by using your phone or computer to log on to your bank account and pay off the bills from there. A side benefit of this is that the bank will maintain accurate records of all your transactions, so you won't ever be left wondering whether or not you paid the most recent power bill!

Finally, having a bank account looks good on rental applications and is often required for various other applications, such as for mortgages, car loans, or credit cards. Banks also offer other services, such as issuing credit and debit cards, issuing cashier or teller checks, loaning money, selling certificates of deposits, and renting safe-deposit boxes.

WORD TO THE WISE

Whatever your current banking needs, when choosing a bank you should also look toward the future. Banks like it when you show yourself to be a loyal customer. A bank manager might give you some leeway down the line if you've done all your banking business with his or her bank. So, let's say you were looking to open your own business sometime in the future. It might be worth your while to look more carefully at the choice of banks and pick one a few blocks away that makes commercial loans rather than the bank around the corner that doesn't.

FINDING A BANK

There is no shortage of banks, so once you decide you want to establish an account with one, how do you decide which bank to go with? Which will be the best one for you? Most people pick a bank near where they work or live. If you find a bank with branches convenient to both work and home, you may want to just go with that one, assuming it offers the services you're looking for.

TIME SAVER

If you live on campus, then a bank that's got a branch on campus will probably suit you best, though that's not always the case. If your parents are the ones putting money into the bank, you may want one that's most convenient for them so that they can't use the "I couldn't get to the bank" excuse if they leave you with an empty wallet.

Of course proximity shouldn't be the *only* factor in your decision. Here are some other things to consider:

- fees for checking accounts, bounced checks, using an ATM, and so on
- balance requirements (Most banks ask that you keep a minimum balance in order to get some services for free, but that minimum varies from bank to bank.)
- costs for using ATMs that are not your bank's
- overdraft protection (If you have this protection, the bank won't bounce your checks for insufficient funds.)
- interest on which type of accounts and at what rates
- credit card fees and rates

If sifting through all the ads or websites for the banks near you seems like a task you'd rather avoid, there's an easier way. There are websites that have **DOWNLOADS** done the legwork for you. You put in your zip code and tell the site what you're looking for and you'll be given a list of the banks near you and the differences among them. Two such sites are **findabetterbank.com** and **bankrate.com**.

Internet-Only Banks

Of course you may want to avoid using a brick-and-mortar bank altogether in favor of an Internet-only bank. These banks don't have the costs that storefronts filled with employees do and so can pass some of these savings on to you by offering a higher APY (annual percentage yield). But obviously if you need to physically go to the bank for some reason, maybe to talk to a banker face to face, that's impossible with a bank that exists only on the web.

And since an online bank has no branches, if you use ATMs to withdraw cash a lot, you'll be hit with extra fees. On the other hand, if you pay for most things with a debit card, this won't be a problem.

 If you're a bit intimidated by the idea of going into a bank and speaking to someone to open an account, an online bank will allow you to avoid this step, though many banks with physical branches will also allow you to open an account online. Some banks, such as Chase, will let you open an account online; then once the account is confirmed, you stop by a branch and just ask to sign your signature card (a document that banks use to confirm your identity).

If you do use an online bank as your only bank, make sure that your money is FDIC insured and ask how long it takes for checks to clear. Some online banks take a very long time to allow you to use the money you deposit.

BANKING BASICS

If you've never had a bank account or paid any attention to banks at all, a short course in banking is in order so that you can understand the terms used in this chapter. There are many different types of bank accounts, and the two most basic are checking and savings.

Checking Accounts

Checking accounts are called so because they were originally created for writing and depositing checks only. Now, of course, you can use your checking account in various ways: writing checks, withdrawing cash, using ATM and debit cards, or paying bills online. Most banks now issue you a primary card that serves as your ATM/debit card (once called a check card) and your bank ID card. You'll use it at ATMs to make deposits or withdrawals at your bank or to make purchases in stores or online.

The difference between writing a check and using your debit card is one of timing. Essentially, both methods remove the specified funds from your account and transfer them to someone else's account. But checks take several days (or maybe weeks) to show up as having been deducted from your account. Debit cards subtract the payment immediately from your account, helping you keep track of your account a little easier.

In exchange for the convenience of writing checks or using an ATM/debit card, banks usually don't pay any interest on a checking account unless you agree to always keep a certain amount of money in the account. This amount varies from bank to bank and can range from $500 to $5,000.

CAUTION You may be charged one or more additional fees for using another bank's ATM to get cash from your account. The bank that gives you the money will charge a fee and potentially so will your own bank. If you intend to use a debit card a lot, make sure that you know the fee structure of your bank and any other bank ATMs you might use regularly.

WORD TO THE WISE Checks are not as widely used as they once were. They take more time and therefore require more accounting in your records, while your debit card transactions show up online very quickly and you can check them anytime through the bank's website or phone app. Choose carefully what things you'll write a check for so you can keep track of them more easily. Rent is the most common reason young people write a check these days.

Savings Accounts

Savings accounts are a useful tool if you want to save money, earn a little bit of interest, and keep your money liquid (meaning you can quickly withdraw it from the bank, unlike money invested in the stock market). The money in a savings account is FDIC insured, and many savings accounts can be started with a fairly small initial deposit. Plus, most banks will link your savings account to your checking account, making it easy to transfer funds between the two.

MONEY SAVER Having a savings account with money in it means you can sign up for overdraft protection at your bank. If you find your checking account overdrawn, but you need to make a purchase or pay a bill, the savings account will cover what your checking account cannot. This is a nice protection to have in place, because without it, you'll be assessed a fee by your bank if your checking account becomes overdrawn.

Savings accounts can be accessed through ATMs to get cash or by going online, where you can transfer money from your savings account to your checking account, if needed. You usually cannot use your savings account to make purchases with your debit card. Because there is less activity in a savings account, the costs involved in maintaining a savings account are lower for a bank, so some of those savings are passed on to you in the form of interest to encourage you to put your money into such an account.

Earning Interest

As I've mentioned earlier, your savings account will earn you interest. Let me explain how that works, in case you're not familiar.

Let's say you had $1,000 in a savings account earning 5% interest. If you left that money untouched for a year, at the end of the year you'd have $1,050, or 5% more than you began with. This extra income can really add up over time. And if you want a higher rate than that offered by the standard savings account, all you have to do is promise to leave your money in the bank for a longer period to lock in a higher rate. Being disciplined about leaving as much money as possible in your savings account can help you grow the account a good deal over time. Then after several years, if you've built up a solid savings account, you can transfer that money into a higher-interest retirement account when you're ready to begin planning for retirement.

Is the money you deposit kept in the bank's vault? A little bit probably is (or placed with the federal government), but most of it is loaned out by the bank. Making loans is how banks make most of their money, be it through an actual loan for a house or car or through credit card charges. And so they encourage you to leave your money in their hands by paying you interest or giving you some service so that they can make money lending your funds out to others. All this money changing hands keeps the economy moving. If everyone kept their savings in a locked box, the economy would come to a standstill!

Depositing Money into Your Account

There are several ways to deposit money into your account. The old-fashioned way, and the way most people still do it, is to visit the bank, sign the back of the check they are depositing (called endorsing), and either give it to a teller with a deposit slip or feed it into an ATM. Your place of employment may allow you to sign up for direct deposit, which means your paycheck will go directly into your bank account without you ever having to handle the check. And if you have the right app in your phone, you can just take a picture of a check and email or text it in order to deposit it into your account.

By the way, don't assume that because you deposited a check that the money goes into your account immediately. It usually takes a few business days for a check to "clear," which means the check you deposit is sent to the bank the check was issued from and the money then goes into your bank. (Electronic transfers are shortening the time it takes for checks to clear, but to be sure, always check with your bank.) If you keep enough money in your bank, whether in your checking account or even in a separate savings account, many banks will count the money you deposit in check form right away. But if your overall funds are low, you will have to remember to allow checks you deposit to clear before spending the money. Otherwise, it will be bounce city for you.

BALANCING YOUR CHECKING ACCOUNT

It's quite possible that after all the years of math classes you've taken you feel as though you really have no use for math. But you're going to need your math skills if you have a checking account. It's true that the only math involved in balancing a checkbook is simple addition and subtraction, but any mistakes you make could have serious real-world consequences, much worse that a red D or F marked on a test paper.

When you write a check or make a ATM/debit transaction, you're supposed to write down in a paper register, or log, that comes with your checks the amount of each check or transaction, the date the check or transaction took place, and the check number (if a check). You then subtract the amount of the check or transaction from your running balance. When you deposit or transfer money into your checking account, you add the amount to your balance and note the date. If you're always accurate with your math, what your register shows as the balance will be the same figure that the bank says you have.

 If you're online and you make a transfer payment, you'll see that your bank balance goes down immediately. But if you tell your bank to pay, say, your phone bill, your balance won't change until the payment actually goes through.

The obvious way to lose track of how much you have in your account is to make a math error—but there are other ways. But what trips up even math geniuses is to not write down ATM cash withdrawals or the money they spend using their debit card. When you write a check, your register is probably right in front of you beside your checkbook, making it likely that you'll enter the amount of the checks you write. But when you go to an ATM or use a debit card in a store, you tell yourself to write down the amount when you get home, but you won't always do so. In fact, you may never do so. But if you're not careful, that's how you can wind up with a bank balance that is in negative territory.

Regularly comparing your register with the transactions listed for your account at your bank's website or on the monthly paper statements you may receive (known as balancing your checkbook) will help you avoid declined cards and bounced checks. Once a month used to be the bare minimum for this, but checking in with your account online several times a week will be worth it when that forgotten café tab or automatic phone payment suddenly comes to mind. And it is so easy to do with the phone apps that are available now.

 If you do all or most of your banking online, you may think that you don't have to worry about such things as check clearing, but you do. The balance amount shown on your computer screen may not be accurate as it won't reflect checks you've written or payments you've made that haven't yet cleared.

CAUTION Relying on the bank's statements to determine your balance means that you trust the bank to always be right. That's true 99.9% of the time, but banks have been known to make mistakes themselves—so even if you don't bother balancing your account to the penny, as some people do, at least make sure you always have a vague idea of what your balance should be. If it seems off, that's when you need to pull out your calculator.

DOWNLOADS Many people use the website service **Mint.com** to handle all their banking calculations. By using such a program, you don't ever have to worry about making a math error. And there are phone apps such as Checkbook, Accounts, PocketMoney, GoodBudget, and Money Monitor for iPhone and Android that are easy to use and work great as a transaction register, if you don't have a traditional check register or don't use checks very often. And all of these programs are very effective at helping you avoid overdrawing your checking account!

Overdrawing Your Account

The main reason you need to keep track of how much money is in your account is that you don't want to bounce any checks (particularly a rent check!). A bounced check means that you sent a check to someone, who then tried to get the money out of your account by depositing that check into his or her account. But when the check was presented to your bank, it said there were insufficient funds in the account to pay the check.

There's any easy way to avoid this hassle. Let's say, for example, you wrote a $65 check to repay a friend for a small loan. You recorded the check in your own personal checkbook register and deducted $65 from your balance. That money is now "reserved." And it needs to stay reserved until it "clears" your bank account and shows up in your transactions—no matter how long it takes for your friend to cash it. Keeping track of checks that haven't cleared is how you avoid bouncing a check.

Obviously, bouncing a check is embarrassing. But it's also costly. Your bank is going to charge you for bouncing a check. The fee varies from bank to bank, but it probably will be no less than $25. And the bank of the check's recipient will also impose a charge, and so the person or company you wrote the check to will probably come after you not only to get the money you still owe them, but to pay off the bank charges as well.

Ask your bank about no-bounce coverage. That means if you ever give a person or company a check for which you have insufficient funds, the bank will accept that check and pay it. Sounds good, right? But the bank will treat this as a loan, so not only will you have to repay the check amount, but you will be charged interest from the day this "loan" is made. If you pay the amount quickly, the cost shouldn't be very much, certainly less than the fee to bounce a check. But if you don't pay it back quickly, then the interest charges can quickly grow.

With a bit of attention to detail, you can protect yourself from ever overdrawing your account. Just get in the habit of routinely logging your transaction and keeping your checking account ledger up to date. Keep track of those pesky checks that haven't cleared your account, and be sure to record transactions you make with your ATM/debit card.

CREDIT CARDS

Banks issue credit cards, which allow you to spend money you don't have. That can be a good thing, if you're careful. Let's say there's a sale on the new bike you've been wanting for commuting to work, but you don't have enough money to buy it right now. You'll have enough money when you receive your next paycheck, but unfortunately that won't happen until three days after the sale ends!

That's where your credit card comes in, giving you a small loan so that you can purchase the bike while it's still on sale. But charging an item on a credit card means you'll be paying a steep interest, possibly 25% or more, if you pay off the charge in monthly installments. Falling behind on your credit card payments—and thereby accruing big interest charges—is a surefire way to get yourself into financial trouble. Millions have fallen prey to this trap, so don't join them!

Always strive to pay more than just the minimum amount due on your bill. And here's the good news: If you pay off your entire credit card bill as soon as you receive it, you won't be charged interest at all. It's like a zero-cost loan. That's why credit cards, when handled with discipline, can be a very convenient tool.

Getting a Credit Card

College students are deluged with offers to sign up for a credit card, even though they often have no source of income and may already be grappling with student loans. (In some cases, parents may have to cosign the credit card application, guaranteeing that they'll pay the money if their son or daughter doesn't.) But other young people who are not in college may find it more difficult to get a credit card, and if you've been delinquent paying off a card or loan, then it can be really difficult.

Some credit cards come with a yearly flat fee, so when you're shopping for a card, don't just look for the card with the lowest interest rate; also be sure to check for low fees. If you intend to use your credit card a lot, then the rates may be the most important factor to you. But if you'll be paying off your credit card bills as soon as they come in, then the lowest fee is what you should be looking for, as the interest rate won't be a factor since you'll never have a balance left over.

Another tactic banks use is to lure you with a low introductory interest rate. Again, if you know you'll be paying off what you owe before the low rate expires, then that can be a good offer. But if you don't, the next rate will probably be a doozy.

DOWNLOADS You can search the web for sites that compare different credit cards, making it easy to see the introductory rates and fees of each card. Use "compare credit card rates" for your search.

FYI Some people play at moving the money they owe from one bank's credit card to that of another bank so that they can take advantage of low introductory rates. It's doable and can save you money if you need to keep a high outstanding balance, but you also have to be careful to keep track of when those initial low rates expire.

Credit Limits

When you first get a credit card, you're given a credit limit. If it's $250, then you can't charge more than that amount until you pay off some or part of your balance. What often happens is that a bank will start you off with a low credit limit and then will notify you when it has raised your credit limit after you've demonstrated for a time that you can pay your bills. And if you plan on buying a big-ticket item, you can also ask the bank to raise the limit, which it may grant. All this doesn't mean you should buy more on credit, but it's good to know that if you need to, you can.

Establishing Credit

One reason to obtain a credit card is to establish your credit rating. If you have a card and pay your bills on time, then you're considered a good credit risk. If you've established good credit, when it comes time to buy something a lot more expensive on credit, such as a car or house, banks will be more likely to grant you that loan. The bank will also be more likely to give you a better rate, which over the lifetime of a thirty-year mortgage could add up to quite a savings.

However, if you misuse your first credit card and run into trouble paying your credit card bills, then not only won't you establish good credit, you'll get a bad credit rating. If you're concerned with your ability to properly handle your credit card, stick with the initial low credit limit, which will cap your ability to get into trouble.

CAUTION Be wary of paying your various monthly bills with your credit card, unless you are always good about paying off your entire credit card bill each month. If you don't, you'll be charged interest.

Alternate Credit Cards

If you've been turned down for a credit card, there are some alternative types that are easier to get, assuming you have some cash to put aside. One type is called a secured card, which offers a good way to establish (or rebuild) your credit rating. You put some money in a bank, agreeing to leave it there as a security deposit (which will earn interest, by the way), and the bank gives you a credit card. The card's limit will probably be about the same as the amount of your deposit. Since most people who need to get a secured card are considered a bad credit risk, the fees are usually higher than normal. Because banks usually do report your payment history with such cards to the credit bureaus, using one properly will help you to build up your credit history. And if you've had problems in the past, this may be one way to repair the damage you've done to your credit rating.

Many banks, such as Chase, offer an online application for a secured card. This is an easy way for you to compare what different banks offer and to get **DOWNLOADS** the process started!

Another option is the prepaid card, which looks like a credit card. But in fact you've put the money you're going to spend in it, making it more like a gift card than a regular credit card. It's a good way to carry around money you want to spend, say, at Christmas, without having to fill your pockets with cash. But there's a charge for getting such a card. Also, banks don't report it to the credit bureaus, so you can't build a credit history with them. You might just as well use your debit card.

Some businesses, such as Walmart and certain check-cashing chains, offer a prepaid card with more services. You can cash a preprinted paycheck and put it on one of their cards, for instance. So if you find yourself in between accounts but need a way to cash your paycheck, this could be an option for the short term. It is not intended for the long term, however, because the fees and hassle can be a nuisance.

Credit Card versus Debit Card Risk

If your credit card is stolen or lost, you aren't liable for more than $50 of any charges made by the thief. The same is true for a debit card if you report the card stolen within two business days. If you wait longer to report a debit card theft, then you're liable for $500, and past sixty days you may be liable for all the money stolen. This risk is one reason why some people prefer to use a credit card, gaining the protection that it offers.

WORD TO THE WISE If you're traveling, write down the phone number listed on your debit card and keep it separate. That way if the card gets stolen, you can easily call and alert your bank ASAP.

IDENTITY THEFT

If your wallet is stolen, you face a greater risk than someone trying to use your credit or debit cards—the thief could attempt to steal your identity. What that means is that the thief opens accounts in your name using your ID and then runs up huge charges that you'll be responsible for, unless you can prove that you didn't do it. Clearing your name and getting your identity back can be a nightmare, but the quicker you act, the less damage can be done and the easier it will be to reverse.

If your ID is stolen (and this can sometimes happen without the theft of physical documents or cards), there are steps that you must take immediately.

- Notify the police. You always want to make sure that there is an official record that you reported a theft of any type, especially identity theft.
- Place a fraud alert on your credit reports and review them.
- Close any accounts that may be compromised.
- File a complaint with the Federal Trade Commission.

For more detailed information on what to do in cases of identity theft, visit the Federal Trade Commission's website: **ftc.gov/bcp/edu/microsites/idtheft/ consumers/defend.html**.

PIERRE SAYS When my daughter got married she moved across state lines. She was required to get a new drivers license and turn in her old one. Somehow that old license turned up in the hands of a crook who patiently waited almost six months, until the Christmas rush, before going from branch to branch of my daughter's bank, taking out thousands of dollars, opening credit card accounts, etc. This story demonstrates that you can't protect yourself 100%, so assume that the worst will happen and take precautions. Here's another government website that tells you how: **www.consumer.ftc.gov/ articles/0272-how-keep-your-personal-information-secure**.

RETIREMENT SAVINGS

If you're setting up your first household, thoughts of retirement are probably far from your mind. But as mentioned in Chapter 1, money that you put into a retirement account comes with tax savings, and yet it can still be spent on some items before you retire, including education and buying a home. Plus, the earlier you get started, the more your money will grow, due to the power of compound interest. Even a slow and modest beginning can result in a substantial retirement account as the years pass. So now's the time to start!

Retirement accounts are a big and somewhat complex subject, so when you feel you're ready to start putting away some money on a long-term basis, a good way to start is to have a talk with your parents.

19 Taxes

How to Prepare for the Different Taxes in Your Life

Learning about Taxes

There's an old adage that says you can never escape two things, death and taxes. This book can't help you to avoid death, though it may help make your life a little easier, nor can it work a miracle and get you out of paying taxes. But in these pages you may find some relief from the second half of this terrible twosome.

Types of Taxes

It's bad enough that you have to pay taxes, but what also upsets many people is that preparing tax forms is so complicated. One reason for this is that you don't pay just one tax. There's federal income tax, there's Social Security tax, there's Medicare tax, and there are potentially state and city income taxes. If you live in one state and work in another, you'll probably have to pay taxes in both states. And all these don't include all the other types of taxes that barrage us, such as sales and property taxes.

WORD TO THE WISE To make taxpaying a little less painful, bear in mind that you do get many things back from the government, such as protection from criminals, fires, and foreign invasions, not to mention the building of roads, bridges, hospitals, schools, and so on. Taxes may be painful, but they're also necessary. On the other hand, if you think your tax dollars aren't being well spent, then you need to become involved in politics, a subject beyond the scope of this book.

FICA Tax

FICA stands for the Federal Insurance Contributions Act tax, which funds the federal government's Social Security and Medicare programs. The FICA tax is split between you and your employer. (If you're self-employed, you have the privilege of paying both halves.) The Social Security portion of the tax is 6.2%, up to an income of $110,100, meaning any income earned that is above that level is not taxed. Your employer pays the same amount. The Medicare tax rate is 1.45%, and again your employer pays the same amount. This tax is not capped, so you pay it on every cent of earned income you make. Note that these rates are often tweaked by Congress and rarely stay the same for very long.

So, are you really going to collect Social Security and Medicare when you retire? Despite all the doom and gloom you may read, the answer is probably yes, though the likelihood is it won't be enough to live on so you have to start saving for retirement as well.

Income Taxes

The word *complicated* is really not strong enough to describe the U.S. tax code, which, by the way, is 73,954 pages long. But you need to understand some basics that we can briefly cover. The first thing is that income tax rates are progressive, so that the more money you earn, the higher your tax rate. As with the FICA tax, federal income taxes are frequently adjusted. Visit **wikipedia.org/wiki/Rate_ schedule_(federal_income_tax)** for an up-to-date table of rates.

The U.S. government isn't the only body that wants a piece of what you make. Many state and city governments will also be dipping into your pocket. Their income tax rates are lower so the pain isn't as great, but when such taxes come on top of the federal taxes, it means the overall bite out of your paycheck is even bigger. However, the good news is that these taxes are usually deductible from your federal taxes, which helps a bit. As discussed in Chapter 1, when you are figuring out your budget, it's vital to estimate the taxes you'll need to pay. Every dollar you allocate to pay your taxes correspondingly reduces your disposable income.

 Not every state or locality has an income tax, which is something to consider if you're thinking about moving. Of course many areas, such as big cities, that do impose income taxes tend to offer higher salaries, so you may not come out ahead by living in a low-tax area. You'll need to decide whether you can earn the same amount of post-tax income doing what you do best in a locality where the tax bite is small, or whether you're better off earning more in a metropolitan area despite having to pay higher taxes.

LOWERING YOUR TAXABLE INCOME

Note that your income taxed is based on your *taxable* income. If your employer pays you $40,000 a year in gross income, that is not your taxable income. You get to subtract certain amounts of income known as tax deductions. The more you can reduce your taxable income, the less in taxes you'll end up paying.

The Standard Deduction versus Itemized Deductions

Everyone who files income taxes gets to deduct some of their income, which means you don't pay taxes on that deducted portion. The standard deduction is currently $5,950 for a single person and $11,900 for a married couple. So, for example, if you're a single person earning $20,000 a year and you take the standard deduction, your taxable income will be reduced to $14,050. Two out of three people filing taxes end up taking the standard deduction. Your other option is to itemize all your eligible deductions and see if by that approach you can deduct more income than with the standard deduction.

If you're using tax software to calculate your taxes, it's pretty easy to get it to do the math both ways. You do have to enter in a bit more information, but if you know you have some deductions, check to see whether they add up to more than the standard deduction.

Even if you do claim the standard deduction, you can, in addition, still deduct certain other items, such as interest on student loans, certain expenses for reservists and performing artists, moving expenses if you move more than fifty miles for work-related reasons, certain expenses that teachers incur, contributions to individual retirement accounts (IRAs) and 401(k)s, and money you put into health savings accounts.

Although it may be a while before you own a home, you'll be happy to learn that a common deduction is the interest you pay on the mortgage of your primary residence. Another way to enjoy significant tax savings, when you're ready, is to invest in special tax-deferred savings accounts, such as IRAs.

Health Savings Accounts and Flexible Spending Arrangements

To encourage you to save money for when illness may strike—and that could mean anything from the common cold to something serious—the government has created accounts that allow you to put aside untaxed money for your health care. An example of this is the health savings account (HSA). With an HSA, whether or not you itemize your deductions, you can deduct money put into such an account from your income. Your school or employer may be able to help you set up an HSA, but if not, a bank or insurance company can act as the trustee. And any contributions your employer makes to your HSA are not counted as income to you.

You may also want to look into flexible spending arrangements (FSAs), which are similar to HSAs. The amount of tax-free money you can put into an FSA is lower, but when you spend it on medical expenses you're paying with tax-free dollars. However, you have to decide ahead of time how much money you'll put in your FSA, and if you don't spend it all, you could lose it.

 Another medical deduction you can take is for the money you spend on prescription drugs. So save your receipts. Often, if you sign up for an online account with a chain pharmacy such as Walgreens, they will email you a document prepared with your prescription drug costs for the year.

PREPARING YOUR TAXES

You have several options when it comes to preparing your taxes. You could download or purchase tax preparation software (some programs are free, at least for basic taxes) and do your taxes on your computer. Or you could use a web-based tax service, fill in the blanks, and let the service's software do the calculations. You could pay a tax preparation service to do the work. Or you could use the gold standard, which is to hire a certified public accountant (CPA). If you're a salaried employee, then your taxes are probably pretty easy to calculate and you can certainly do them yourself, especially with the help of software. But if you have a variety of income sources, do a lot of freelance work, or have property or investments, your taxes can get a bit complicated. The more unique your situation, the more help you'll need. But keep in mind, the professional help you pay for may actually end up saving you money in the long run, as well as time and aggravation.

Deciding How Much to Withhold

If you are working for one employer, as opposed to freelancing, then each pay period your employer will take out of your pay the taxes you owe and send them to the government. This process is called withholding. The money remaining after your employer removes your taxes constitutes your paycheck.

To some extent, you can control exactly how much your employer withholds from your paycheck through what are called exemptions. The more exemptions you take, the less tax money your employer withholds. Everyone is entitled to claim one exemption. If you have dependents, either children or adults for whom you are financially responsible, you can also claim these individuals as dependents, and so even less money will be taken out of your paycheck.

Note that just because withholding taxes are taken out of your paycheck doesn't mean you might not still owe additional taxes by April 15 each year. It all depends on how closely the amount withheld throughout the year matches your ultimate tax bill. Some people hate the idea of owing this money and would prefer to receive a tax refund from the government. If you're this sort of person, it means you'd prefer to overpay your taxes during the course of the year, so you should tell your employer you want to take zero exemptions. This may be a safe approach to take when you're just starting out. You won't have to worry about a tax bill each year and will instead look forward to receiving a refund of some amount. But over time, as you become a whiz at paying taxes and a master at budgeting, you may discover you're uncomfortable with the government hanging on to all that money for so many months. If this is the case, start taking some of the exemptions you qualify for. Your paycheck will increase in size as the amount withheld decreases. Just be sure that come April 15, you have enough money saved to pay your tax bill.

If this is all a bit confusing, I suggest speaking to someone at your place of employment who can take the time to explain it to you.

 You might be wondering how long you need to hang on to receipts and financial statements. The IRS offers some handy guidelines at **www.irs.gov/ Businesses/Small-Businesses-&-Self-Employed/How-long-should-I- keep-records**. Above and beyond what the IRS cares about, you'll want to permanently retain certain documents, such as birth certificates and wills.

For the Self-Employed

Maybe you're a musician or freelance writer, or you work for several companies as an independent contractor—like a painter who paints a different house each week. If so, then you're considered self-employed. Since you don't draw a fixed salary, there's no employer to withhold your taxes, and so your tax scheme is different. Self-employed people pay their taxes on a quarterly basis rather than in a lump sum by April 15 each year. It's up to you to calculate what your taxes will be at the end of the year and pay one-quarter of that amount every three months. That takes a certain amount of guesswork if you're working freelance, particularly since your income may go up and down considerably each quarter—but as long as you can show that you paid at least what you owed in any given quarter, you'll be OK.

On average, young freelancers put about 15% of each paycheck into their savings account earmarked for their taxes. Since they usually don't make more than $35,000 a year, it generally covers the tax bill. Of course some self-employed people spend all the money they bring in as they make it, neglecting to set any aside to pay their taxes. The IRS is not an agency you want to fool around with. It can garnish your wages (take a portion of your paycheck until the tax bill is paid off), put a lien on a home or car you own (take possession of it to pay back what you owe), and prevent you from qualifying for business or educational loans in the future. In short, the IRS can put a halt to your financial future at too young an age.

PIERRE SAYS What happens when self-employed people don't earmark tax money and pay it out each quarter? Here's a sobering true story about a friend of mine that will give you a taste of what it's like being on the IRS's bad side. After ten years of ignoring his tax bills, a freelance computer programmer found himself audited by the IRS. Liens were placed on the condo he had purchased five years earlier and the car he had purchased three years earlier. After consulting with a legal CPA, he went into negotiations with the IRS, which was asking for $52,000 in back taxes, plus a fee of $10,000. The CPA managed to get the IRS to let go of the car and the fee. The programmer, however, had to pay back his tax bill in monthly payments of $500 over the next ten years—and he still lost his condo. He was thirty-five years old.

CHAPTER 20 LEGAL ISSUES

How to Deal with Law Enforcement, Contracts, Jury Duty, and More

DEALING WITH LAW ENFORCEMENT

In a practical sense, most of your "legal issues" will concern day-to-day laws and, hopefully, only very occasional interactions with law enforcement.

Speeding Tickets and Traffic Violations

Most people will receive a speeding ticket or traffic violation at some point in their driving careers. For every violation you receive, points will be assessed against your driver's license. Too many points and you could see your car insurance rates go up and possibly lose your license. The best way to manage violations is to not ignore them. If you believe you were ticketed wrongly, show up on your court date and explain your case. It may be dismissed.

If that's not the case, be certain to clear your obligations with dispatch. If you're eligible for traffic school, sign up and complete the requirement as soon as possible. Sometimes you can even do it online. If you owe a fine, take care of it promptly. If the fine is too large to pay in one go, call the traffic court and ask if you can make a number of payments. Often, the traffic court will be willing to work with you if you are upfront, honest, and expeditious about taking care of the ticket.

CAUTION If you ignore a traffic ticket for a long period, you could be racking up additional fines. Eventually, a warrant for your arrest could be issued, and if a police officer pulls you over again, you could be taken in. Alternatively, it is possible that your license will be suspended until you pay all of your fines—which will leave you without legal transportation.

But you can easily avoid all of this by (a) driving carefully and legally and (b) communicating with the court in a timely fashion and arranging to pay your fines.

Drinking and Driving

This is a major violation that can really mess up your plans for the future. At the very least, if you are pulled over by an officer or stopped at a DUI checkpoint and you test over the blood alcohol limit, you could lose your license for at least a year and spend the night in jail to boot. If you are in an accident or if you injure someone while driving drunk, you could find yourself facing some serious criminal charges. Time in prison could be on the table. Even if you manage to settle the criminal case, you could be on the hook for tens of thousands of dollars in fines and probation. Not to mention the guilt of having injured or killed another human being.

It is best to have a designated driver who doesn't drink at all during your nights on the town with friends. Store the phone number of several local taxi services. A ride home usually won't cost you too much, and you can come back for your car in the morning. There are also designated driver services in many areas that you can call for a pickup for both you and your car. Go to **bemydd.com** or google the various sober and safe ride programs to see what is available in your area. Keep their contact info on you for when you need it.

Interacting with Police Officers

In our day and age, most law enforcement officials are on heightened alert for criminal activity. They want to protect both their communities and themselves. To keep encounters with the police on the safe and sane side, a few guidelines will help.

If you are stopped in your community or in your vehicle:
- Keep a level head and your voice low. Use polite language and cooperate so that the officers can complete their assignment and you can get on with your day.
- Cooperate with their reasonable safety requests. If they ask you to sit down or step aside, do so. This way the officers can maintain everyone's safety and gather their information peacefully.
- Be respectful, even if you feel the officer isn't respectful of you. Both of you wish to resolve the situation peacefully. Avoid using the word *cop*; say *officer* instead.
- Answer questions respectfully, honestly, and simply. Don't elaborate. Don't become argumentative with an officer. Ask the officer only questions of clarification if you need to do so; for example, "Why must I stop my activity? Am I in violation of a law?"

- Don't ever accuse or complain directly to an officer. If you need to do so, you can request to speak to his or her supervisor or watch sergeant.

If you are detained for questioning: The police may question anyone. Even if you are not under suspicion or arrest, police may ask you questions. However, **you have the right to remain silent and do not have to answer police questions or agree to an interview.** Be quiet and polite, and cooperate if the police ask to question you. If you are questioned regarding an investigation, do give your name, address, and date of birth. You may answer any questions you feel comfortable answering. If you no longer feel comfortable answering, you can request any further questioning be conducted in the presence of an attorney. You can also ask for permission to leave.

If you are arrested: Stay calm and cooperative in your actions. However, maintain your right to silence until an attorney is there to represent you.

Creating a rapport with your local officers: It is better to have your local law enforcement with you than against you. Take time to talk to police officers you see in your community. Get to know the officers who frequently work in the area where you live, work, and play. Often, if officers feel that their efforts are appreciated by the community, they will be more respectful of community members. A sense of mutual cooperation and investment is created when both officers and citizens work together.

CONTRACTS

Up until now your parents may have acted as your legal guardians, but for this chapter we're going to assume that you're old enough to sign legal papers such as contracts.

When you sign documents to get electrical, gas, or cable service, or to rent a car, you're signing a contract that's enforceable under the law. But there are many instances when you don't even have to sign actual paperwork to be party to a contract. For example, if you call your electric utility and ask them to turn on service to your home, whether or not you sign anything, there is an implied and legally enforceable contract that obliges you to pay for the electric service that is delivered.

Employment Contracts

When you're being offered a new job, your employer may give you a contract that spells out the many rules and regulations that regulate working for that specific company. Usually when you are offered an employment contract it means that you're working for a large company that has an army of lawyers who draw up such documents. Once you and the person hiring you have agreed on a salary, trying to change the rest of the contract you're given is almost impossible because a whole host of people would have to agree to it. But that doesn't mean that you shouldn't read the contract carefully. Here are some terms you may encounter:

Exclusive employment: This contract clause usually stipulates that your employer doesn't want you to also work for another company, be it a competitor or not. Stay alert for this language if you plan on working more than one job.

 In some industries, the pilfering of employees happens all the time, despite signed contracts, and what usually happens is that the company hiring away the employee pays the company that lost out a certain sum as compensation.

No authority to contract: This means that as an employee you can't enter into a contract on behalf of your employer that would be binding on your employer.

Termination: Just because you have a contract doesn't mean you can't get fired. A job termination clause spells out the company's policies with regard to firing as well as how much severance pay you might receive and so on.

Confidentially agreement: This agreement prevents you from disclosing company information to anyone outside the company. If your employer found that you were communicating such information to anyone else, not only would you lose your job, but more than likely you'd be sued.

Noncompetition agreement: To prevent you from taking information you learned at the company and applying it to a new job at another company or your own start-up, the contract you sign might include a noncompetition agreement that would prohibit you from doing that for a certain period. Usually, the more valuable you are to a company, the longer the time period.

Arbitration: This means that if the contract parties disagree, rather than go to court they must go in front of an arbitrator. Arbitration is a less complex and less costly way of settling disputes.

A company that signs new employees to a contract will usually have someone in human resources whose job it is to handle contract matters. If you have questions about the contract being offered to you, you probably should check with someone from HR, as he or she will be more familiar with the ins and outs of the company's contract.

 Many jobs don't involve a contract. If you're hired and you're not offered a contract, your employment is "at will," which means you can be fired at any time and for no particular reason. Even if you've worked at a firm for ten years, that doesn't mean that the company has to continue to employ you.

BEING AN INDEPENDENT CONTRACTOR

An independent contractor or freelancer is someone who does work for many people for a short period and is not considered an employee. Many people work exclusively as freelancers or freelance to supplement the income they receive from a job they have with an employer.

If you're a freelancer, in some ways you have fewer legal obligations than regular employees who signed a contract with a company. But you also have fewer legal safeguards. In order to guard against clients who refuse to pay for your services or who abuse your position as a freelancer (by dragging out a project so that it takes three times as long as it usually would), be certain to think through what you can do to protect yourself. Here are some ideas:

- Document, document, document. At the end of the day, record all of the hours you spend working on the project you're hired for and what you did for it. Keep an official "billable hours" log with the title of the project, client name, dates, hours, and tasks. It may seem like a hassle, but if you're questioned by a client regarding a bill, it is a quick and easy way to make your time concrete to them.
- Clearly list the services you'll provide, how much they cost, and how many hours these services will require. For example, a graphic design of a poster might be one design and six hours of work, charged at $20 an hour, along with two additional corrections/changes at no charge. Any changes or corrections beyond those six hours and two free corrections/changes will be an additional $25 per hour up to three

hours. Spelling out what clients receive and where your boundaries are in advance will keep clients focused and help remind them that you aren't their official employee. You take jobs and clients at your own will.

- Once clients are interested in your services and have agreed to a price and terms (feel free to negotiate these), have them sign a contract agreement for services that spells it all out for both of you. That way if they refuse to pay when you invoice them, you have a signed agreement you can use against them, especially if you wish to take them to small-claims court. Your contract agreements should do the following:

    1. State what you're charging for a particular job. "Project YES will take no fewer than four hours and no more than six hours at $25 per hour." This protects both you and your clients. You know the minimum you'll get paid and they know the maximum they'll pay.

    2. Spell out the payment and invoicing agreement. Do you invoice at the end of the month for all work? Do you require a deposit on the fee and the rest when finished? Do clients have a certain amount of time to pay? Is there a penalty for paying late? Can they pay in installments? Spell it all out.

    3. Name one client staff member you will take direction from on the project. Having a single point of contact keeps the feedback and accountability filtered through one person, avoiding confusion.

    4. Specify a cancellation fee. Sometimes freelance projects are canceled before they're finished. To ensure you are paid something for your valuable time, list a cancellation fee for the job. Usually this is between 25% and 50% of the agreed-upon fee.

    5. If you are a writer, spell out how many revisions and rewrites you provide for free on a single project (usually two or three). If the project requires more than that, state how much each revision will cost or draw up a new contract for an entirely new project and discuss the terms with the client. This will help you avoid doing more work outside the scope of the original project.

    6. State that you own copyright until final payment is made. List

any other ways you'd like permission to use the work after clients have paid for it (inclusion in your portfolio, public displays of your work, competitions, and so on) and have them agree to allow it, if possible.

7. Set the final deadline and put it in writing. This will prevent you from delaying an important project for your client and will keep the client from moving the deadline up when you are unprepared for it.

- Know your copyright rights. If clients refuse to pay you for a creation you've made for them (such as a graphic design, written copy, and so on), it is illegal for them to use the work until they've paid you. But once they've paid you, you don't always have copyright on that design or writing. If it is "work for hire," most of the time you don't have automatic copyright on it. You can, however, put in the agreement that you can use the work in your portfolio or show it publicly as your work, thus giving you the right to display your work. Become familiar with copyright law and limitations by reading up at **copyright.gov**.

JURY DUTY

One way you're almost certain to make contact with the legal system is when you're called to jury duty. The summons usually arrives at the most inopportune time, though in most cases you'll be able to reschedule a more convenient time, assuming there is such a thing. Since each state has different rules regarding how to get out of jury duty, read the summons carefully. Not only will there be rules you have to follow, but you may have to follow them in a timely manner or else you could lose the chance to reschedule.

CAUTION Don't ignore a jury duty notice because at some point the court will track you down and give you no alternatives.

Some people believe that the state finds them because they have a driver's license or have registered to vote. But these days, states are using all sorts of records to identify potential jurors, including utility bills, so there's no point in altering your life in an attempt to avoid jury duty. Deciding not to obtain a driver's license won't save you from getting called. (And really, is the hassle of not having an ID or giving up your voting rights worth it? While some people may consider jury duty to be a nuisance, many others find it to be a very rewarding experience.)

ESTATE PLANNING

If you're single and have very little in terms of assets, you might understandably assume you don't need a will, and in most cases that would be true. If you were to die, your assets, whatever they were, would most likely go to your parents. If your parents had both passed away, then your assets would go to your nearest relatives, such as your siblings. However, if you have absolutely no family, then your assets would go to the state. If you'd prefer to have them go to some charity, then you would need to stipulate that in a will.

WORD TO THE WISE

A will is key to making sure that in the event of your death, your possessions will go to the exact people you want them to go to. If you have any feuds going with certain family members and don't want them to inherit your goods, your will can specify this. Similarly, if you want your comic book collection to go to your eight-year-old nephew, your will can help make that happen.

While young people with few assets may not need wills, that's not true of certain other legal documents, especially if you're single. A **power of attorney** (POA) means that you designate someone to handle your affairs if you are incapacitated. For example, if you were in an accident and ended up in a coma, who would pay your rent? Without a POA, you might find yourself healed but out on the street. But if someone you designated had POA, he or she could have your bank issue a check to your landlord while you were unconscious.

A **health care proxy** allows you to appoint someone to make medical decisions for you if you can't, which could be very important if you live far from any family. For example, you can appoint your best friend, girlfriend, or boyfriend to tell doctors what course of action to take. If you don't appoint a health care proxy, no doctor will pay any mind to what your friend has to say.

A **living will** states the medical treatment that you would prefer if you become mentally or physically incapacitated and cannot speak on your own behalf. For example, your living will may request that doctors refrain from prolonging your life artificially if an accident puts you in a vegetative state. However, the instructions in such documents have to be on the vague side and so are not always followed, which is why appointing a health care proxy is the better means of accomplishing what you want.

You can find some of these documents online, and if you get them notarized, they might serve their intended purpose—but such boilerplate or one-size-fits-all documents aren't as good as ones prepared just for you by an attorney. Of course attorney fees are high, so high that at this point in your life the benefits may not outweigh the costs. Just bear in mind that as you grow older, and accumulate both family and possessions, you shouldn't trust such homemade documents to protect you; instead, you should invest in having an attorney prepare a new, personalized set.

DOWNLOADS You can find free legal documents with step-by-step instructions at **free-legal-document.com**. Another alternative is **LegalZoom.com**. LegalZoom's personal documents usually cost around $35–$50 to prepare, but they are highly rated and correctly prepared. So if it is very important for you to have a will, power of attorney, or a health care proxy, this is a low-cost option.

A Note on Notaries

Nearly every town has a local notary public, an official who can authorize that your legal document is authentically yours. Your local bank may well offer this service. Otherwise, most law firms and government offices have notaries. You can also find independent notaries in your local phone book. The cost for a notary to authenticate your document is usually under $50. Very important: Have your witnesses sign the document in the presence of the notary, not before!

PIERRE SAYS The older you get, the higher the odds that something is going to happen to you that will render you incapacitated. Sure, at this stage of your life you don't need to worry much about this, but you do have your parents to think of. I'm working on a project called 5@55 which aims to get everyone to have five critical estate planning legal documents set up by no later than age 55. Are your parents protected by documents such as wills and health care proxies? Have they ever talked to you about their affairs? You might wonder why I'm bringing up your parents in a chapter about *your* legal health. The reason is simple: Your parents' situation affects you! If they don't properly set up their estate, it's you who will have to deal with the fallout at some point. So have a conversation with them and find out what's up. Otherwise you could get stuck with a very big headache—and possibly heartache, as well.

ATTORNEYS

For most of what we've covered in this chapter, having access to an attorney would be beneficial but is not absolutely necessary. However, life sometimes throws you a curve and you find yourself in a situation where you positively need an attorney.

The first thing you need to know about attorneys is that most specialize in a particular area of the law. If you are accused of committing a crime, you need to find yourself a criminal attorney who knows his or her way around the criminal courts. If you get into an accident and need to sue, then you need a negligence attorney. For wills, POAs, and other aspects of what is called estate planning, you need an estate planning attorney. And if you buy a house or apartment, you need a real estate attorney. Some attorneys handle more than one type of situation, but if you've been accused of committing a crime, you definitely need a specialist defending you.

While there is no shortage of attorneys in the United States, finding the right one can be tricky. Attorneys are all members of a state bar association, so if you need to find a specialized attorney, the website of the bar in your state can help guide you in finding the right type of attorney. Of course, getting personal recommendations is always the best way to find a professional in whom you can trust in any field.

If you need a lawyer and can't get a personal recommendation, there are websites that can help you to narrow down your search including **Lawyers. com** and **ZeekBeek.com**.

If you are arrested on a criminal charge and can't afford an attorney, the U.S. Supreme Court has ruled that you must be given a court-appointed attorney to defend you.

INDEX

Acknowledgments

I have to begin by acknowledging how much I learned that was useful in putting together this book from assisting my two children, Peter Lehu and Gabrielle Frawley, to get launched from our own little family nest into the big, wide world. Thanks also to Melissa Sullivan, Jim Frawley, and the ever-adorable Jude Sullivan Lehu. My wife, Joanne Seminara, deserves her own page of thanks, but this sentence will have to do for my partner in everything, love of my life and best friend. And thanks go to the whole Seminara clan for their support and warm welcome over the years.

I've been the acknowledged Minister of Communications to Dr. Ruth Westheimer for over 30 years, so here I must acknowledge my gratitude for the title, for giving me the opportunity to jump into the field of professional writing and for her vow to make me laugh at least once a day.

Having my name on the cover of so many books, and also helping others to do the same as a literary agent, I've met many people in the field of publishing— but the connection that has been the most rewarding has been the one with a company that resides on the other side of the continent from me, Quill Driver Books. First with Steve Mettee, who then sold the company to Kent Sorsky. Both these gentlemen invest a tremendous amount of energy and skill in the projects they take on and the work that Kent and his team have done has added so much value to the goal of this book—to help the next generation make a successful transition out into this incredible world. Thank you.